Scottish Primary Mathematics Group

Primary Mathematics

A development through activity

Stage 1 , Second Edition

Teacher's Notes

Heinemann Educational Books

London and Edinburgh

Heinemann Educational Books Ltd
22 Bedford Square, London WC1B 3HH

LONDON   EDINBURGH   MELBOURNE   AUCKLAND
HONG KONG   SINGAPORE   KUALA LUMPUR   NEW DELHI
IBADAN   NAIROBI   JOHANNESBURG
EXETER(NH)   KINGSTON   PORT OF SPAIN

ISBN 0 435 02806 5

© Scottish Primary Mathematics Group 1975, 1984
First published 1975
Second edition 1984
Reprinted 1984

Filmset by Advanced Filmsetters (Glasgow) Ltd
Printed and bound in Great Britain by
Spottiswoode Ballantyne Ltd,
Colchester and London

Primary
Mathematics

List of authors

Douglas L. Alder	Lecturer in Mathematics of the former Hamilton College of Education, Hamilton
John T. Blair	Lecturer in Mathematics, Jordanhill College of Education, Glasgow
James Carpy	Senior Lecturer in Mathematics, Jordanhill College of Education, Glasgow
Ian K. Clark	Lecturer in Mathematics, Craigie College of Education, Ayr
Aileen P. Duncan	Lecturer in Mathematics, Jordanhill College of Education, Glasgow
Peter S. Henderson	Formerly Principal Lecturer in Mathematics, Craigie College of Education, Ayr
Archie MacCallum	Principal Lecturer in Mathematics, Craigie College of Education, Ayr
David McCulloch	Formerly Lecturer in Mathematics, Craigie College of Education, Ayr
David W. A. McInnes	Lecturer in Mathematics of the former Callendar Park College of Education, Falkirk
John Mackinlay	Lecturer in Mathematics of the former Callendar Park College of Education, Falkirk
Catherine D. J. Preston	Lecturer in Mathematics and Primary Education, Moray House College of Education, Edinburgh
William W. R. Tait	Senior Primary Adviser, Tayside

Contents

Introduction to the course

The course, *Primary Mathematics: A development through activity*, had its origins in a working party on mathematics in the primary school (National Primary Mathematics Project) which was formed to examine the structure and content of a mathematics course for children in Scottish primary schools. The working party recommendations provided the framework for 'Curriculum Paper 13, Primary Education in Scotland: Mathematics', which was published by the Scottish Education Department on the advice of the Consultative Committee on the Curriculum and '. . . serves as a handbook of guidance to the teacher in the primary school . . .'.

These recommendations also served as the basis for a curriculum project in schools. Teachers in these schools were asked to assess the project materials. Discussion of the teachers' comments and their own classroom observations enabled the working party members to revise the materials in the light of this experience. Stages 1 to 5 of *Primary Mathematics: A development through activity*, which are suitable for children aged 7 to 12, were subsequently published.

Later developments

As a result of frequent requests from schools for material designed to lead directly into Stage 1 of *Primary Mathematics*, a pilot project was developed for children aged 5 to 7 years. This resulted in the publication of *Infant Mathematics: A development through activity*, First Stage and Second Stage. Also, to meet a growing demand for enrichment materials suitable for pupils aged 10 to 14 years, four topic books entitled *Topics and Activities in Mathematics* were published, again following extensive piloting.

Over the years teachers and the authors have continued to work together, reviewing the material and exchanging experiences of using *Primary Mathematics* in school. Valuable suggestions have thus been incorporated in the second edition, which also takes account of currency changes and the infant material available. One important outcome of these consultations is the provision of assessment material for each stage of the course, from Stage 2 onwards.

Features of the course

As the sub-title '*A development through activity*' implies, two important features of the course are:
 (i) the development of a progression of work within a particular topic from stage to stage of the course
 (ii) the emphasis placed on practical work to help children acquire concepts and understand particular techniques.
Number (which includes money and pictorial representation), measure and shape form an essential part of each stage of the course, and the integration of these is another important aspect of the series.

Number

The general approach to number work is that emphasis is placed on the use of practical material, including structured number material, diagrams, and number lines, and on problem solving, number patterns, and games.

The approach to the teaching of each of the four whole number operations involves the use of Tillich material and adopts the following pattern:
  (i) manipulating the material to find an answer which is recorded
  (ii) linking the manipulation to the written technique
 (iii) practising the written technique
 (iv) consolidation of the technique by reference back to the material.
In *subtraction*, language and activities involving 'take away' and the comparative ideas of 'how many more' and 'difference between' are emphasised.

The decomposition method of subtraction has been used since it arises naturally from the use of material and can be fairly easily understood by young children. This method has been fully described in the *Teacher's Notes*. Although the workbooks show structured apparatus used in this way, the examples themselves could be used by children who had been taught another method of subtraction.

In *division*, sharing and grouping activities are used to introduce the topic.

The division technique is introduced using structured number apparatus which leads to the children sharing out the material. The written technique and associated language are thus based on the sharing aspect of division. The grouping aspect of division has not however been neglected. Many examples involving grouping language are included throughout the course.

The use of material has had an influence on the authors' initial interpretation of the ' $\times$ ' sign. Four sets with three articles in each set is seen as four threes or 4 times 3 or 4×3. Some teachers write four sets with three articles in each as 3×4 which they read as 3 multiplied by 4. With young children, the authors (and others) take the view that four sets of three or four threes is better symbolised as 4×3 rather than 3×4 which reverses the factors. Once the principle of the commutative law has been understood, 4×3 and 3×4 are seen to be equivalent.

The approach to *fractions* starts with the use of diagrams and number lines which are later used to illustrate operations involving fractions.

Money work is integrated with the number work, e.g. place value to 99 is followed by laying out amounts to 99p.

Pictorial representation has a definite progression from the pictograph approach in Stage 1 to straight line graphs in Stages 4 and 5. Emphasis is placed both on drawing and interpreting graphs. Each time a new aspect of graphical work is introduced it is done in the number section. Thereafter, applications appear in the measure and shape sections.

Measure

Throughout Stages 1 to 5 practical work is advocated to secure concepts, give practice in measuring skills, and develop meaningful language associated with length, weight, area, volume and time. In the early stages some of the learning occurs at a perceptual level.

The development of each aspect of measure is treated in a broadly similar way. It is recognised however that a certain concept in one aspect of measure can be grasped at an earlier age than a comparable concept in another aspect, e.g. the concept of a metre is introduced before the concept of a litre.

Each aspect of measure is developed along the following lines:

  (i)   comparing and ordering experiences to develop relationships and meaningful language

  (ii) the use of arbitrary standards (e.g. spans) to quantify measure and to show the need for a standard measure

  (iii) the use of standard measures (e.g. the metre) in estimating and measuring activities

  (iv) the use of fractional parts of the conventional standards, leading to an awareness of the approximate nature of measure.

At the beginning of the course, separate sections on length, weight, area, volume and time have been produced, but in later stages the various aspects of measure are integrated in single sections where the emphasis is on experimentation and problem solving. Where appropriate, the measure work is integrated with shape and number, including pictorial representation.

Shape

Practical informal activities to develop children's recognition of shapes and awareness of some of their properties occurs regularly throughout Stages 1 to 5.

Emphasis is placed on the children handling, examining, sorting, and building solid (3D) shapes, and cutting out, fitting, moving, folding, sorting, and examining flat (2D) shapes. Plasticine, cardboard, nailboards, paper and Meccano-type strips are used to make shapes.

The aesthetic and recreational appeal of coloured patterns, tiling work, shape puzzles, curve stitching, bilateral and rotational symmetry is recognised by including these aspects at appropriate stages.

The shape work, which can be broadly classified under the headings of solid (3D) shape, flat (2D) shape, symmetry, and angles, shows a progression within each of these topics as the course develops.

It is important that all children are given ample opportunity to experience this shape work; indeed children who have difficulty with number work often gain confidence through their achievement in shape work.

Format of the material

The choice of format was determined by two main considerations:
 (i) Children should be presented with a variety of ways of completing written work and recording the results of practical work. Thus the children's material consists of workbooks, workcards, and textbooks.
(ii) Teachers should be provided with ample suggestions for teaching and learning situations. These suggestions should include references to teaching aids, games, cut-out shapes, etc. Thus the teacher's material consists of the *Teacher's Notes* and an optional *Teacher's Materials Pack*. Answer books are also provided.

The use of expendable material is particularly suitable for younger children. Four workbooks each containing number, measure and shape are supplied at each of Stages 1 and 2. The workbooks in Stage 2 are shorter than those in Stage 1 but are supplemented by a textbook. Each of these Stages also has a set of workcards.

In Stages 3, 4, and 5 most of the work is presented in a textbook format, one textbook for each Stage. A workbook and a set of workcards are also supplied for each of these Stages.

Each of the Stages 1 to 5 also has a *Teacher's Notes* book, an *Answers Book* and an optional *Teacher's Materials Pack*. To assist the teacher in record keeping a 'Record of work' grid is incorporated in the workbooks. Written assessment material has been supplied from Stage 2 onwards. This should not, however, replace the oral, informal discussion between teacher and child, which in itself is a valuable form of assessment.

Introduction to Stage 1

In determining the starting point for Stage 1, account has been taken of the fact that the children have different backgrounds and abilities. Initially, there is provision for revision and consolidation of work which has probably been dealt with in earlier years. Those children who have used the course *Infant Mathematics: A development through activity* should find the changeover straightforward, since there is planned continuity between the two courses.

For the **number work**, it is assumed that children have a reasonable knowledge of number in its cardinal and ordinal aspects. This would include the ability to recognise, name, write, and order numbers up to 20. Also it is assumed that the process of counting is understood and, in particular, can be applied to collections of up to twenty objects. The concepts of addition and subtraction will have been established and the children should have a reasonable knowledge of the composition of numbers up to 20.

In **measure** it is assumed that language will have been developed through activity, for example 'make a *long* bead necklace', 'spread the paint over the *surface* of the paper', 'pour water from the bottle into the jug to see *which holds more*'. The variety of language associated with measure becomes meaningful when it arises in the context of practical work. Such work could have included experimenting with containers in the sand tray and sink, and with a balance to determine 'heavy' and 'light'.

For **shape**, it is expected that the children will previously have used building blocks of various shapes and sizes. They will have counted them, built with them, and arranged them according to size, colour and shape. Jig-saw puzzles, fitting into holes, plasticine modelling, tiling work, picture making, and using pegboard and pegs are typical activities used to encourage the development of language associated with shape work. 'Curved', 'straight', 'block', 'box', 'ball', 'cone', 'square', 'rectangle', 'triangle', and 'circle' are some of the important words which may have occurred quite naturally during these experiences.

Format of Stage 1 material

Stage 1 has four expendable workbooks and 35 double-sided non-expendable workcards. There are several advantages to be gained from using expendable workbooks for this age group:
  (i) a model layout is provided
 (ii) recording is simplified
(iii) more work is possible in the time available
 (iv) a record of work done is readily available
  (v) some worthwhile practical activities are best presented in this way.

Approximately half of each workbook consists of number work, which can be subdivided into short sections of a few pages each. These should be tackled in the order in which they are presented. On completion of any short section of number work a group of children could proceed to any of the independent sections on measure and shape which make up the rest of the workbook. It is not intended that all the number work should be completed before the measure and shape sections are attempted. Sections on measure and shape are found in all the workbooks and these make up a sequence of work. In this way there is continuous development of these topics. Sections on money and pictorial representation appear within the number work. All the work within a single workbook should normally be completed before moving to the next workbook.

A 'Record of work' grid is supplied on the cover of each workbook and this can be used for checking progress during the year. The teacher may (i) tick each box to indicate that the child's work was satisfactory, (ii) use a coded grading system in the boxes to indicate the degree of success achieved by the child, (iii) tick each box to indicate work which is to be attempted by the child.

At the top of each workbook page there is a title for the children and one for the teacher. The latter acts as a reminder to the teacher of the type of work which is being tackled.

Number   Revision to 10

Add or subtract

Workcards

In Stage 1 there are 35 double-sided workcards which are non-expendable. Card references, which give the workcard numbers and their content, are supplied on the appropriate workbook pages. On the completion of a section of work in the workbook the child is often directed to some workcards. These may contain further practice material, which might be needed by some children, or they may present more difficult and challenging work, which is useful for a more able child. Sometimes they may ask the child to do certain practical activities on shape or measure.

Ask your teacher if you should do Length Cards 11, 13, 15, 17, 19.

The workcards themselves are arranged in batches of five or ten and are of equal difficulty within the batch, so a child may start with any one of them. It is not necessary, of course, for one child to do all the cards in one batch. The advantage for the teacher is that a given batch of non-graded workcards can provide work for at least five children, and sometimes as many as ten, at any one time.

Teacher's Notes

The *Teacher's Notes* form an essential part of this course. They contain many suggestions for practical activities to be done before the workbook pages and cards. They also describe additional activities, oral work, and games, together with extra cards and worksheets which could be made by the teacher. Lists of contents and materials are given for each workbook, together with detailed notes relating to individual workbook pages. Teaching notes for the workcards appear at the point at which they are referenced from a workbook. Reference is also made at appropriate points in the *Teacher's Notes* to the *Teacher's Materials Pack*.

Answers

An *Answers Book* is supplied in which photo-reductions of workbook pages appear. The workcard answers are in a separate section at the end.

Teacher's Materials Pack

This pack is available as an optional extra and consists of useful resource material which is closely related to the work contained in the workbooks and workcards. Included are teaching aids, demonstration apparatus, and games for all the aspects of mathematics dealt with at this stage.

Using the course: getting ready

Teachers will find it helpful to refer to the materials list at the beginning of the teaching notes for each workbook so items are available when required.
It is also suggested that workcards relevant to a particular workbook should be sorted into batches ready for use as required.
It is recommended that reference be made to the appropriate section of the *Teacher's Notes*. This will help the teacher to make optimum use of the children's material.
For those teachers who intend using the *Teacher's Materials Pack* it would be beneficial if the relevant parts of the pack were prepared before they were needed.

Using the course: classroom organisation

Teachers try to cater for the needs of all children, whether they be very able, of average ability, or slow learners. Very able children will inevitably complete more work, more quickly than children of average ability. They are at risk in that they may become bored and lose interest. The teacher, on the other hand, has to decide to what extent, and at what time, they should be allowed to go ahead to the next section of a workbook or even to the next workbook. Such children may sometimes be given enrichment material associated with a topic they have been studying. This kind of work is to be found in some of the workcards and workbook pages.

The range and extent of the work in any one Stage is such that a child of average ability may be expected to complete it in a school year. It is not intended, however, that every child will complete every workbook page and workcard in the course of the session. The teacher will still have to provide extra material for practice or enrichment when this is thought to be necessary, but at the same time, there will be workcards and workbook pages which may be too difficult for some children of average ability. Slow-learning children can always benefit from more teacher help and often require help and encouragement with number work. It is important for teachers to appreciate that such children will not manage to complete all the work and a selection will have to be made. This need not be restricted to number work only, since children who are poor achievers in number sometimes cope very well with work on measure and shape.

Each workbook and its associated workcards have been compiled in a way which helps the teacher to organise the work to suit individuals, groups of children, or even the whole class. The normal starting point in each workbook is with the number work but, at the appropriate time, the teacher should direct a group of children to do one of the measure or shape units. The availability of apparatus and the nature of the practical activity may determine just how many children can tackle any one of these units at one time. Another group of children may be asked to do workcards associated in some way with the number work in the workbook. The workcards chosen may contain more practice work or perhaps something more challenging such as puzzles or number sequences.

Games and other activities suggested in the notes may be organised for other groups.

After children have completed a particular measure or shape unit, or the workcards, they should return to the number work section and proceed to the next part of it. Clearly it is not envisaged that all the children work from the beginning to the end of every workbook in the page order.

It is intended that preliminary teaching should be done before workbook pages and workcards are attempted, and also that regular 'mental' work should form an integral part of the course.

Development of Stage 1

	Number							
Work-book	**Place Value** **Addition** **Subtraction**	**Multiplication**	**Division**	**Fractions**	**Money**	**Graphs**	**Other topics**
1	Revision to 20 of: Place value Addition Subtraction				Revision to 10p	Picture graphs	
2	Place value to 99 Addition to 99				Revision to 20p 20p coin 50p coin Money to 99p		Puzzles Odd and even numbers
3	Subtraction within 99	Concept of multiplication The × sign 2 times table		Halves and quarters	Addition and subtraction of money to 99p	Block graphs	
4		2, 3, 4, 5 times tables	Concept of sharing and grouping into 2, 3, 4, 5 The ÷ sign				Puzzles

	Measure					Shape	
Work-book	Length	Weight	Area	Volume	Time	Solid shape	Flat shape

1	Language
	
	Arbitrary
	standards
					Hours
					Half hours
					Days of the week
					Duration (hours)
						Recognition:
						  sorting
						  naming	

2		Language
		
		Arbitrary
		standards
			Language				Recognition:
							  square
							  rectangle
							  triangle
							  circle
							  pentagon
							  hexagon

3	Metre Half metre Quarter metre			Language			Nailboards Folding
4			Arbitrary standards		A quarter past A quarter to Ordering Months	Faces of solids	

Stage 1   Workbook 1

Stage 1   Workbook 1

Introduction

This workbook is arranged so that different sections of the work can be tackled at the same time by different groups within the class. It is not intended that the children should work through the workbook in the order in which the pages are printed, nor is it necessary or even desirable for every child to do all the work on every page. The more able children can be guided quite quickly through the revision and practice work but care should be taken to prevent the less able spending excessive time on one piece of work and so never reaching valuable work in length, time and shape.

Although some of the early number work may seem too simple for some children, it is important to realise that it is the language associated with number which is being emphasised as well as the revision aspects of numbers to 20.

Pages 1 to 22 of the number section would normally be tackled in the order in which they are printed, but the work could conveniently be grouped in the following way:

Pages 1 to 4	Revision of addition and subtraction to 10
Pages 5 to 9	Picture graphs
Pages 10 to 14	Revision of money to 10p
Pages 15 to 22	Revision of addition and subtraction to 20
Workcards 1, 3, 5, 7, 9	Revision to 20
Pages 23 to 25	Counting and number names to 100

After any one of these small sections has been completed, it should be possible to ask children to attempt any of the sections on length, time or shape. The shape work requires a certain amount of advance organisation to ensure an adequate collection of the necessary shapes.

Obviously the overall approach to the workbook will be affected by the availability of materials. In particular, apart from the desirability of grouping the children by ability for the number work, it is likely that group working will be essential when doing the practical money work, some of the length section, and when using shapes in the shape section.

The workbook should not be regarded as a 'programmed text'. Generally some teaching is necessary before children attempt the workbook pages and cards.

Contents

Time

Shape

Materials

Counting materials such as beads, buttons, counters, cubes, pegs, straws, or
  any other suitable objects
Interlocking cubes
Tillich-type material with tens and units
Coins – plastic, cardboard or real (1p, 2p, 5p, 10p)
Scissors, glue, coloured pencils, crayons
Number lines, number strips
Flashcards of numerals and number facts
Large sheets of paper for wall charts
12 sticks or canes about a metre long
Straws, string, paper clips
Demonstration clockface with moveable hands (geared if possible)
3D shapes – cubes, cuboids, cylinders, cones, spheres, triangular prisms

The teaching notes for each page list the specific material required and offer
suggestions for alternative materials where appropriate.
The following items from the *Teacher's Materials Pack* will be useful for this
work:

Space game	Cards 1, 2 and 3
Notation cards	Card 5
Number line 1 to 100	Cards 10, 11, 12, 13
Clock	Card 26
Castles: a length game	Cards 28, 29

Number	**Revision to 10**	**Pages 1 to 4**

Content and development

This first section of Workbook 1 revises addition and subtraction facts
within 10 and should help the teacher to determine how well the children can
recall these basic facts.
The section begins with addition and subtraction presented in various
formats. This is followed by 'adding on' or 'complementary addition'
examples of the type $4 + \square = 7$, and examples on the comparison aspect of
subtraction, i.e. the ideas of 'how many more' and 'difference between'. The
section ends with further 'complementary addition' examples, of the type
$\square + 4 = 7$, and with examples of the addition of three numbers.
Because it has been impossible to cover all the addition and subtraction facts
within the four pages, teachers may wish to provide extra examples (see
additional workcards and worksheets on pages 16 and 17) especially those
involving zero facts, for example $7 + 0 = 7; 6 - 6 = 0$.

Further revision work on addition and subtraction within 10 but related to money is covered in Workbook 1, pages 10 to 14.

The extension of the revision work to addition and subtraction within 20 is dealt with in Workbook 1, pages 15 to 22.

Introductory activities for Page 1

It is to be hoped that at this stage most children will have a firm grasp of the basic addition and subtraction facts within 10.

It is important to link the associated addition and subtraction facts. A child should be familiar with the various addition and subtraction combinations for three numbers. For example:

$$2+5=7; 5+2=7; 7-2=5; 7-5=2.$$

Revision of this work should be demonstrated or even carried out by a group of children using counters, beads, interlocking cubes, etc. For example:

1 Using gummed circles

to revise the various stories of 7.

Seven gummed circles are stuck on to a piece of card.

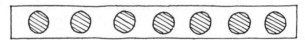

A pencil is then laid across the card to show:

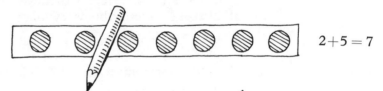

$$2+5=7$$

The card is then turned round to show:

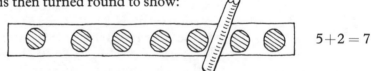

$$5+2=7$$

Covering up one set of circles would give:

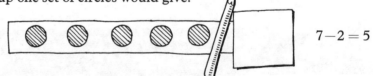

$$7-2=5$$

Covering up the other set of circles would give:

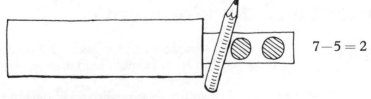

$$7-5=2$$

The other stories of 7 would be linked together and revised by changing the position of the pencil.

2 Using interlocking cubes

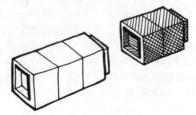

to show $3+2=5$
$2+3=5$
$5-2=3$
$5-3=2$

3 Lining up children

to show $4+3=7$
$3+4=7$
$7-3=4$
$7-4=3$

4 Using beads or other similar materials, for example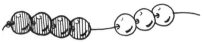

Teachers should remember to include examples involving the zero facts, for example $7+0=7; 0+7=7; 7-0=7; 7-7=0$. These facts will be important later when dealing with additions and subtractions of tens and units:

$$\begin{array}{cccc} 47 & 20 & 67 & 37 \\ +30 & +57 & -30 & -27 \end{array}$$

For many children a quick revision of the number stories for 3 to 10 will be all that is necessary.

For the less able child who does not have a complete grasp of these facts it might be advisable to carry out this revision work in stages:

   (i) stories of 3, 4, and 5
   (ii) stories of 6 and 7
   (iii) stories of 8, 9, and 10

Each stage should be followed by appropriate worksheets which should be fairly simple. Here are two examples. In example (a) the children have to insert a number in each box so that the pair add up to the centre number.

(a) 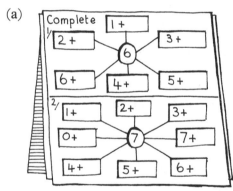   (b)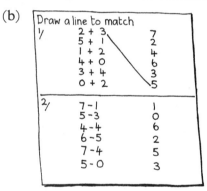

Window cards would also be useful. Instructions for making these are given on page 16.

Page 1   **Add or subtract**   · **Number   Revision to 10**

Materials   counters, beads, etc. if required

This page provides practice examples using different formats: mapping diagrams, examples recorded horizontally, examples recorded vertically, and problems.

The first example in question 1 has been completed to show children what they are expected to do.

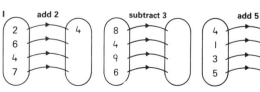

For the subtraction examples in questions 2 and 3 the appropriate language would include '8 take away 6' or '8 subtract 6'. Teachers may feel that they should give children more word problems to reinforce the meaning of such phrases as 'How many are left?', 'How many altogether?', etc. It should be noted that the word 'total' is not used in the problems on this page and is used for the first time on Page 4.

Page 2	Adding on	Number Revision to 10

Materials   counting materials if required

Whereas the addition examples of Page 1 dealt with the combination of two groups to form a total group $(5+2 = \boxed{7})$, the examples on Page 2 revise the idea of 'what has to be added on' to make a known total, that is, $5+\square = 7$. Most children should be able to cope with this idea by recalling known addition facts. To find the answer to $5+\square = 7$, the child would recall that $5+2 = 7$ and would insert 2 in the $\square$. However, the less able child may need to find the answer in a practical way using materials. For example, to find the answer to $5+\square = 7$, counters could be used. The child would lay out five counters of one colour.

and then put down more counters of a different colour to make a total of seven

The child would then see that he or she needed to add 2 to 5 to make 7. Questions 1 and 2 are very similar to the counter example given above. In question 1, the answer is found by drawing extra mugs, etc. and in question 2 by drawing dots. It is hoped that the answers to questions 3 to 7 would be found by recall of basic facts.

Introductory activities for Page 3

The practical revision work for Page 1 concentrated on the 'take away' aspect of subtraction. Although this page is headed 'How many more?' it deals with both the comparative ideas of subtraction – 'How many more?' and 'difference between'. This can be a difficult idea for many children and some preliminary work is suggested.

1   The idea of 'How many more?' could be introduced as follows:

David has 9 sweets and John has 5 sweets. How many more sweets has David than John?

(i) The two rows of sweets would first be drawn on paper:

(ii) The sweets would then be matched by drawing lines:

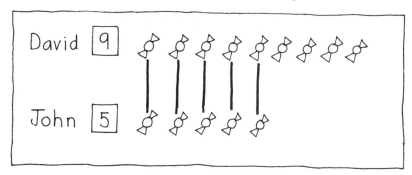

(iii) The unmatched objects give the answer to 'How many more?'.

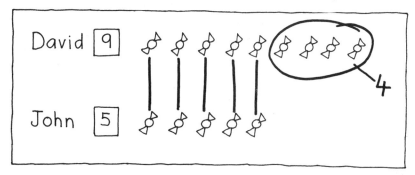

(iv) The link is then made with the subtraction fact which the children already know.
David has 9 sweets.
John has 5 sweets.
David has 4 sweets more than John. $9 - 5 = 4$

2 The idea of 'difference between' could be introduced using the example above but changing the language:

David has 9 sweets and John has 5 sweets. What is the difference between the number of sweets that they have?

Again a link is made with the known subtraction fact:
David has 9 sweets.
John has 5 sweets.
The difference is 4 sweets. $9 - 5 = 4$

Page 3	**How many more?**	Number Revision to 10

Materials   none

The answers to questions 1, 2, 4, and 5 can be found by counting the unmatched objects. It should be pointed out to children that care must be taken when drawing the objects in questions 2 and 5 so that they can be matched easily:

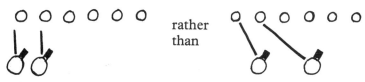

In questions 3, 6, and 7 the children should realise from the 'difference between' and 'How many more?' language that subtraction is involved and recall the appropriate subtraction fact to find the answer.

Introductory activities for Page 4

The 'complementary addition' examples on Page 2 contained examples of the type '4 and what make 7?' ($4 + \square = 7$). It is hoped that children found the answer by recall of the appropriate fact, but the answer could have been found by counting on.

Questions 1 and 2 of Page 4 also deal with 'complementary addition' but with examples of the type 'What and 4 makes 7?' ($\square + 4 = 7$). Again it is hoped that the answer will be found by recall, but because of the commutative nature of addition ($\square + 4 = 4 + \square$), the answer could again be found by counting on. Many children may be encountering examples of the type '$\square + 3 = 8$' for the first time, and it would be desirable to give them practice in these before attempting Page 4.

Page 4 also revises the addition of three numbers. The technique for doing this should be discussed with the children. The answer to $3 + 2 + 4 = \square$ would be found by saying '3 and 2 makes 5', and then '5 and 4 makes 9'. Some children may find it necessary to put in a crutch figure for the first few examples: $3 + 2 + 4 = 9$.
$_5$

The children should also be given practice in examples which are set down vertically and should be encouraged to add both 'up' and 'down'. This serves as a useful check. Crutch figures may be necessary here as well.

$$\begin{array}{r} 3 \\ 1 \\ +5 \\ \hline 9 \\ \hline \end{array}$$

Page 4	**Adding**	**Number Revision to 10**

Materials   none

Although some children may find the answer to question 1 by drawing in the dots and counting on, it is hoped that others will find the answer by recall of the appropriate fact, then draw in the dots and check their answer by counting the total number of dots.

In question 3 the answers to the top row of examples could be found by counting, using the illustrations, but it is hoped that the answer will be found by adding the numbers in pairs.

In question 5 the word 'total' is used. This may need some explanation.

Additional workcards and worksheets

Examples of different types of cards and worksheets which could be made are given below. These should include 'zero' examples.

Window cards   A piece of paper is placed between the folded halves of a card. The answers are written on the paper through the slots in the card. After correction the paper can be removed and a new piece inserted for another pupil.

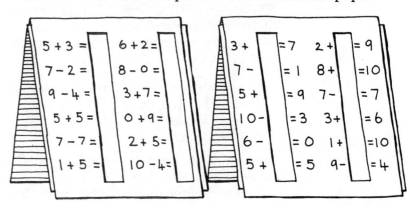

Worksheets   Various types of worksheet, suitable for the more able pupil, could be made.

(a)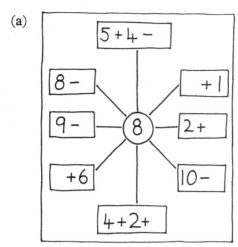

(b)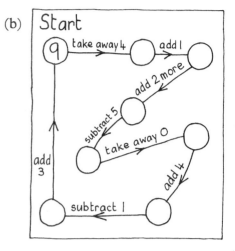

This type of worksheet gives practice in the composition of a particular number, in this case 8. The children have to find the missing number in each box so that the answer is 8.

This is a self-correcting worksheet. If completed correctly the pupil should finish with the starting number.

(c)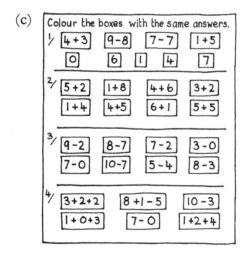

(d)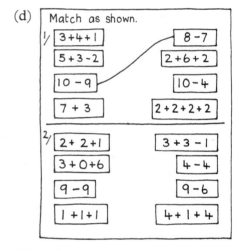

In this type of worksheet the pupils colour the boxes which have the same answer. There need not be the same number of boxes in each row. An extra box could be inserted as a distractor.

Here the pupils connect the boxes which have the same answer with a line. Again extra boxes can be inserted as distractors.

Workcards   Different types of cards, in which the pupil has to copy the example into an exercise book, should be made up. These should be of different levels of difficulty, as shown below:

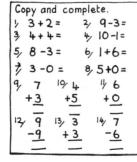

Copy and complete.
1/ 3 + 2 =   2/ 9 − 3 =
3/ 4 + 4 =   4/ 10 − 1 =
5/ 8 − 3 =   6/ 1 + 6 =
7/ 3 − 0 =   8/ 5 + 0 =

9/ 7   10/ 4   11/ 6
   +3   +5   +0
   ──   ──   ──

12/ 9   13/ 3   14/ 7
   −9   +3   −6
   ──   ──   ──

Copy and complete.
1/ 2 + 3 + 4 =   2/ 5 + 1 + 1 =
3/ 2 + 2 + 6 =   4/ 1 + 7 + 1 =
5/ 3 + 0 + 3 =   6/ 2 + 6 + 0 =
7/ 5 + 1 + 2 =   8/ 6 + 3 + 1 =

9/ 4   10/ 3   11/ 7
   3   3   1
 + 2   + 3   + 2
 ──   ──   ──

Copy and fill in the missing number.
1/ 3 + □ = 2 + 6
2/ 10 − 3 = 6 + □
3/ 3 + 5 = 10 − □
4/ 4 + 2 = □ − 3
5/ 2 + 2 + 5 = 3 + □
6/ 5 + 2 = 1 + 3 + □
7/ 10 − 3 = 2 + 2 + □
8/ 6 − □ = 2 + 2 + 2

Additional activities

Games to consolidate addition and subtraction facts within 10 are given in *Infant Mathematics, First Stage, Teacher's Materials Pack.*

Graphs   **Pages 5 to 9**

Content and development

The graph work (pictorial representation) at this stage is used to supplement the money and number work. The graphs are picture graphs and show both horizontal and vertical displays. Some are for interpretation but others should be constructed by the children, by cutting out pictures of objects and sticking them on to the page.

Some children may have done no formal graphical work before this, but it is likely that they will have lined up concrete materials while sorting and counting. For example, they may have built up a number stair in a graph-like display:

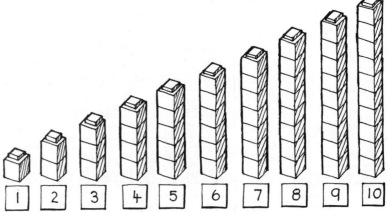

In subtraction, the comparison aspect is introduced using concrete materials which are lined up. Later, pictures of objects are used like this:

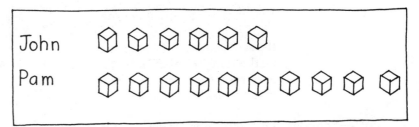

This pictorial representation helps children to find 'the difference between', 'How many more?', 'How much more?', etc. The move from this to three or more rows or columns of data should be within the scope of most children. In Workbook 3, the graph work is developed further using boxes on squared paper instead of pictures to represent data.

Introductory activities for Pages 5 to 9

Before proceeding to the graph pages it would be worth doing some sorting exercises with concrete materials such as toys. Let the children line them up and then ask questions about the display. This would revise the language, for example, 'Which do we have most of?', 'How many more?', 'How many altogether?'. It would also ensure that the children fully appreciate the 'lining up' principle.

Initially, some children might put the cars bumper to bumper. On the graph the car and the lorry will have to occupy the same space although in reality the lorry is much larger.

| **Page 5** | **A coin graph** | Graphs |

Materials   at least thirteen 1p coins, either real, plastic or card (stick-on coins could be used)

In the first graph the children are expected to lay the coins on the circles to show the amount of money each child has. They then have to answer the questions. The number work involved is all revision of addition and subtraction facts within 10. However 'How much money altogether?' involves addition of three numbers and this revision appears on Page 13, for example $3+6+4 = 13$. Children who find the addition of three numbers difficult could find the answer by counting all the coins on the graph.

Introductory activities for Pages 6 and 7

Teachers may wish to create a large 'Our pets' graph with the help of the children. One way to do this is to decide on the four or five most popular pets in the class and ask some children to draw their favourite pet on a rectangle of paper provided by the teacher. These drawings of pets should be stuck on the graph to create the 'Class pets graph'. The children can then be asked questions about it.

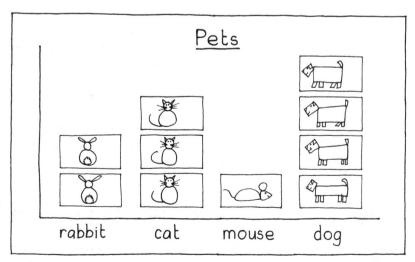

The rectangular pieces of paper make the lining up relatively easy.

Page 6   A picture graph   Graphs

Materials   none

This is another simple interpretation graph but this time a picture is used to represent each pet. Discussion along the lines of the introductory activities above would be a suitable introduction to this page.

To answer question 4, the children should *count* all the pictures on the graph. When answering question 5, the children should be encouraged to count the 'extra' dogs from the graph rather than to subtract.

Page 7   Your picture graph   Graphs

Materials   scissors, glue, pets pictures (cut from the bottom of the page)

This graph has to be constructed by the children. They should cut out the animal boxes along the red lines and then stick the small rectangles on the grid. All the rectangles are the same size, which will assist the children in lining them up on the grid.

The children could find 'How many altogether?' by counting the pictures on the graph. This time there are four things to add, for example, $3+5+3+4 = 15$.

Page 8   A toys graph   Graphs

Materials   none

This graph is similar to the pets graph on Page 6, although the display is horizontal. Some children may have problems with the word 'fewer' in question 6. Teachers should make sure that children associate 'How many fewer?' with subtraction, in a similar way to 'How many more?'.

Page 9   Your farm graph   Graphs

Materials   scissors, glue, farm animal pictures (cut from the bottom of the page)

This horizontal display has to be constructed by the children themselves using the farm animals cut from the bottom of the page. As for Page 7, they should cut along the red lines to make small rectangles which can then be stuck in the appropriate rows.

The children should be encouraged to write 'stories' which involve mathematical statements about the graph. For example, 'There are 2 cows, 3 hens' etc.; 'There are more pigs than sheep'.

Additional activities

1   Discussion with the class might produce other 'favourite' topics which could be dealt with as in the introductory activities for Pages 6 and 7. Remember that the total number of children involved with each graph should not exceed 20, since this work is revising addition to 20. Possible topics for favourite graphs are comics, ice creams, sweets, TV stars, chocolate biscuits, fruit, drinks, TV programmes.

2 Extra worksheets could be made up like the ones below, where pictures of objects are given and the children have to draw them on the graph and answer questions.

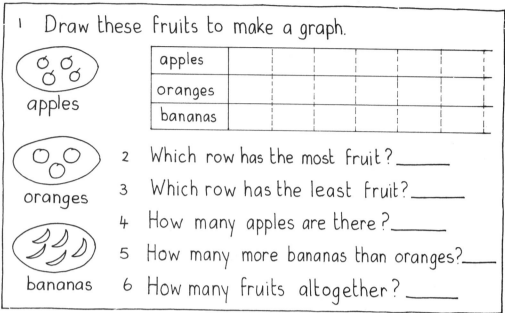

1 Draw these fruits to make a graph.

apples						
oranges						
bananas						

2 Which row has the most fruit?_____

3 Which row has the least fruit?_____

4 How many apples are there?_____

5 How many more bananas than oranges?____

6 How many fruits altogether?_____

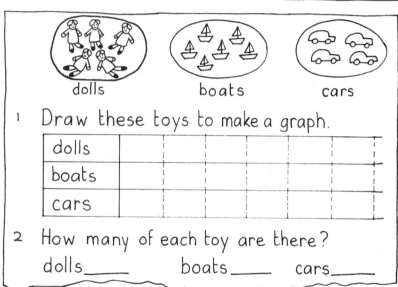

1 Draw these toys to make a graph.

dolls						
boats						
cars						

2 How many of each toy are there?
dolls____   boats____ cars____

Money to 10p   Pages 10 to 14

Content and development

In this workbook it is assumed that children have already been introduced to the 1p, 2p, 5p, and 10p coins and that they are familiar with laying out coins for amounts to 10p, addition and subtraction to 10p, and giving back change from 5p and 10p. Such work is to be found in *Infant Mathematics: A development through activity*, Second Stage. All of this work is revised and consolidated in Stage 1, Workbook 1 of *Primary Mathematics*. Emphasis is placed on laying out coins following an addition or subtraction activity, and on language work, including 'difference in price' and 'How much more?'. Giving back change from 5p and 10p concludes the work of this section. Further work on money to 20p and to 99p occurs in Stage 1, Workbook 2.

Introductory activities for Page 10

1 The 1p and 2p coins   The teacher should remind the children that two 1p coins can be changed for one 2p coin. He or she may wish to put out coins and a flashcard as shown.

  can be changed for

The teacher should then discuss various ways of paying for articles priced 3p and 4p. The children should put out the coins each time, for example:

   or

   or

or

2 The 5p coin   The teacher should remind the children that five 1p coins can be changed for one 5p coin.
Various ways of paying for an article priced 5p should be shown, for example:

   or

or   or

The children should then be asked to put out coins for articles priced 6p to 9p, for example:

   or

or

It should be pointed out that for these amounts it is best to start with a 5p coin, i.e. a coin with as great a value as possible.

3 The 10p coin   The teacher should remind the children that ten 1p coins can be changed for one 10p coin.
Various ways of paying for an article priced 10p should be shown. Particular

emphasis should be put on and   as ways of paying.

4 The 1p, 2p, 5p and 10p coins

Various other activities related to these coins could now be carried out by the children.

(a) The children could be asked to sort a box of coins into sets of 1p, 2p, 5p, and 10p coins.

(b) Coin rubbings could be made using real coins, and the various designs on both faces discussed.

(c) A class shop could be set up with articles priced 1p to 10p and the children invited to buy and pay for one of the articles. Alternatively, they could be invited to choose two articles with a total cost of 10p or less, and to pay for these.

(d) Cards could be made, each of which shows the price of an article. The child should be asked to put out the appropriate coins for each article. They should be encouraged to use as few coins as possible. So for 6p they should put out 5p and 1p rather than 2p, 2p, 1p, and 1p.

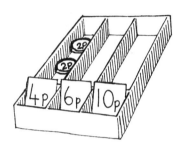

(e) Sorting boxes could be used as follows:
The children could be asked to put the appropriate money in each part. The children could be given the box with money in each part and asked to pick cards to show how much money there was in each section (totals 10p or less). *This last activity is a particularly important one.*

The two alternatives in (e) could be combined in the following manner. The box could initially be put out with the amount cards. The first child would put out coins for each amount. The cards would then be removed and the second child asked to find the appropriate cards for the coins laid out. The coins would then be removed and so the activity would continue. At first the teacher could check after each child had carried out the task, but later it would be interesting to see if any changes had occurred after a number of children in a group had been involved. The teacher should encourage the group to work carefully so that the 'game' works.

Page 10	Shopping	Money to 10p

Materials   1p, 2p, 5p, and 10p coins

This page gives the children further practice in laying out coins for amounts to 10p.

Find the cost. Put out coins.

1   The apple costs [6] p   (5p) (1p)

---

2   The chocolate costs [4] p   (2p) (2p)

In question 1 the children are meant to place coins on the outline drawings of coins, and then to record their answers as shown above.
In question 2 the children should put out coins in the space provided and then record their answer by drawing round the coins, as shown above.
Alternatively, once the coins have been laid out, they could write down their answer as '2p, 2p', or could stick on gummed paper coins to record their answer.

In questions 3 to 7 the children have to find the total cost of two articles before laying out the coins for the total cost. Some children may lay out coins for each article separately. For example, in question 4 the child may lay out

  and   initially. They should be

encouraged to see that   would be better.

Page 11	**Subtract**	**Money to 10p**

Materials   1p, 2p, 5p, and 10p coins

This page revises the 'take away' aspect of subtraction and 'difference in price'.

The teacher should relate this work to the class shop, prior to the children trying Page 11.

An article could be taken from the class shop,

for example:

and the children invited to 'take 3p off' the price. Once the new price has been established, they could then be asked to pay for it using coins. Several examples like this should be tried.

Two articles could then be taken from the class shop and the fact that their prices are 'different' be established. For example:

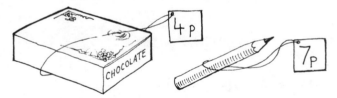

To find the difference in price it may be necessary for some children to lay out 1p coins and match them, for example:

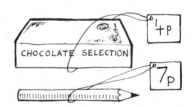

However, every effort should be made to establish that the difference in price can be found by subtraction, i.e. that the difference in price is $7p - 4p = 3p$.

The children should now try Page 11.

As in Page 10, space has been left in questions 1, 2, and 3 for the children to put out coins for the new prices. They should record their results by drawing round the coins and writing on them ②p ①p or by writing '2p, 1p', or by sticking on the appropriate gummed paper coins.

Questions 5 to 8 are meant to be done by subtraction. However, it may be necessary for some children to lay out and match 1p coins for each article in order to find the difference in price.

Materials   1p coins if required

This page revises the phrase 'How much more?'.

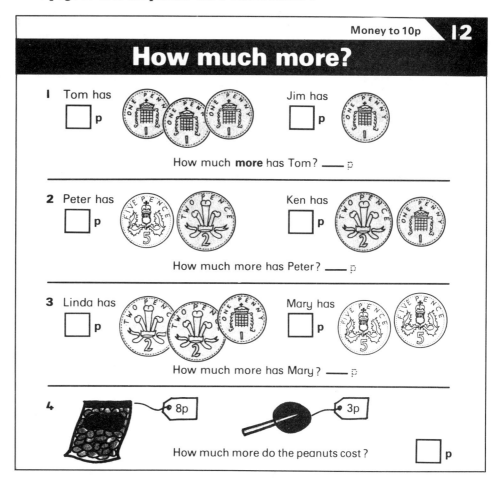

The teacher should do some preliminary teaching or revising before the children try this page.

He or she should give five 1p coins to one child and two 1p coins to another and then establish, by matching the coins, that one child has three pence more than the other. The teacher should also point out that the answer could have been found by subtraction, i.e. 5p − 2p = 3p. The teacher should do several examples like this.

Two articles could then be taken from the class shop, for example:

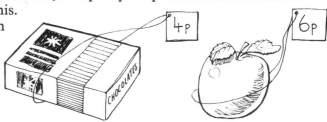

and the question posed 'How much more does the apple cost?'.

The answer should be found by subtraction, though it may still be necessary for some children to lay out 1p coins and match them to find out how much more the apple costs.

The children should now try Page 12.

In questions 1 to 3 they should write over the broken 'p'. It is important to emphasise the phrase 'How much more?' in all of the questions.

It may be worth pointing out in question 2 that although Peter and Ken have the same *number* of coins, Peter has more money than Ken. Similarly, in question 3 Mary has more money but fewer coins than Linda.

Introductory activities for Pages 13, 14

Giving change from 5p and 10p

Although giving change from 5p and 10p may have been introduced to children previously, for example in *Infant Mathematics*, Second Stage, it is possible that some children were not able to cope with this topic at that time. Consequently, this work may be new for some children.

1 Giving change from 5p

This activity should be linked to the class shop and the method of giving back change taught systematically.

It may be easiest to start with an article priced 4p and to find the change from 5p. For example:

(i) I have 5p.
4p and *what* to make 5p?
Child from the group or teacher puts out

Then proceed to articles priced 3p, 2p, and finally 1p. For example:

(ii) I have 5p.
2p and *what* to make 5p?
Child from the group or teacher puts out

As each coin is put out the child could say

'2p and 1p makes 3p'   '3p and 2p makes 5p'

As an intermediate step for some children, it may be best to put out 1p coins as change, for example:

'2p and *what* to make 5p?'

'2p and 1p makes 3p'   '3p and 1p makes 4p'   '4p and 1p makes 5p'

The next step would be:

'2p and 1p makes 3p'   '3p and 2p makes 5p'

2 Giving change from 10p

As with change from 5p, change from 10p should be revised or taught systematically. It may be easiest to start with an article priced 9p and to put out the change from 10p. For example:

(i) I have 10p.
9p and *what* to make 10p?
Child or teacher puts out

Then proceed to articles priced 8p, 7p, 6p, and so on to 1p. For example:

(ii) I have 10p.
6p and *what* to make 10p?
Child or teacher puts out and says

'6p and 2p makes 8p'   '8p and 2p makes 10p'

Difficulties will probably occur with the lower priced articles, for example:

(iii) I have 10p.
2p and *what* to make 10p?

'2p and 1p makes 3p'   '3p and 2p makes 5p'   '5p and 5p makes 10p'

Children should be encouraged to make the amount up to 5p and then to 10p.

3 Giving change from 5p and 10p

(i) The class shop could now have articles priced from 1p to 10p. The children could be given a 5p or 10p coin and asked to *select* an article from the shop, for it is important that children realise what they *can* buy with the money they have.
The 'shopkeeper' should give back the change. The 'customer' then becomes the 'shopkeeper' and so on.
If it is to be worthwhile, this activity should be supervised by the teacher to ensure that the correct change is in fact given.

(ii) The children could 'buy' their pencils (or straws or milk, etc.) with a 5p or 10p coin and the 'shopkeeper' could then give back the appropriate change. The prices could be changed from day to day.

Pages 13 and 14   Change from 5p and 10p   Money to 10p

Materials   1p, 2p, 5p, and 10p coins

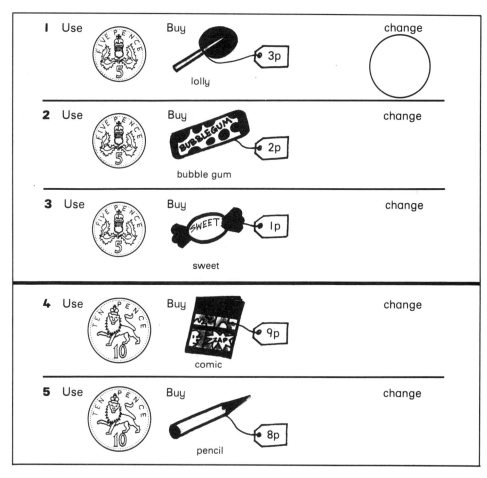

Page 13 deals with giving back change from 5p or 10p after purchasing *one* article, while Page 14 deals with change from 5p or 10p after purchasing *two* articles. The examples on giving back change from 10p on Page 13 are probably easier than those on Page 14, because on Page 13 the buying price is relatively close to 10p. For example, in question 5, Page 13, the buying price is 8p and the change 2p, while in question 5, Page 14, the buying price is 3p, and the change 7p.

As in previous pages, space has been left for the children to put out coins for change. They should draw round these coins, or write down the value of the coins, or stick gummed paper coins, in the space provided.

Additional activities

A set of shopping cards with articles priced from 1p to 10p would be very useful. Several cards for each price might be provided and they could be used in various ways. For example:

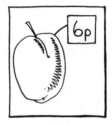 

1 The child selects a card and puts out the money for the article.
2 Two cards (total 10p or less) are selected and the child puts out the money to buy both articles.
3 The child selects a card and puts out the change which would be received from 10p if this article were bought.
4 Two cards (total 9p or less) are put out and the child asked how much the two articles cost. He or she then puts out the change received from 10p if these two articles were bought.
5 'Take 2p off', 'Take 3p off', etc. are written on the back of each card and the child asked to put out coins for the new price.
6 Two cards are selected and the child asked to find the difference in price or how much more one article costs than the other.

Number	Revision to 20	**Pages 15 to 22** **Cards 1, 3, 5, 7, 9**

Content and development

This section provides revision examples in addition and subtraction within 20. Number stories from 11 to 13 and then from 14 to 20 are revised systematically using cubes, counters and number lines as illustrations. The last two pages and the cards referenced from the end of the unit provide mixed revision examples involving totals from 11 to 20.

Examples such as $13+6 = 19$ and $18-5 = 13$ are not included, as it is felt that they need not be memorised by the children and will ultimately be tackled by the usual technique involving place value, where units are dealt with first and then tens. Additions and subtractions of this type are introduced in Workbooks 2 and 3 of Stage 1.

A number of different ways of recording addition and subtraction are used in this section. Most of these were used in the Second Stage of *Infant Mathematics: a development through activity* but they may be new to some children. Vertical settings include:

$$
\begin{array}{cccc}
14 & 15 & \square & 5 \\
-\ 6 & -\ 7 & +\ 8 & 7 \\
\hline
 & & \overline{13} & +\ 3 \\
\hline
 & & & \\
\end{array}
$$

Corresponding horizontal settings also appear:

$14-6=\square$ $15-7=\square$ $8+\square=13$ $5+7+3=\square$

Examples of the type $\square+6=12$ are also included. These were introduced for the first time on Page 4 of Workbook 1. Arrow diagrams appear on Page 21.

The pages and cards contain a variety of 'word problems'. In particular, different aspects of subtraction such as 'taking away' and 'difference between' are dealt with in this way.

Introductory activities for Pages 15 to 19

This unit deals with revision of number bonds in distinct sections as follows:

Stories of 11, 12, and then 13
Stories for totals from 14 to 20
Miscellaneous practice for totals from 11 to 20.

Suggestions for oral work, the use of practical materials, and individual activities for pupils are given below. It is likely that teachers will wish to do such work for each number story as they come to it and before the pupils start on the appropriate workbook pages. The suggestions below are all concerned with the story of 13 but the ideas can be adapted to other totals when teaching at various stages within the unit. Teachers might choose to use *some* of these ideas or to use their own as they see fit. Some teaching will be necessary to revise the ideas before pupils start on the written work. Some pupils might profit from 're-discovering' the number bonds related to 13 from a teacher demonstration using apparatus.

1 One possible method for a group lesson is to use a large sheet of paper and counting materials as follows:

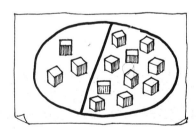

Allow the children to count out 13 cubes and place 3 of them in one part of the diagram. The other cubes are counted to establish that $3+10=13$. One cube could then be transferred to the left hand section to establish $4+9=13$ and so on until all the relevant number stories are listed.

$$
\begin{array}{ll}
3+10=13 & 10+3=13 \\
4+\ 9=13 & 9+4=13 \\
5+\ 8=13 & 8+5=13 \\
6+\ 7=13 & 7+6=13 \\
\end{array}
$$

It would be worthwhile pointing out the 'twin' facts

$$10+3=13 \qquad 3+10=13$$

and other commutative facts like these.

Subtraction stories involving 13 can be derived from the same situation by covering up or removing the appropriate number of cubes.

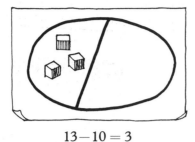
$13-10=3$

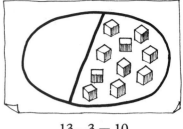
$13-3=10$

2   Other possible ways in which a teacher could revise stories include:

(i) large cardboard strips rather like Cuisenaire rods

$3+10=13$
$4+\ 9=13$
$5+\ 8=13$
and so on.

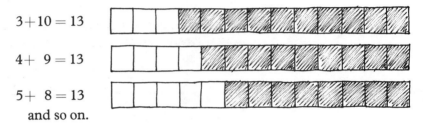

(ii) cut out cardboard figures

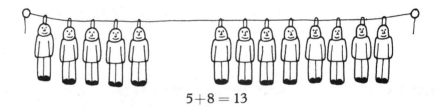
$5+8=13$

(iii) drawings on a blackboard

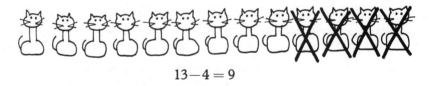
$13-4=9$

(iv) less able children might find it easier to work through 10, i.e. $7+5$ as $7+3$ and then add on the other 2. A *number line* might help them to do this.

3   A particular story could be revised with a group of children by the teacher holding up one of a set of cards with numbers on them. The children should be asked 'How many more would make 13?' (in this case 6). This would continue using each of the cards until all the 'stories' had been covered.

4   There are also a number of ways in which individual children can use practical materials to revise number stories.

(i) Unifix cubes

$10+3=13$

(ii) Cuisenaire rods

$10+3=13$
$9+4=13$
$8+5=13$
and so on.

Cuisenaire rods are particularly useful for examples of the type

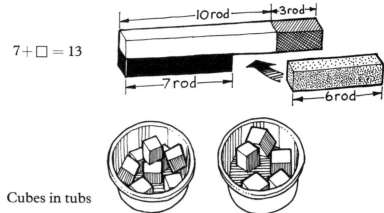

$$7 + \square = 13$$

(iii) Cubes in tubs

(iv) Matching cards could be used to revise facts without counting in ones. Answers would be self-checking because of the way the cards fit together.

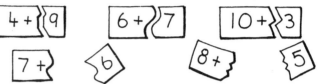

For subtraction, a different pattern of card would be needed.

| **Page 15** | **Eleven and twelve** | **Number   Revision to 20** |

Materials   cubes or counters if required

A lot of oral work is needed so that the children have speedy and accurate recall of the basic facts of arithmetic. The language used in oral work should include the various phrases which occur in the children's work:

5 and 6 make(s), give(s), equals 11
5 and what make(s) 11?
What must be added to 6 to make 11?
11 take away 6 gives 5
11 subtract 6 equals 5
and so on.

Phrases such as 'Altogether there are', 'What is the difference?', 'How many more to make?', should also be used.

The children should be asked to check the number of cubes shown at the top of question 1. They should be shown how to place a pencil to help them find the answers.

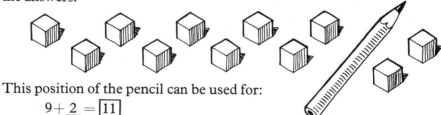

This position of the pencil can be used for:

$$9 + 2 = \boxed{11}$$
$$9 + \boxed{2} = 11$$

and $11 - 2 = \boxed{9}$ where the two cubes on one side of the pencil are covered up.

Question 1 contains most of the basic addition and subtraction facts for 11. There are, however, only three examples in each of the four different formats used in the question, i.e.

$$9 + 2 = \square$$
$$7 + \square = 11$$
$$11 - 2 = \square$$
$$\square + 8 = 11$$

Question 2 deals in a similar way with the addition and subtraction facts for 12. Questions 3 to 6 are word problems involving a variety of language and should be answered by recall of the facts for 11 and 12. Less able children could use cubes or counters to help them to answer the problems, particularly if the work is given orally.

| Page 16 | Thirteen | Number   Revision to 20 |

Materials   interlocking cubes or counters if required

As for Page 15, a lot of oral work is needed to enable children to memorise the addition and subtraction facts for 13. This oral work should include the words and phrases 'and', 'add', 'and what', 'take away', 'How many more?' and so on, which are used in the children's work.
Question 1 collects the basic facts for 13, except 10, in quartets, each of

$$+\ \underline{3}$$

which contains a pair of addition and a pair of related subtraction facts. The facts are presented in a vertical layout. The oral work should highlight each related quartet of facts. Unifix type material could be used if required.
Question 2 asks for *three* more stories for 13. The only quartet of facts not used in question 1 is that based on

$$\begin{array}{r} 10. \\ +\ \underline{3} \end{array}$$

Some children may also make use of

$$\begin{array}{rr} 11 & \text{and} \quad 12. \\ +\ \underline{2} & +\ \underline{1} \end{array}$$

However, if a horizontal layout and more general stories such as $4+6+3$ are acceptable, many answers are possible. Children could find many such stories using the cubes.
Question 3 may be done by adding upwards or downwards. In either case a form of complementary addition using '9 and what make 13?' or 'What and 9 make 13?' will probably be used. Some children may notice the pattern of the answers which will help them.
Questions 4 to 6 are illustrated word problems which use the language of difference. It is intended that they should be solved by recalling the facts of 13. Some children might answer these problems more easily if they are given orally.

Page 17	**Eleven to thirteen**	Number Revision to 20

Materials   interlocking cubes or counters if required

This page gives further practice in addition and subtraction in the range 11 to 13.
The number line at the top may be used to find the answers to all the questions on the page. The teacher could demonstrate, with the children's involvement, how the number line can be used by moving a finger along it.

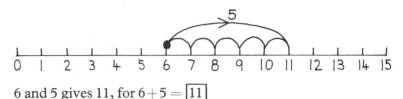

6 and 5 gives 11, for $6+5 = \boxed{11}$

13, then back 7 gives 6, for $13-7 = \boxed{6}$

Many children will find the answers to questions 1, 2, and 3 by recalling the facts and will just use the number line to check their answers.
The dartboard scores of question 4 should help children to appreciate the important 'associative law of addition'. The three numbers, added in any order, give the same total score. Some discussion of this property of the addition of numbers would be a valuable experience for children. Pam's score can be found as:

2 and 4 (which is 6) and then 5 more gives 11
or   2 and 5 (which is 7) and then 4 more gives 11
and so on.

In question 5 this same property of adding the three numbers in any order can be used both to find the answers and to check them, using a different order of adding. Less able children may need to use cubes or counters to find the answers. Again the three groups of cubes may be added in any order.

Page 18	**Fourteen and fifteen**	Number Revision to 20

Materials   cubes and number lines if required

The top section of this page deals with number pairs which add to 14 and the corresponding subtraction facts. The arrangement of examples is deliberate in that an attempt is made to associate an addition fact such as

$8+6 = 14$

with the related addition fact $6+8 = 14$ (emphasising once more the commutative nature of addition) and the two related subtraction facts

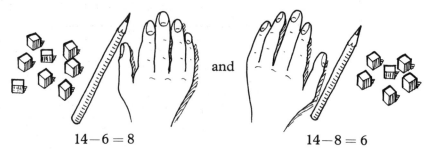

14−6 = 8   14−8 = 6

Using cubes in this way would be a suitable introduction to this page. Some children may need to use concrete materials or partition the 14 cubes drawn on the page. Others will be able to do the examples by mental recall. Number lines are used to introduce a similar revision of number stories about 15 in the lower half of the page. The largest number line can be used as an aid when finding answers to the examples at the foot of the page. When doing an example such as $15−6 = \square$, the pupils could find 15 on the number line and then count back 6 to reach the answer 9.

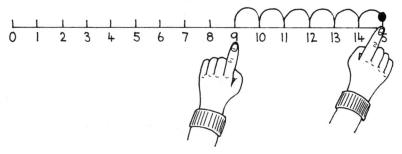

Teachers may wish to provide some less able pupils with duplicated sheets of number lines so that they can use a new number line for each example. More able children should have memorised these addition and subtraction facts and should be able to do the page without using cubes or number lines. Some teachers may wish to give pupils more practice with the stories of 14 and 15 before moving on to Page 19. Suggestions for extra practice are given below.

Additional cards and worksheets – stories of 14 and 15

1 The two cards shown below would provide extra practice in addition and subtraction involving 14 and 15. The format shown is that of a 'window card' where a piece of paper is placed between the folded halves of the card and answers are written on the paper through the slots. The paper can be removed after correction and a fresh piece inserted for the next pupil.

8 + 6 =	15 − 6 =	10 + 4 =	14 − 10 =
10 + 5 =	15 − 8 =	5 + 9 =	14 − 4 =
8 + 7 =	14 − 7 =	6 + 8 =	15 − 9 =
9 + 6 =	14 − 5 =	7 + 8 =	14 − 6 =
7 + 7 =	15 − 10 =	6 + 9 =	14 − 8 =
9 + 5 =	14 − 9 =	4 + 10 =	15 − 7 =

Paper to be inserted between the two 'halves' of the card.

2 The four worksheets shown below give further practice with the stories of 14 and 15 but the recording format is more difficult. Such sheets might provide varied practice for more able children.

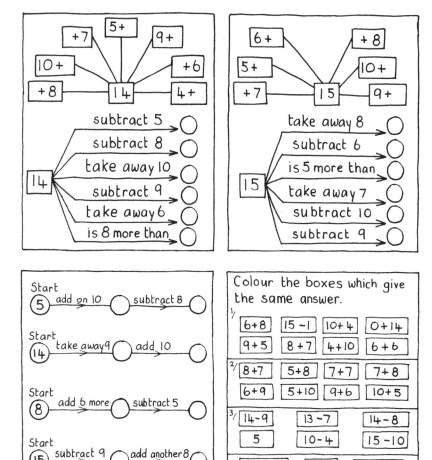

Materials counters, interlocking cubes or other counting materials if required, number lines if required

The stories of 16, 17, 18, and 19 are covered here in a similar way to those on Page 18. Counters, Unifix cubes, and number lines are used to illustrate some of the number facts. Some pupils may need to use such apparatus or alternative concrete counting material. Again it is hoped that as many children as possible will do the examples by mental recall.

For children who do use counters to help them with the examples in question 1 it might be worth providing a cardboard sheet showing a partitioned set or two separate sets on which they can rearrange the counters.

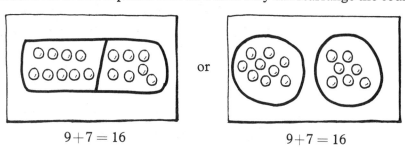

9+7 = 16   9+7 = 16

In question 2 the illustrations show Unifix cubes being used, with the different coloured cubes indicating the numbers being added and subtracted. The arrangement shown can be used to emphasise commutative pairs such as $7+10 = 17$ and $10+7 = 17$, and to show that the subtraction $17-7 = 10$ is related to the addition $7+10 = 17$.

The examples on this page are given in vertical format. This one can be read as 'Ten and what make sixteen?' or 'What do we add to ten to give sixteen?'.

$$\begin{array}{r} \Box \\ +\,10 \\ \hline 16 \end{array}$$

The remaining number facts for 20, $10+10 = 20$ and $20-10 = 10$, appear as examples among the mixed revision of Pages 20 and 21.

Additional worksheets – stories of 16 to 20

Some teachers may wish to provide additional worksheets or cards giving practice in addition and subtraction with totals of 16 to 20 before going on to the more general revision of Pages 20 to 23. The ideas used for stories of 14 and 15 on pages 34 and 35 are also suitable for 16 to 20. A few more sample worksheets are given below.

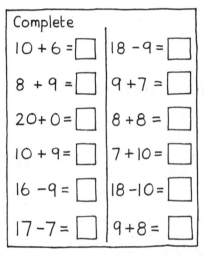

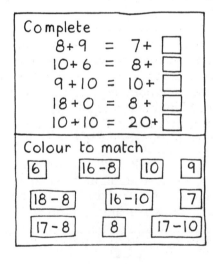

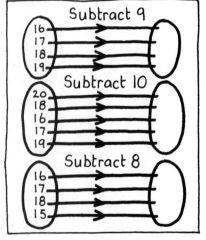

Page 20   **Stories 14 to 20**   Number   Revision to 20

Materials   counting materials or number lines if required

The top part of the page provides further revision examples in a vertical setting for the number facts covered in Pages 18 and 19. Cubes or other counting materials should be available for those children who have difficulty recalling the number stories.

The bottom part of the page contains a mixture of different types of 'word and picture' problems. Question 2 deals with 'taking away' while questions 5, 6, and 7 deal with the 'comparison' aspect of subtraction, using the phrase 'How many more?'. Pupils having difficulty with this type of example could lay out cubes or counters and line them up to represent

17 mice

and   9 mice

They can then count the extra ones in the top row to find that Ian has 8 more mice than Peter.

The remaining two questions, 3 and 4, are both about addition involving the use of the word 'more'. Some oral work in which the teacher lays out 6 cubes and then adds 9 'more' would help pupils having difficulty with the words used.

Page 21   **Stories 11 to 20**   Number   Revision to 20

Materials   counting materials if required

This page provides further practice in the addition and subtraction stories already dealt with on Pages 15 to 20. Two particular types of example are involved. The top half contains 'arrow' diagrams which allow the repeated addition or subtraction of the same number. Some pupils may have to be reminded to look back at the instruction at the top of the diagram and to carry it out for *each* number in the set. Pupils who have used *Infant Mathematics: A development through activity* should be familiar with this type of recording.

The lower half of the page gives practice in addition of three numbers. In most cases, the first two numbers which the children add give a total of 10 or less no matter whether they add from the top 'down' or the bottom 'up'. This allows them to use the number stories they should have memorised when adding on the third number. There is one exception to this, a total of 11 where the third number to be added is 1.

Some children may find it useful to write an intermediate total beside their sum after adding the first two numbers.

$$\begin{array}{r} 7 \\ 3\ _8 \\ +5 \\ \hline \end{array}$$

Page 22   **Problems**   Number   Revision to 20

Materials   counting materials if required

The examples on this page provide further revision in number bonds from 11 to 20 but concentrate on the phrases 'difference between' and 'How many more?'.

For question 1, some children may have to lay out counters or use a number line if they cannot remember the appropriate number facts. For $7 + \square = 16$ they could lay out 7 counters and then find how many more were needed to make 16.

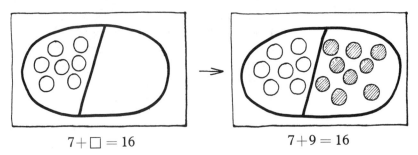

$7 + \square = 16$ $7 + 9 = 16$

Cuisenaire rods are also useful for this type of example. Questions 2 and 3 are similar to the 'How many more?' examples on Page 20 and could be treated in a similar way.

Questions 4, 5, and 6 use the phrase 'difference between'. Pupils who have difficulty with this should compare the sets in questions 4 and 5 by joining pairs of objects and then count the 'extra' objects in one of the sets.

It is important that the children are made aware that the answers to the 'difference' problems can be found by subtracting. The children should do the workcards referenced at the foot of Page 22 at the teacher's discretion.

Number cards 1, 3, 5, 7, 9   Revision to 20

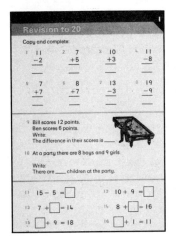

These five cards all have similar layouts and contain questions of comparable difficulty, so they may be done in any order. Each card gives practice in addition and subtraction for numbers from 10 to 20. Questions 1 to 8 consist of a mixture of additions and subtractions all of which are presented in a vertical format. Questions 9 and 10 are word problems (often illustrated) which are more difficult because of the variety of language and ideas they contain. For example:

He needs ____ more to make 20.
Sue is ____ years older.

The children are expected to write and complete each coloured answer sentence. Less able children would probably need to have these problems read and explained to them.

The third section of each card comprises six questions in horizontal layout. The variety in these questions makes them more difficult than the eight questions in the first section of each card.

Additional activities for revision to 20

1 Stories cards   These cards could be displayed in the classroom and used in regular oral sessions.

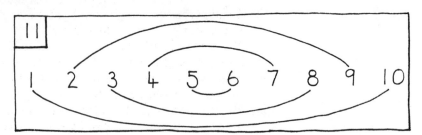

The card above summarises the basic addition and subtraction facts to be memorised for 11.

$$10+ 1 = 11 \qquad 2+9 = 11 \qquad 3+8 = 11$$
$$1+10 = 11 \qquad 9+2 = 11 \qquad 8+3 = 11$$
$$11- 1 = 10 \qquad 11-2 = 9 \qquad 11-3 = 8$$
$$11-10 = 1 \qquad 11-9 = 2 \qquad 11-8 = 3 \qquad \text{and so on.}$$

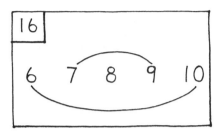

This card summarises the basic facts for 16. Some teachers may prefer cards which summarise *more* than just the basic facts.

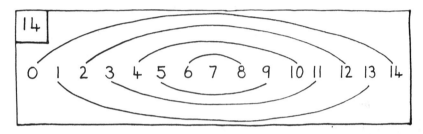

Answers to
$$2+12 = 14 \qquad 14- 2 = 12$$
$$12+ 2 = 14 \qquad 14-12 = 2$$
can be obtained by 'counting on' or 'counting back'.

Some children may have sufficient understanding of the place value aspect of, for example, 12 as $10+2$, and of the fact that numbers may be added in any order, to see that $12+2$ is $10+2+2$ which gives 14.

2 Flashcards A range of flashcards could be made and used in regular oral work with the children.

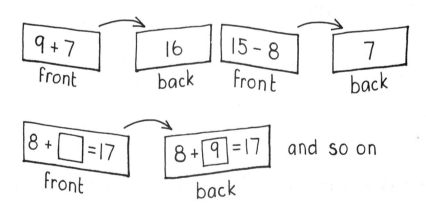

3 Oral work (i) Doubles, for example, $7+7$, and near doubles, for example, $7+8$, which can be thought of as 1 more than double 7 or as 1 less than double 8.

(ii) Examples involving 9 which can be done mentally by adding or subtracting 10 and adjusting the answer by 1. For example, $9+6$ thought of as $10+6$, which is 1 more than the correct answer 15. Also, $17-9$ thought of as $17-10$, which is 1 less than the correct answer 8.

(iii) Place value ideas, for example, 14 is thought of as $10+4$, so $14+3$ is $10+4+3$, which gives 17.

(iv) Working through 10 in two steps, so that $7+5$ is thought of as $7+3+2$, which is $10+2 = 12$. Also, $8+\square = 14$ can be found as $8+\boxed{2+4} = 14$.

4 Window cards Window cards could be made to suit both vertical and horizontal layouts.

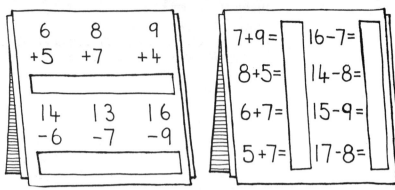

5 Games A game using prepared number cards will motivate some children. An appropriate set of 12 cards which are used in pairs would be:

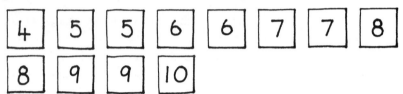

The teacher or a child should hold up two cards and ask for the total. Alternatively, the teacher could call out a total, say 17, and a child would respond by holding up two cards, for example:

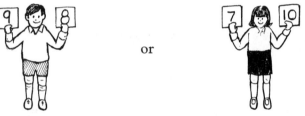

or

A suitable set of twelve cards which are used in threes would be:

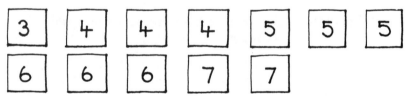

The cards should be placed face down and picked up at random.

The children should be asked to write down the numbers and find the total each time. These sets of cards could be used by an individual child or by a small group of children. In this case the cards could be laid out face down and two cards or three cards turned over. The children should record each result and the results could be checked later.

$$\begin{array}{r} 7 \\ +6 \\ \hline 13 \end{array} \quad \text{or} \quad \begin{array}{r} 6 \\ +7 \\ \hline 13 \end{array}$$

6 Dice   Dice, which give practice in adding and subtracting two numbers, could be made.
One cube should be marked 4, 5, 6, 7, 8, 9 and another marked 5, 6, 7, 8, 9, 10.
These could be thrown to give random additions with totals from 9 to 19.
This could also be done using cards with numbers on them.
Another pair of cubes, one marked 17, 16, 15, 14, 13, 12, and the other 3, 4, 5, 6, 7, 8, could be thrown, and the subtractions recorded.

$$\begin{array}{r} 14 \\ -6 \\ \hline 8 \\ \hline \end{array}$$

Teachers whose schools have been using *Infant Mathematics: A development through activity* will find cards in the Second Stage *Teacher's Materials Pack* appropriate for revision of addition and subtraction to 20.

| **Number** | Numbers to 100 | **Pages 23 to 25** |

Content and development

This section deals with numbers in the range 20 to 100. It is assumed that the children have had some experience of recognising, reading, writing and ordering these numbers. Also the children are expected to be able to count sets of more than 20 objects. Work of this nature is provided in the Second Stage of *Infant Mathematics: A development through activity*.
Pages 23 and 24 of the workbook provide revision of these important aspects of number work.
For the questions on Page 25 the children have to be able to read number names from 'twenty' to 'one hundred'. For many children this will be new work.

Introductory activities for Page 23

Before asking the children to do Page 23, the teacher should take the opportunity to carry out some revision of the numbers to 100. At this stage, a child should be able to recognise a given number, name it, and write it down correctly. Also, the child should be able to name the number after or the number before any specified number. For this the child must have some knowledge of order within the range of numbers to 100.
Much of the revision will be oral, although it can be accompanied at any time by practice in writing the numbers. The following suggested activities may be useful for revision purposes. A number strip or number line which clearly displays all the numbers from 1 to 100 would be useful here.

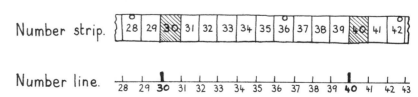

It is advised that the decade numbers, 20, 30, 40, etc., should be shaded or coloured to highlight each range of ten numbers. This also helps the children to locate numbers more easily and, apart from anything else, helps the visual presentation of such a long row of numbers.

Cards 10 to 13 of the Stage 1 *Teacher's Materials Pack* can be cut and assembled to form a complete number line.

Activities

1 The teacher points to the actual numerals or sequences of numerals on a number line or number strip and the children have to say the name of each numeral as indicated. The children should listen to patterns of names and should realise that the sequence of names 'one, two, ... nine' is used over and over again. Common oral sequences are:

   (i) twenty, twenty-one, twenty-two, ... twenty-nine, followed by thirty, thirty-one, thirty-two, ... thirty-nine
  (ii) ten, twenty, thirty, ... ninety, one hundred
 (iii) twenty-one, thirty-one, forty-one, ... ninety-one.

Practice can also be given in writing these sequences of numbers, at first by copying from the number line or number strip and later without reference to the teaching aid.

2 The teacher can name a number, for example 'thirty-four', and ask a child to point to it. The child may also be asked to point to and name the number before thirty-four and the number after thirty-four.

These activities can be made more difficult by obscuring one or several numbers, for example:

'Which number is hidden?'

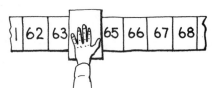

'What is the number after 63?'
'What is the number before 67?'
'Write down the missing numbers'.

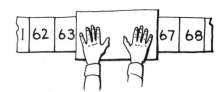

3 Although the numbers 1 to 100 are displayed in order and questions like 'What is the number after twenty-four?' require a knowledge of order, it is worthwhile testing the child's ability to arrange numbers in their correct order. Suggestions for this include:

  (i) Drawing 'dot pictures' by joining up a sequence of numbers correctly.

  (ii) Sorting into the correct sequence number cards which have been spread out at random.

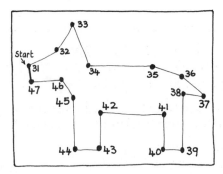

(iii) Picture puzzle cards can be made by the teacher (or the children) and these can cover various ranges from 1 to 100. When the parts are fitted together in their correct order a complete picture is formed.

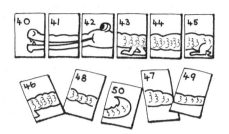

Page 23	**Missing numbers**	Numbers to 100 Revision

Materials   none

For questions 1 and 2 on this page the children must recognise and complete sequences of numerals. Some children may still need to use a number strip (or number line) for reference.

In questions 3 and 4 the children are given a number and have to write down 'the number before', 'the number after', or both.

The final two questions are exercises in ordering sets of numbers. This is done by joining numbered dots in the correct order to complete a simple picture.

Introductory activities for Page 24

There are only five counting activities provided on Page 24 and it is advisable to give the children the chance to do some counting, preferably using real objects, before doing the page. As well as counting the number of objects in a given set, the children should be asked to put out, count out, or even draw sets which contain specified numbers of objects. Because of the larger numbers involved, it is easiest to use small objects such as marbles, straws, pencils, rubbers or pegs. Classroom containers like boxes, bottles and jars are also useful, and counting might often be into or out of such containers.

An advantage in using real objects for counting is that during the counting process the child can arrange the objects into tens or fives. For example, the eleventh object (or the twenty-first, etc.) can be placed as the start of another group of ten while the child is counting. This makes it easier to check or recount the total.

Here are some possible introductory counting activities:

1 Containers are provided in which there are a number of objects. The child counts the objects and records the totals. As a check the objects can be counted as they are returned to the container.

2 The teacher might ask the children to put out certain numbers of objects. Simple instructions (oral or written) could be:

'Put out 30 straws'
'Make a wall using 25 bricks'
'Count out 40 pegs'
'Put 28 pencils in the box'.

3 Drawing and painting activities can involve counting larger numbers. For example:

> 'Draw 21 apples on the tree'
> 'Draw a garden with 32 flowers'
> 'Draw a snake with 28 spots'.

Apart from these activities, there are many day to day opportunities for counting. For example:

> 'How many children are in class today?'
> 'How many cards are in the pack?'
> 'How many dominoes are in the box?'
> 'How many words are written on the blackboard?'

Page 24	Counting	Numbers to 100 Revision

Materials   none

This page provides five sets of objects to be counted by the children. The squares, triangles, and apples may be numbered by the children as they count. For example:

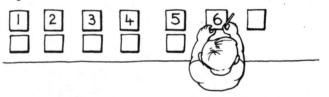

Alternatively, each object may be ticked or crossed off as it is counted.

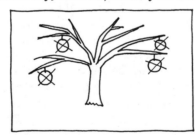 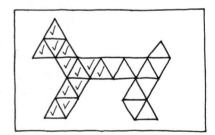

This makes the counting easier as it reduces the likelihood of omitting one item or counting one more than once.

Question 3 shows birds arranged in twos. It is hoped that the teacher will show some children that they can count the birds in twos by saying 'two', then 'four', then 'six', etc. An intermediate step might be to say 'two', 'four', 'six', etc. more loudly, though still reciting every number. Other exercises, such as counting eyes, hands, feet or ears in the class, will give further practice in counting in twos.

Introductory activities for Page 25

Children may have had previous experience of reading number names from 'one' to 'twenty', for example in *Infant Mathematics: A development through activity*. On Page 25 of this workbook there are exercises which require the children to read number names in the range 'twenty' to 'one hundred'. Each of these number names has to be recognised and matched to its appropriate numeral. It can then be associated with the set containing the correct number of objects. The following teaching suggestions may be helpful in dealing with these new number names.

1 Flashcards   A set of flashcards with the number names 'twenty', 'thirty' ... up to 'one hundred', and a set with the number names 'one', 'two' ... up to 'nine' would be very useful for this work.

twenty	thirty	forty	fifty	sixty	seventy	eighty	ninety	hundred
one	two	three	four	five	six	seven	eight	nine

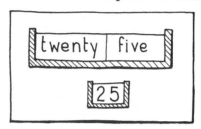

By selecting one card from each set the teacher can present any name between 'twenty' and 'one hundred'. A pocket or board on the wall to display the pairs of cards would be useful. The display might also include the numeral. The children could put the cards in the display themselves or could be asked to complete the display when some cards are missing.

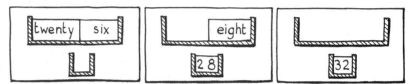

Children find most difficulty in reading the 'ten' words, that is 'twenty', 'thirty', etc.; they are already familiar with the words 'one' to 'nine'. The teacher may wish to concentrate on one decade of numbers at a time, so the children can practice one particular 'ten' word.

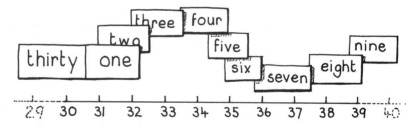

2 Oral work   Much of this number name work can be done orally. The teacher could hold up a number name and ask questions like: 'What does it say?', 'Find the correct number for this name', 'Write the number', 'Point to this number on the number line'. Conversely, the teacher may point to a number and ask the children to find the correct name.

Page 25   **Number names**   **Number names to 100**

Materials   coloured pencils

In question 1 all the answers can be seen on the given number line and it might be helpful for some children to refer to a number line or strip while doing the rest of the page.

For the work on this page the children must be able to read each number name correctly and write or recognise the appropriate numeral.

Length

Pages 26 to 32
Cards 11, 13, 15, 17, 19

Content and development

Two major stages in the development of length are covered in this section. Initially the activities are designed to develop the qualitative aspect of length. The work is concerned with the language involved in the simple comparisons of pairs of objects and the ordering of more than two objects. Later, the children deal with length quantitatively. They are introduced to the idea of measurement using arbitrary standards such as rods, straws, cubits, spans, the length of a foot, and sticks.

The language involved in this topic is extensive and the selection included here – long, short, tall, thick, thin, high, low, wide, narrow – has been chosen to consolidate the children's experience in earlier classes. Those children who have used *Infant Mathematics: A development through activity* should be familiar with most of this language. It should be possible to cover this ground fairly rapidly and if desired additional vocabulary can be introduced. Much of the work with arbitrary standards will be new to the children. These introductory experiences of measurement are important and some time should be spent on them. An important aim is to recognise the need for a conventional standard (the metre) and this will be used as the starting point for the next section on length which appears in Stage 1, Workbook 3.

It should be noted that these major stages, language and arbitrary standards, are paralleled in the developments of weight, area, and volume.

Introductory activities for Pages 26 to 28

Much of the language associated with length which occurs in these pages will already have been encountered by the children. Nevertheless, prior to any teaching associated with individual pages, it would be well worth while involving the children in practical activities designed to cover the range of language in the workbook.

1 Comparison of two objects

Initial activities could be limited to the direct comparison of two objects with discussion using the appropriate vocabulary. Some examples are given below:

(a) A ruler and a pencil could be compared, one being described as 'short' and the other as 'long'; one is also 'longer than' or 'shorter than' the other. Such pairs of objects can be laid on a desk and labelled using cards thus:

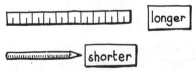

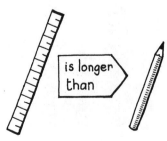

This anticipates the diagrams which appear in the workbook pages.

An alternative arrangement might be:

(b) A picture could be drawn on the blackboard and the children invited to draw in arrows meaning 'is higher than' or 'is lower than'. This could be followed by a discussion of the position of some classroom objects, for example, 'The door handle is lower than the light switch'.

(c) A set of objects could be sorted. For example, if several objects are compared to a straw for thickness then the sorting might look like this:

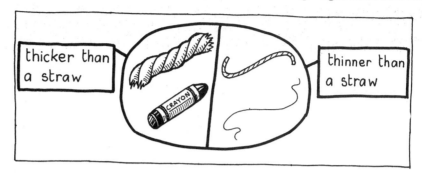

(d) *Teacher's Materials Pack* Cards 28 and 29 provide a game involving the comparative language of length.

2 Ordering of three or more objects

(a) The above activities could be extended to include the ordering of three or more objects, again using the appropriate vocabulary in discussion. The teacher might compare the width of a cupboard with other widths. The cupboard may be 'narrower than' the blackboard or the window but 'wider than' the classroom door; the window may be 'widest' or 'broadest' and the door may be 'narrowest'.

(b) Three objects could be set out on a desk and labelled using cards thus:

Again, this anticipates the diagrams which appear in the workbook pages.

(c) A picture could be drawn on the blackboard and the children asked to label it appropriately. The children could also make drawings of their own and label them:

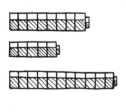
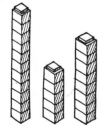
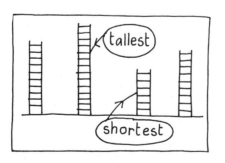
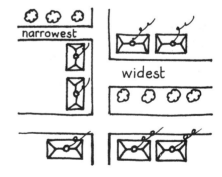

(d) Interlocking materials could be laid out and discussed, using 'is longer than', 'is shorter than', 'longest', and 'shortest'. The material can then be rotated and the language becomes 'is taller than', 'is shorter than', 'tallest', and 'shortest'. This more subtle use of language may be difficult for some children. Only with experience over a period of time will they become confident in the choice of words.

(e) A group of children might be asked to carry out a comparison of their own foot lengths. This could be done by drawing round the outside of the foot, cutting out the foot shape and ordering a set of such shapes on a display chart. Discussion including 'longer'/'shorter', 'longest'/'shortest', and possibly 'is about the same length as' should follow.

Page 26	**Comparing**	Length Language

Materials   crayon

For each activity on this page the child must make a perceptual comparison between two objects. The vocabulary covered includes 'long', 'longer', 'short', 'shorter', 'tall', 'taller', 'thick', 'thicker', 'thin', 'thinner', 'high', 'higher', 'low', 'lower'. In questions 1, 2, and 4 the child must *record* the appropriate word and this is an important aspect in developing vocabulary. It is equally important that the child *hears* the words and is given the opportunity to *use* them. Consequently preliminary discussion should take place with the children before they attempt the questions.

Questions 1, 2, and 3 are concerned with 'taller' and 'shorter'. Note that the objects in each pair differ in one aspect – length or height – only, for example, the pencils differ in length but not in thickness.

Questions 4 and 5 are concerned with the relations 'thicker than' and 'thinner than'. Appropriate objects, for example a telephone directory and a notebook, should be used to emphasise these relations. In question 5 the effects of thick writing and thin writing can be achieved using a crayon and a pencil.

The relations 'higher than' and 'lower than' are used in question 6 and many children will require guidance concerning the required form of recording. A blackboard drawing like Figure 1 could be used and the position of the children on the stairs discussed using statements such as 'Jim is lower than Mary' or 'John is higher than Mary'. When arrows meaning 'is lower than' are added to give Figure 2, the teacher should emphasise the direction of the arrows. Some discussion of relative positions of objects in the classroom should also take place.

Figure 1

Figure 2

Additional workcards

The following cards could be prepared and used to supplement the work of Page 26.

These cards could be varied considerably, for example, 'things shorter than my pencil', 'things thinner than my desktop', 'things higher than the bookshelf'.

Page 27	**Longest, shortest, tallest**	Length Language

Materials   each child's own pencil, crayon, and shoe

On the previous page, comparative terms only were considered. Now the children have to compare three objects at a time and so use superlatives like 'longest', 'shortest', and 'tallest'. Inevitably these words will have been used in the past and it should be possible for the children to do Page 27 without much prior discussion with the teacher. A little guidance may be helpful, however. In question 2 each child has to work with two friends. The teacher may decide to determine the trios in advance. In question 3 it may happen that one child has both the longest shoe *and* the longest pencil. The diagram might then look like this:

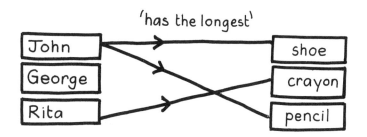

In question 4 the children are given pictures of three objects, each differing from the others in one dimension, height, only. They have to identify the tallest and shortest objects out of the three and label them appropriately. The extra requirement compared to similar questions on Page 26 is that the children have to attach the labels to the objects by drawing lines.

Should the teacher wish to give some follow-up work using superlatives a workcard on the following lines could be prepared:

---

1 Work with the others in your group.
  Who is tallest?
  Who is shortest?
  Write some sentences about the heights of your group

2 What is the highest part of your classroom?

3 What is the lowest part of your classroom?

This card allows practical comparison and ordering based on the children's heights. It forces the use of the word 'height' if this has not occurred previously. If help is needed with the sentences, the teacher might make some initial suggestions, for example, 'John is the shortest', 'Ann is taller than Graham'. The card also anticipates the use of the superlatives 'highest' and 'lowest' which appear on Page 28.

Page 28	Widest, thickest, highest	Length Language

Materials none

A range of comparative terms was used on Page 26 and some of these were extended to their superlatives on Page 27. The other comparative terms are now extended giving the superlatives 'thickest', 'thinnest', 'highest', and 'lowest'. To begin with, however, some new language is introduced – wide, wider, widest, narrow, narrower, narrowest. It is suggested that some preliminary discussion should take place before the children use the new language in questions 1, 2 and 3. A possible approach would be to draw three or more rectangles which have the same length but a different width, as shown below:

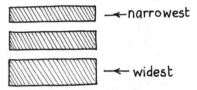

These rectangles could be discussed, making full use of the new language, which should then be applied to objects in the classroom. It seems inevitable in any such discussion that other language will be used – broad, broader, broadest, breadth, width, length – and this should be encouraged. The rectangles should now be re-arranged as shown:

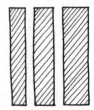

This new arrangement could lead to discussion about the heights of the rectangles and which is tallest. They are, of course, all the same height but now they differ in width. The apparent inconsistency in language will no doubt lead to some difficulties and children should not be expected to cope immediately with the subtle differences in meaning. They should, however, be made aware of the vocabulary used in such situations and, through time and with further experience, they should gain confidence in using the appropriate terms.

The remaining questions, 4, 5, and 6, require the children to record the terms 'widest', 'narrowest', 'thickest', 'highest', and 'lowest'. Questions 4 and 5 use the familiar matching format of Pages 26 and 27 and little difficulty should be encountered. The use of H (for highest) and L (for lowest) in question 6 may require discussion.

A possible follow-up workcard is as follows:

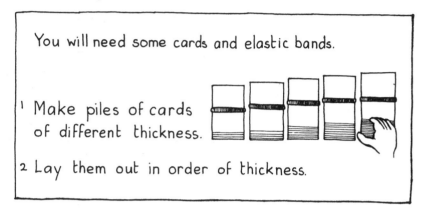

You will need some cards and elastic bands.

1 Make piles of cards of different thickness.

2 Lay them out in order of thickness.

To gain maximum benefit from this workcard, the teacher should discuss the order which the child creates. Questions such as 'Which pile is thickest?' and 'Which pile is thinner than this one?' could be asked.

| **Page 29** | **Comparing lengths** | Length Comparing |

Materials scissors and string

All the comparisons carried out in Pages 26 to 28 have been 'visual' and have involved only the pairs of objects being compared. On this page the comparisons remain 'visual' but the idea of using an intermediate object to facilitate the comparisons is introduced. In questions 1 and 2 the children have to find objects in the classroom 'narrower than', 'wider than', and 'about the same width as' the door. This is achieved by cutting a piece of string to match the width of the door and then comparing other objects with the piece of string. It is suggested that the children work in pairs. The teacher may wish them to work in groups. Whatever organisation is adopted, the children should be given clear instructions. They should also be told to record lengths as '*width* of the blackboard' or '*height* of my desk' and not merely as 'blackboard' or 'desk'.

Children completing questions 1 and 2 should be able to proceed without teacher intervention to questions 3 and 4. Although these questions again concern direct comparison, they also introduce an important new idea. The children are asked to *guess* if an object is longer or shorter than a pencil before the direct comparison is made. This will lead in Workbook 3 to the important idea of estimation.

Some teachers may prefer to do some group or class work before letting the children move on to questions 3 and 4. If so, the children could be asked to guess which objects in the classroom are 'longer than', 'shorter than' or 'about the same length as' an object such as the blackboard pointer. A check by direct comparison could then be made and one or two tables of results, like those in questions 3 and 4, written on the blackboard.

Page 30   Rods and straws   Length   Arbitrary standards

Materials   about twelve rods (Cuisenaire orange or multibase 'tens' or similar), about ten drinking straws, string, two paper clips (note: it must be possible for the string to slide easily through the straws)

Length   Arbitrary standards   **30**

Rods and straws

Work with a partner. You need rods.

> The length of my desk top measures about 6 rods.

1 Guess first and then measure with rods.

Object	Number of rods	
	My guess	My measure
Length of my desk		
Length of my atlas		
Length of the table		
Length of my schoolbag		

2 Complete: The **longest** object is _____

The **shortest** object is _____

On Page 29 the children were introduced to the idea that direct visual comparison of lengths can be difficult or even impossible. One method of dealing with such a situation was introduced. Now, on Page 30, another method is used. This involves laying a supply of identical objects (units) end to end alongside *each* length to be compared. The numbers of identical objects used are then counted: the higher count indicates the longer length. This important idea should be introduced by the teacher as a class or group lesson. Certainly, some preliminary discussion of the word 'measure' will be necessary.

Questions 1 and 2 require the measurement of four lengths using rods. It may well be possible to decide the longest and shortest objects before using the rods and if so question 2 should confirm whether or not this preliminary decision was correct. Note that the children are asked to guess the number of rods in each length before measuring. This again anticipates the important idea of estimation to be associated with the metre in Workbook 3.

Questions 3, 4, and 5 repeat the pattern of questions 1 and 2 but this time the children construct a crude measuring instrument to measure four 'widths'. The straws are strung together and each end is secured with a paper clip, producing a simple measuring 'tape' which should prove easier to handle than a supply of loose straws.

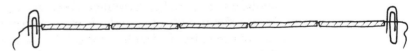

In these measuring activities the problem of the 'extra' length that will not 'fit' will arise. At this stage children should be encouraged to use phrases such as 'and a bit', 'just over', 'just under', 'nearly', and 'about' in their recording. For example, '2 and a bit rods' or 'about 2 rods' or 'just over 2 rods'.

Page 31   **Cubits, spans, and feet**   Length   Arbitrary standards

Materials   cardboard (two different colours), scissors, sticky tape

On Page 30 lengths were compared using a supply of identical objects as measuring units. It is obviously possible to measure a single length using this method, the length being expressed as a number of the identical objects. The identical objects can then be adopted as standard units. This important idea of a standard for measuring lengths should be discussed with the class or group before they are asked to tackle the work of Page 31 which is based on the use of parts of the body as arbitrary measuring units.

For questions 1 and 2, groups or pairs of children can make their own 'measuring tape' by cutting strips of card to match the cubit of a chosen child. The strips are then joined using sticky tape, alternating the colours as shown:

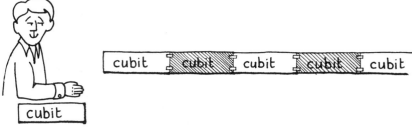

For questions 3 and 4, similar 'measuring tapes' could be made for 'spans' and 'feet', but it is suggested that measurement in spans is carried out by alternately placing hands along the objects to be measured and measurement using feet can be by the 'heel-to-toe' method.

Throughout this page the problem of the 'extra' length that will not 'fit' should be dealt with as in Page 30.

Page 32   **More measuring**   Length   Arbitrary standards

Materials   about twelve sticks approximately one metre in length (note: a stick could be dowelling, garden cane, stiff card or even an unmarked metre stick)

In questions 1 and 2 the children have to measure four lengths using their spans. The lengths have been chosen to make visual comparisons difficult, so to answer question 2 it is likely that the measurements taken in question 1 will have to be used. The cartoon illustrates the method of alternately placing 'spans' along the length to be measured. Note that this question requires the individual child to use his or her own span, whereas on Page 31 the span of only one child may have been used to construct the 'measuring tape' used by a whole group.

In questions 3 and 4 another step is taken in developing the children's measuring skills. Firstly, in question 3, the children use sticks which are set end to end alongside the lengths being measured; the sticks can then be counted. Secondly, in question 4, the children measure using a *single* stick repeatedly. If some children have difficulty using a single stick they could be allowed to use *two* sticks which can be set alternately end to end.

It is useful to have sticks which are approximately one metre in length, for two reasons. Firstly, it allows the children to measure long lengths which would require very large numbers of rods, spans, etc. Secondly, it anticipates the introduction in Workbook 3 of the first conventional standard, the metre. Indeed, even at this stage, some teachers may wish to refer to these as 'metre sticks'.

The children should do the workcards referenced at the foot of Page 32 at the teacher's discretion.

Length cards
11, 13, 15, 17, 19   Language and arbitrary standards

The work on these cards extends that on Pages 26 to 32 of the workbook. The order of working is not important. However, it should be noted that although no new language is introduced, the work with arbitrary standards introduces the measurement of curved lengths and links length with graphs, as well as giving further experience of measuring.

Card 11   Comparing Ann and Sue

Materials   large sheet of plain paper, coloured pens

The activity on this card requires the use of some comparative vocabulary – thicker, longer, wider, shorter, and taller. The children are given two simple sketches as shown to copy. They then add arms, legs, and so on, which are specified as thicker, longer, etc. in either Ann or Sue. It is suggested that the plain paper be A4 in size and that it be used in the position shown. Most children would enjoy colouring in the completed figures.

Card 13   Comparing houses

Materials   none

This card is also concerned with language, this time mainly superlative words – tallest, narrowest, widest, thickest, highest, lowest. The comparative words 'wider' and 'narrower' are also used. The children have to write out eight sentences about the dimensions of a row of houses. This may be too much for some children and the teacher should decide how much is appropriate for each child. Indeed, for some children it may be better to use this card as a basis for discussion. In question 9, some children may not have a 'high' and a 'low' window in their own house. They could use a relative's house if suitable, or the classroom, or some well known local building such as a church.

Card 15   Arm lengths

Materials   string, scissors, wallchart paper, glue

Clearly, by its nature, much of the work in measurement is practical. An important aspect of such practical activity is the recording of results. On this card the children work in groups and cut string to measure their arm lengths. They are shown a possible form of recording and are asked to produce a similar chart using the data gathered within their own group. Finally they are asked to complete sentences about the information displayed in their chart.

Card 17   Length round things

Materials   scissors, string (or tape or paper streamer), two large sheets of paper

Like Card 15, this card is concerned with recording the results of a practical activity. The work on the card also introduces the children to the comparison of curved lengths. Initially the children have to cut a piece of string 'so that it measures round your wrist'. If desired, the teacher could use the term circumference for the length around a curved object, for example, the circumference of a wrist. In questions 1 and 2 the children work in pairs to make it possible for them to make the measurements and cut the string. Each child now has pieces of string measuring his or her wrist, ankle, and neck circumferences. In question 3 it is possible for each child to make a chart similar to the one on the card.

For questions 4 and 5, the children should be put into groups. Each child cuts string to measure his or her chest circumference. The lengths of string are then pooled and used to make a 'poster' entitled 'Our chests'. When the children have completed the graphs in questions 3 and 5 they could be asked to write about their graphs. For example, appropriate sentences for question 5 would include:

The length around Bill's chest is the longest.
The circumference of Mary's chest is longer than Ann's.
The distance around Ann's chest is the shortest.

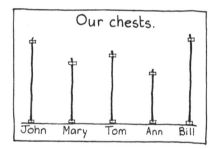

Some teachers may prefer not to use the word circumference in this connection.

Card 19   Heel to toe

Materials   none

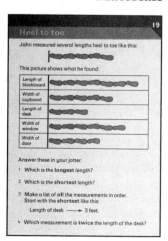

Like Cards 15 and 17, this card is concerned with data recorded as a result of practical measurement. This time, however, the children are *given* a pictograph (showing lengths of classroom objects measured in foot lengths) and they are asked to interpret it. Children should be encouraged to write answers fully, for example they should write 'length of blackboard' for question 1 and not just 'blackboard'.

Additional workcards

Some teachers may wish to give individual children more opportunity to measure using their own spans, cubits, and foot lengths as in question 1 of Page 32. The following cards could be made as a number of individual cards or, with suitable modification, combined together to make a single worksheet. Note that these cards extend further the variety of recording methods already used by the children.

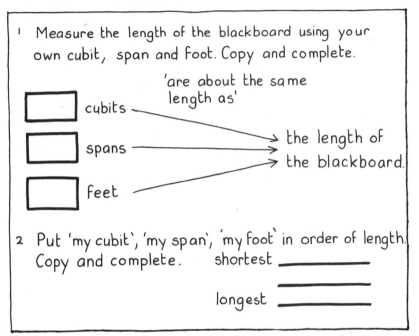

Clearly the objects being measured can be varied, for example the width of the window, the length of the table, the width of the cupboard, and so on. An alternative recording for question 1 might be used:

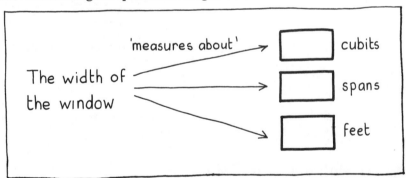

Time   Pages 33 to 37

Content and development

This section revises and consolidates earlier work which is included in most infant courses. Such work on time is introduced in *Infant Mathematics: A development through activity*, Second Stage.
In particular the revision deals with:

1 the ordering of events in a daily routine using the words 'before', 'after', 'first', 'last', and the sequence 'morning, afternoon, evening and night'
2 the reading and writing of clockface times with emphasis on 'o'clock' and 'half past'

3 the days of the week as a repeating cycle, together with the words 'today', 'tomorrow', and 'yesterday'.

The work is extended by including:

1 the duration of events from 'start' to 'finish'
2 the words 'earlier', 'later', 'fast', and 'slow' in relation to clockface times
3 the idea of 'just before' and 'just after' specific times.

Further work on time occurs in Stage 1, Workbook 4.

Page 33	**Our day**	Time Order of events

Materials   none

This page deals with some words which are associated with the order of events. In their daily lives, both in and out of school, the children should have heard and used a range of words related to the order of events. The children now have to be able to read these phrases and to understand them. The words on the page, 'before', 'after', 'first', 'last', 'morning', 'afternoon' and 'night', should be well known to the children.

The teacher could prepare the children for the page by discussing some relevant time sequences with them. Discussion about the order of dressing for school and undressing for bed would prepare them for question 1. What they do in an ordinary school day from the time they get up until they go to bed would help them with the other questions.

After some general discussion, flashcards similar to those shown for Jill's day could be made. They could perhaps be augmented by cards for

breakfast , play , tea , and so on. These cards could be used to

make ordered sequences. In questions 3 to 6 the children are expected to answer by writing the appropriate caption, for example 'gets up', for each pictured event.

Introductory activities for Pages 34 and 35

1 The teacher should use a large real clock (or a plastic model with gears) to show how the hands move round in the direction indicated by the numbers: 1, 2, 3 . . . . 12.

2 The hands should be moved slowly to show that the long (minute) hand moves faster and further than the short (hour) hand. The minute hand goes from 12 right round to 12 while the hour hand only moves from one number to the next.

3 A real or geared clock should be used to show how each hand moves as time passes. Starting at 3 o'clock, the hands could be moved slowly round while the features which are needed by the children at this stage are pointed out.

At 3 o'clock the minute hand points to 12 and the hour hand points to 3.
Just after 3 o'clock the minute hand has passed 12 and the hour hand has just passed 3.

At half past 3 the minute hand has gone half-way round and points to 6 and the hour hand points half-way between 3 and 4.

Just before 4 o'clock the minute hand is approaching 12 and the hour hand is very nearly at 4.

Some teachers may prefer to deal with each hand separately. Commentary on one full turn of the minute hand could be followed by commentary on the corresponding movement of the hour hand. A cardboard clock with removable hands is supplied in the *Teacher's Materials Pack*, Card 26. To prepare the children for Page 35 the terms 'hour hand' and 'minute hand' will have to be used rather than the more informal 'short hand' and 'long hand' which were used earlier.

4 The children should be involved in a lot of oral work dealing with both 'telling the time' and 'setting the hands to show a time'. The teacher could tell a story using a lot of different times and as the story progresses, the children have to put the clock to each correct time. Alternatively the teacher could put the clock to each time and the children have to give the time as each part of the story is told.

5 The oral work should extend the language of time. Morning, afternoon, evening, night and even noon (midday) and midnight are important at this stage. This vocabulary will bring in the fact that there are two cycles of 12 hours (twice round the clock) in a whole day of 24 hours.

6 A clockface stamp could be used to make a set of cards (24 cards would give good coverage) showing the kind of times used on Pages 34 and 35.

Matching labels would be needed.

These cards, or selections from them, would give the children some useful 'matching' and 'ordering' activities.

7 It is important that 'telling the time' should be related to events in the child's day. Drawings could be made or pictures used for a wall display associating events with time.

Materials   none

The introductory activities outlined above should provide adequate preparation for the work on this page.

In question 1 the children have to write the time shown on each clockface. The cartoon pictures are intended to make the work more interesting. The teacher could use the pictures to ask questions such as 'What is happening at 1 o'clock?' and 'At what time were the children painting?'. This could be part of the discussion after children have completed the page.
The abler children could be asked to write the story shown by the times and the pictures.

3 o'clock   **after 3 o'clock**   **before 4 o'clock**   **4 o'clock**

These four clockfaces from the middle of Page 34 show part of the sequence of movement of the hands which is recommended in part 3 of the introductory activities. It is important to emphasise 'just before' and 'just after' certain o'clock times.
Questions 2 and 3 give written practice on this aspect. Telling the time in this way is fairly common. The hands of a clock are frequently 'just after' or 'just before' an exact o'clock time. The phrase 'coming up to' is often used instead of 'just before' and 'just past' instead of 'just after'.

Materials   none

The teacher should check if a child is able to attempt this work by selecting appropriate cards and labels for the child to match from the set suggested in part 6 of the introductory activities. Questions 2 and 3 refer to the hands, for the first time, rather more formally as the *minute* hand and the *hour* hand. This may prove to be an added difficulty for some children.
The cartoon pictures in question 4 allow questions such as 'What is happening at half past 4?' and 'At what time did John get up?'. The abler children could be asked to write the story of John's day shown by the pictures. Questions 5 and 6 require the children to write a phrase or sentence. These questions should help children to realise that a complete day from midnight to midnight consists of two 12-hour circuits by the hour hand of a clock.

Introductory activities for Page 36

The ideas on this page will require very careful teaching. An understanding of the passage of time, the duration of events, and the concept of an interval of time, takes a long time to develop.
1 The teacher could draw the children's attention to a clock at, say, 2 o'clock

and then from time to time until 3 o'clock. In this way children should come to realise that an hour is a long time. This activity should be repeated on different days and at different times. Children have to know that from 2 o'clock to 3 o'clock takes one hour and also from 12 o'clock to 1 o'clock and so on.

2 Using a real clock (or a geared model clock) the teacher could set the hands at, say, 2 o'clock, then move them slowly to 3 o'clock which is one hour later, and then to 4 o'clock which is another hour later. After some discussion the children should come to realise that from 2 o'clock to 4 o'clock takes two hours.

The abler children, particularly, should be made aware of durations of time which 'bridge' 12 o'clock. From 11 o'clock to 12 o'clock takes one hour and from 12 o'clock to 1 o'clock takes another hour.

The other ideas on Page 36 are one hour before, one hour after, one hour earlier, one hour later, and clocks being 'fast' or 'slow'. Most of these ideas should be within the everyday experience of the children.

3 The teacher could set the clock to show, say, 3 o'clock and then ask what the time was one hour before 3 o'clock and then what the time will be one hour after 3 o'clock. Able children should also deal with half an hour before and after given times.

Flashcards $\boxed{\text{I hour before}}$ $\boxed{\text{I hour after}}$ could be made. One child sets the clock to an o'clock time and another child picks a flashcard, says what the new time would be, and adjusts the clock accordingly.

4 School starting one hour later than 9 o'clock or finishing one hour earlier than 4 o'clock should be within the children's experience. Going to bed and getting up both earlier and later could also be used to clarify their understanding. Again, half an hour earlier and later should also be considered by able children.

5 The idea of a clock being 'fast' or 'slow' is a difficult one for some children. A careful explanation will be needed, perhaps along the following lines. When a clock does not show the correct time it is said to be 'fast' or 'slow'. A clock which is 'fast' shows a time ahead of the correct time. If the correct time is 2 o'clock, a clock which is one hour fast will show 3 o'clock.

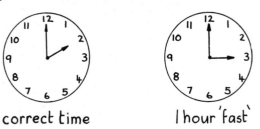

correct time   I hour 'fast'

Similarly, a clock which is 'slow' will show a time behind the correct time. If the correct time is 2 o'clock, a clock which is one hour slow will show only 1 o'clock.

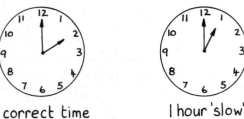

correct time   I hour 'slow'

Children should be asked to set a clock to show one hour fast and one hour slow for different correct o'clock times. Questions could be asked such as 'If the clock is one hour fast, what time does it show when we start school/finish school?' and so on.

6 Children will require a lot of oral work based on the kind of questions on Page 36.

Page 36   **Problems**   Time   Duration and language

Materials   none

This page is probably best suited to children who have good reading ability. Other children will have to be given the work orally.

In questions 1 and 2 the 'starting' and 'finishing' times have been restricted to o'clock times so that the durations are a whole number of hours. Children should be reminded to count on in hours from the starting time to the finishing time. In question 1 a step by step demonstration may be needed. From 4 o'clock to 5 o'clock is one hour and from 5 o'clock to 6 o'clock is another hour, so John walked for two hours. In questions 3 to 6 it is necessary to read the time shown on each clockface before answering each question. The introductory activities recommended above for this work would allow most children to make a reasonable attempt at the questions.

Additional activities for Page 36

1   A clockface stamp could be used to make a set of graded cards on the duration of time from 'start' to 'finish'.

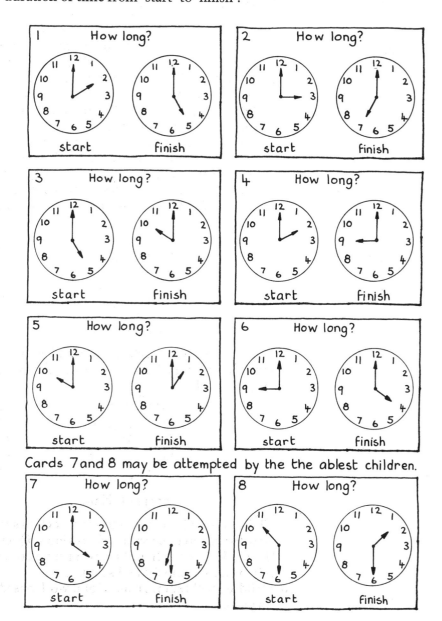

2 Further practice on the time one hour 'before' and 'after' and one hour 'earlier' and 'later' could be provided on worksheets like these.

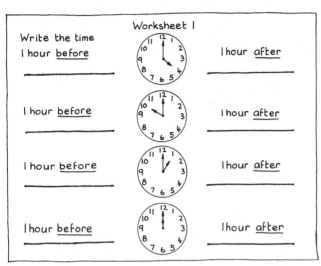

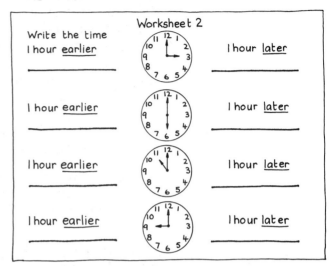

3 Worksheets or cards could provide further work on clocks which are 'fast' and 'slow'.

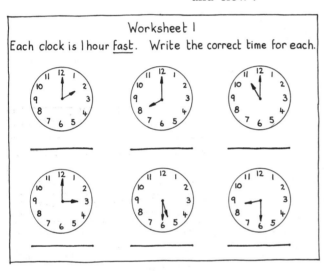

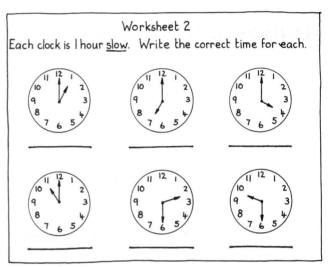

Page 37   **Days of the week**   Time   Days of the week

Materials   none

This page revises the days of the week. This should be ongoing throughout the year and is included in most courses for infant schools. *Infant Mathematics: A development through activity*, Second Stage deals with this work. The language involved means the children have to be good readers. Many more children could do the work if it were given to them orally. Flashcards showing the days of the week as well as day before day after yesterday today tomorrow would be useful in preparatory work. The days of the week cards could be placed in a circle to highlight the repeating nature of the cycle.

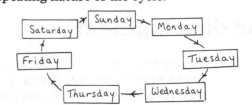

The sequence of the days can be started at any day. One or more of the cards could be turned over and the children asked to name the 'hidden' days. The introductory oral work should include all the words and ideas the children will need to know before they attempt the page. One child could choose any day card, for example ⎢Tuesday⎥, and other children select the correct cards for ⎢day before⎥ and ⎢day after⎥.

Similar work should be done using pairs of cards

|today| |tomorrow|

|Saturday| ?

and later ⎢yesterday⎥ |today|

? |Friday|

The names of all of the days of the week appear somewhere on the page so the children should be encouraged to check that they have written their answers correctly.

Additional activities for Page 37

1 Recording each day on a prepared card.

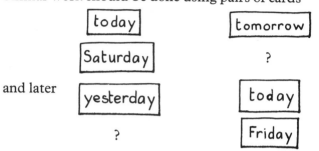

2 Changing a wall-chart daily.

3 Keeping daily absences.

4 Writing each day in a diary or exercise book.
Today is _____.

Solid shapes   **Pages 38 and 39**
Cards 2, 4, 6, 8, 10, 12, 14, 16, 18, 20

Content and development

During their first two infant school years most children will have been encouraged to sort, build with, and name solid shapes using junk material such as cartons, tubs, tins, boxes or shapes obtained from educational suppliers. Those children who have used *Infant Mathematics: A development through activity*, Second Stage will have become familiar with cubes, cuboids, cylinders, and cones.

Work involving these four shapes is found in Pages 38 and 39 of this workbook and in Workcards 2 to 20 (even numbers). This work is also extended to include the sphere, egg-shape, and triangular prism. The work continues to be informal, but includes comparison of rolling shapes and non-rolling shapes, reference to faces, stability, components of composite shapes, and the nature and number of component parts, and early experience of the conservation of mass and volume.

The work is developed further in Workbook 4 when the faces of solid shapes are dealt with.

Introductory activities for Pages 38, 39 and Cards 2 to 20 (even numbers)

Before children are asked to do Pages 38 and 39, the teacher should provide all the lettered shapes which will be required – see materials listed for Page 38 of the workbook, on page 65 of the *Teacher's Notes*.

Children should be given an opportunity to handle the shapes and to sort them. Here are one or two possible ways of sorting into two sets:

  (i) a set of shapes that roll and a set of shapes that do not roll
 (ii) a set of shapes with *only* flat faces and a set of *other* shapes (This will produce the same two sets as in (i) above.)
(iii) a set of shapes that can roll in a straight line and a set of shapes that cannot roll in a straight line
(iv) a set of shapes with no corners or edges (sphere and egg-shape) and a set of the *other* shapes.

Children might be chosen to *roll* the sphere, the egg-shape, the cylinder, and the cone and this could trigger off a good deal of useful discussion during which the following points should emerge:

  (i) the sphere rolls and may also be spun on the spot
 (ii) the cylinder can be made to roll in a straight line
(iii) the cone rolls too but in a *circular* path
(iv) the egg-shape rolls in a 'wobbly' manner and tends to move in a circular path. This might lead to a discussion of some seabirds' eggs which, because of their more conical shape, roll round in a small circle and are thus prevented from rolling off a cliff ledge!

Although children's ability to *name* the shapes is perhaps not the first priority, the teacher should ensure that they get to know the correct name of each solid. Names such as 'sphere' and 'triangular prism' will be quite new to most, if not all, children. Young children usually like using new words and there is an advantage in their being able to refer, without ambiguity, to specific shapes: a 'round shape' might refer to a cylinder, a sphere or a cone but a 'cylinder' refers to a specific shape.

Further discussion should focus on the different kinds of flat faces that the solids have: the circle face of the cylinder and cone, the square faces of the cube and of *some* cuboids, the rectangle faces of cuboids, and the triangle *and* rectangle faces of the triangular prism.

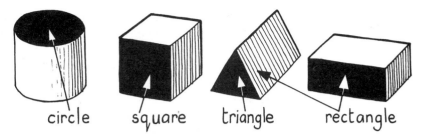

circle   square   triangle   rectangle

Children should appreciate that *some* cuboids may have square faces as well as rectangle faces but in the case of a cube *all* the faces are squares. It is, of course, true that the set of squares is a sub-set of the set of rectangles but the writers have decided that for children involved with *Primary Mathematics: A development through activity*, a rectangle *with all sides equal* is referred to as a square.

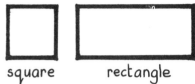

square   rectangle

Similarly, cuboids with *all* of their faces square are referred to in this course as *cubes*.

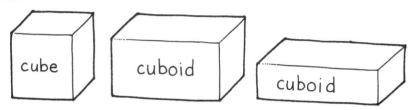

cube   cuboid   cuboid

Children should also appreciate that some of the solid shapes have curved surfaces, for example the sphere, egg-shape, cylinder, and cone. This could lead to wider discussion about other curved surfaces, for example the surfaces of bottles, balloons, arms, and legs.
In this way the children's vocabulary is enriched and their awareness of shape in the environment fostered.

Page 38   Sorting shapes   Solid shapes   Sorting

Materials   one or more boxes containing shapes which are clearly lettered. Each box of shapes should contain the following:

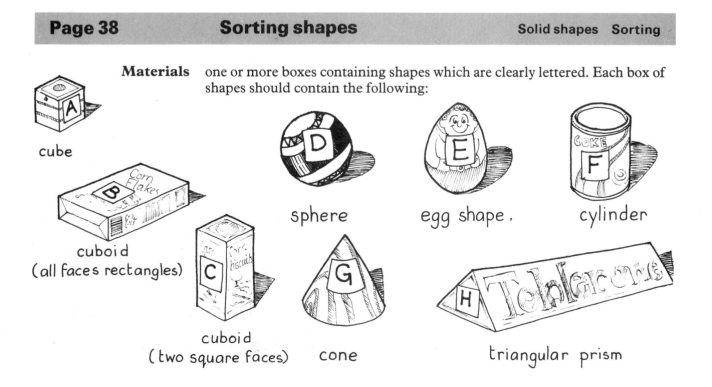

cube

cuboid
(all faces rectangles)

cuboid
(two square faces)   cone

sphere   egg shape.   cylinder

triangular prism

Note: B and C could be empty cartons or boxes, D could be a small ball, F could be a soft drink can, H could be a 'Toblerone' chocolate packet.
    A plastic or wooden cone would be best since it has to be rolled.

Each box should be used by a small group of children. The number of groups working on Page 38 at any given time will depend on the material available.

It is essential that children be allowed to handle actual shapes. They should not be asked to complete the page as a 'pencil and paper' exercise without having first worked with actual shapes.

In response to question 1, children should make a set of shapes that roll, comprising sphere, egg-shape, cylinder, and cone – that is the shapes with curved surfaces

and a set of shapes that do not roll, comprising cube, cuboids, and triangular prism – that is the shapes having *only* flat faces.

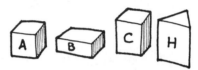

Question 2 should give the 'straight line' set, comprising cylinder and sphere

and another set, comprising egg-shape and cone.

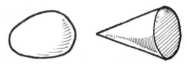

Question 3 should result in the same two sets obtained for question 1 since the shapes which do not roll are the same as those having only flat faces. Teachers may find it worthwhile to consolidate the ideas covered so far by discussing the answers for this page after it has been completed.

Page 39	**More sorting**	Solid shapes Sorting and naming

Materials   one or more 'shapes boxes', each box containing the following shapes:

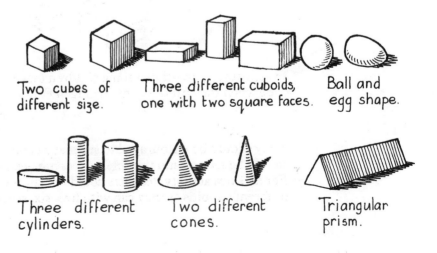

Two cubes of different size.

Three different cuboids, one with two square faces.

Ball and egg shape.

Three different cylinders.

Two different cones.

Triangular prism.

Each box should also contain a name card to match every solid, for example cuboid , cylinder .

Each box should be used by a small group of children. Again it is stressed that children should not be asked to complete the page as a 'pencil and paper' exercise but that they should have access to the actual shapes.

Shape cards 2, 4, 6, 8, 10 12, 14, 16, 18, 20   Solid shapes

These cards provide further experience of solid shapes in an informal context. They may be tackled in any order.

Card 2   Cuboids

Materials   a 'cubes box' containing eight small, identical cubes and three larger cubes of different sizes

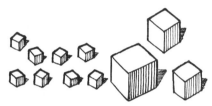

Note: Tillich or Cuisenaire cubes would do but they are on the small side for young children to handle and cubes a little larger would be preferable.

Although the three larger cubes are not required for this workcard, they *are* required for Workcard 4. Teachers may prefer to have separate boxes for Workcards 2 and 4, one containing only the eight identical cubes for Workcard 2 and the other with the three larger cubes as well to be used with Workcard 4.

The children should find that the four cubes may be arranged to make cuboids in different ways, for example:

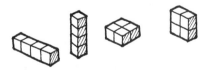

In attempting question 5 some children may think that they have made a cube when they produce this arrangement:

They should be encouraged to see that a cube shape requires that *all* faces should be *squares* and that *eight* cubes are needed.

For an extra activity, teachers could ask children to try making as many different cuboids as they can with five, six, seven, or eight cubes.

Card 4   Cubes and towers

Materials   a 'cubes box' as described in the notes for Workcard 2

This card involves children in:

  (i) ordering by size
 (ii) building a stable arrangement of cubes
(iii) building an unstable arrangement of cubes

Teachers should encourage general discussion about loads on lorries, high walls, factory chimneys, etc.

Card 6   What shape?

Materials   a 'shapes box' as described in the notes for Page 39 of the workbook

This card is concerned with a 'lucky dip' kind of activity which, as well as being fun, leads to worthwhile experience of the shapes. For example, a child can only identify a cylinder by feeling its rounded surface and its flat faces which are themselves identified as circles by feeling round the circular edges. This activity might also take the form of a game with two teams of, say, three players who take it in turn to feel and identify shapes.

Card 8   Twin shapes

Materials   a 'twins box' containing pairs of identical shapes as follows:

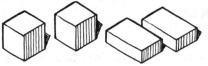

two cubes   two cuboids   two cylinders two cones

This is an informal activity which highlights the nature of cubes, cuboids, cylinders, and cones. The children should discover that:

(i) two cubes do not make a cube shape since all faces of the composite shape are not squares

(ii) two identical cuboids fit together to make another cuboid

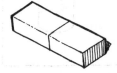

(iii) two identical cylinders fit together to make another cylinder

(iv) two cones fit together to make an interesting composite shape which is not a cone.

It is, of course, true that in the case of the cuboids and cylinders the two shapes which are put together need only have the same cross-section, that is, the faces which are placed together must be identical but the lengths of the two original shapes may be different.

Teachers might wish to discuss this point with the children or even consider the situation where there are not any faces which can be matched. In this case composite shapes result which are *not* cuboids or cylinders.

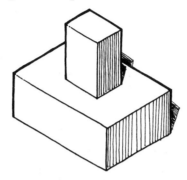 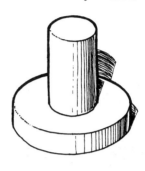

Card 10   Towers

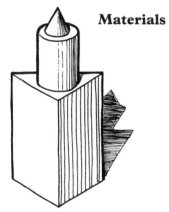

Materials a 'shapes box' – see notes for Page 39 of the workbook

In this card the children build a tower. This is a straightforward activity but one which should help children to appreciate that:

(i) cones will only sit *on top* of the tower

(ii) spheres and egg-shapes are not used for building towers since they have no flat faces.

Card 12   Rocket

Materials a 'shapes box' – see notes for Page 39 of the workbook

In this activity children have freedom to choose their own building shapes. Any composite model which looks rocket-like is acceptable.
The children are not expected to produce adult-standard, '3D' drawings.

Card 14 　　Names and numbers

Materials　a 'shapes box' – see notes for Page 39 of the workbook

This activity helps to consolidate children's ability to name shapes correctly and to recognise the written form of these names.

Card 16 　　A church

Materials　a 'shapes box' – see notes for Page 39 of the workbook

This activity is similar to that of card 12. The children have freedom to select their own shapes. Models with or without steeples are acceptable but the child must name correctly each shape which is used to make the model.

Card 18 　　Changing shapes

Materials　plasticine, small pieces of hardboard or short rulers for patting and rolling the plasticine

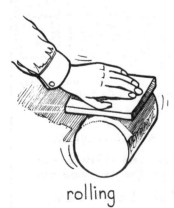

rolling

In this activity the child should start with one lump of plasticine and make with it, in turn, the four different shapes. At any given moment the child will have *only one* shape. The activity provides informal experience of conservation of mass and volume.

Each shape, in turn, has the same mass, weight and volume as its predecessor, since the same lump of plasticine is used for each shape. Children should discover that a ruler or small piece of hardboard makes the creation of a cylinder quite easy. Rolling the plasticine back and forth, then patting to achieve flat faces soon produces a recognisable cylinder.

patting

Card 20   Naming shapes

Materials   plasticine, small pieces of hardboard or short rulers for patting and rolling the plasticine

This activity helps to consolidate knowledge of solid shapes and their names. Its value, however, lies also in experiencing properties of the shapes through *making* the shapes. A child who has patted a ball of plasticine to make reasonably square faces and then a sausage of plasticine to make rectangular faces probably appreciates the difference between a cube and a cuboid better than a child who has only handled and looked at cubes and cuboids.

Something like a cone can be made with a little practice, starting with a cylindrical lump and rolling it to a point between the outer edges of the hands.

Teachers might follow up this work with discussion about what happens when plasticine solids are sliced through. In fact some actual slicing might be done. Children could consider, for example, which solids would result when cubes, cuboids, cylinders, and cones are sliced through.

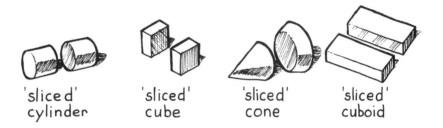

| 'sliced' cylinder | 'sliced' cube | 'sliced' cone | 'sliced' cuboid |

Additional workcards

These six workcards could provide further useful activities for some children. A supply of small cubes is the only material necessary. Tillich or Cuisenaire cubes would do.

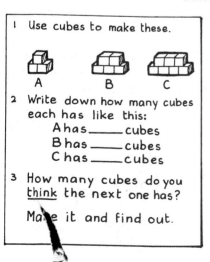

1 Use cubes to make these.

A   B   C

2 Write down how many cubes each has like this:
A has_____cubes
B has_____cubes
C has_____cubes

3 How many cubes do you think the next one has?

Make it and find out.

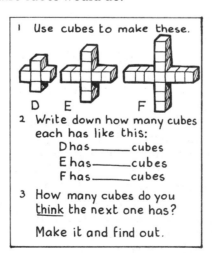

1 Use cubes to make these.

D   E   F

2 Write down how many cubes each has like this:
D has_____cubes
E has_____cubes
F has_____cubes

3 How many cubes do you think the next one has?

Make it and find out.

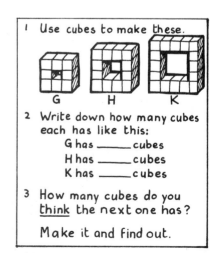

1 Use cubes to make these.

G   H   K

2 Write down how many cubes each has like this:
G has_____cubes
H has_____cubes
K has_____cubes

3 How many cubes do you think the next one has?

Make it and find out.

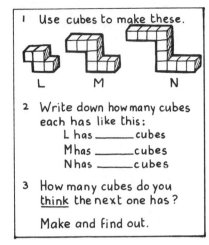

1 Use cubes to make these.

L M N

2 Write down how many cubes each has like this:
   L has _____ cubes
   M has _____ cubes
   N has _____ cubes

3 How many cubes do you think the next one has?

Make and find out.

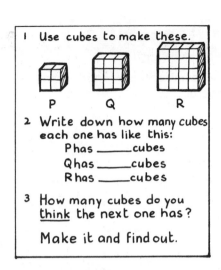

1 Use cubes to make these.

P Q R

2 Write down how many cubes each one has like this:
   P has _____ cubes
   Q has _____ cubes
   R has _____ cubes

3 How many cubes do you think the next one has?

Make it and find out.

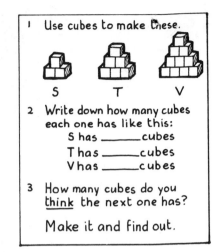

1 Use cubes to make these.

S T V

2 Write down how many cubes each one has like this:
   S has _____ cubes
   T has _____ cubes
   V has _____ cubes

3 How many cubes do you think the next one has?

Make it and find out.

The six workcards could be tackled by less able pupils who will look, build, count, probably *guess* the answer to question 3, and finally make and count as instructed. More able children should be encouraged to look for a number pattern and try to *think* what the next number of cubes would be in answer to question 3. They are then able to check by making the next one.
The number patterns for the numbers of cubes are:

A, B, C ..... $\longrightarrow$ 3, 5, 7, 9, 11 .....
D, E, F ..... $\longrightarrow$ 5, 9, 13, 17, 21 .....
G, H, K ..... $\longrightarrow$ 8, 12, 16, 20, 24 .....
L, M, N ..... $\longrightarrow$ 4, 7, 10, 13, 16 .....
P, Q, R ..... $\longrightarrow$ 4, 9, 16, 25, 36 .....
S, T, V ..... $\longrightarrow$ 3, 6, 10, 15, 21 .....

Additional activities

To help consolidate the children's ability to recognise and name solid shapes, here are two games and other possible activities.

1 Snap This is a game for 2, 3, or 4 players. The 24 cards are dealt so that each child starts with 12, 8, or 6 cards as the case may be. The cards are kept face down in the player's hand. Each player in turn places a card face up on the table. When two consecutive cards appear with the same shape or shape name, the first player to call 'Snap' takes all the cards on the table and adds them to the bottom of his or her hand.
The game proceeds until one child has all the cards or until a set time limit is up, when the child with most cards is declared the winner.
On page 73 are two possible sets of cards. Other selections of four different shapes could also be made up.

2 Sets The 24 cards could also be sorted by an individual child or by a small group of children, all the cube pictures and cube name cards forming a set, all the cone pictures and cone name cards forming another set, and so on.

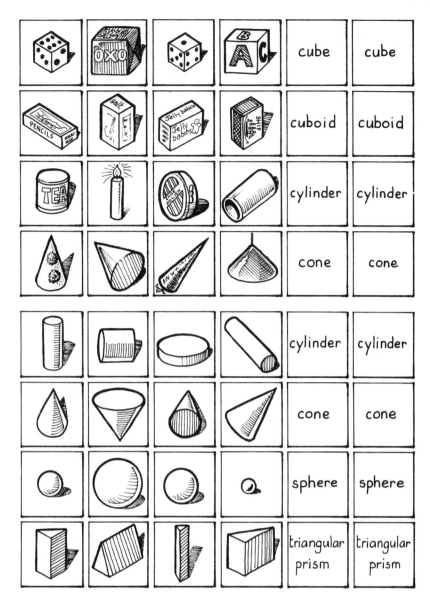

				cube	cube
				cuboid	cuboid
				cylinder	cylinder
				cone	cone
				cylinder	cylinder
				cone	cone
				sphere	sphere
				triangular prism	triangular prism

3 Solid shapes dominoes

This is a game for 2 or 4 children. It is played like ordinary dominoes. The set of 28 dominoes are:

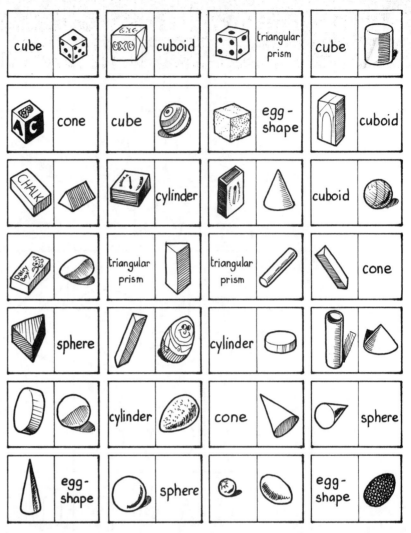

4 Looking for shapes in the environment

Children should be encouraged to look for examples of solid shapes in the world around them and to talk about these solid shapes. For instance, there are many examples of cylindrical shapes which are seen in everyday life: pencil, milk straw, circular biscuit tin, can containing soup, fruit or soft drink, petrol tanker, oil drum, chimney, boat funnel, garden roller, and so on.

5 Class 'shape books'

Children could contribute pictures, drawings or writing to a class book of solid shapes. For example, the book might have a picture of a garden roller cut from a gardening catalogue and have the accompanying writing: 'A garden roller is a large cylinder'.

Stage 1   Workbook 2

rkbook 2

...ion to Workbook 1, at any one time groups of children within the class can ... ...ons of the work. It is not intended that the children work through all the numb... ...pting any of the measure and shape pages. Individual circumstances with respect to c... ...isation and availability of materials will affect the order in which the work is attempted by grou... ...hildren.

In Workbook 2, the part on number work forms several natural sections.

Pages 1 to 5	Money work to 20p
Pages 6 to 11	Place value to 99
Pages 12 to 19 and	Addition of tens and units
Workcards 21, 23, 25, 27, 29	
Workcards 31, 33, 35, 37, 39	Addition puzzles and patterns
Pages 20 to 22	Money work to 99p

After any one of these sections is completed, children could try any of the other sections on area, weight or shape. It is not advised that every child should attempt all the work on every page or workcard. The more able children can be guided quite quickly through the revision and practice work but, at the same time, the less able should not spend excessive time on some piece of number work and thus be prevented from tackling measure and shape work.

A certain amount of material is required which should ideally be collected before work starts on this workbook. This applies particularly to structured apparatus for place value and addition of tens and units.

Teachers are again reminded that, in general, preliminary teaching is necessary before workbook pages and cards are attempted.

Contents

Materials

Plastic, cardboard or real coins (1p, 2p, 5p, 10p, 20p, 50p)

Counting materials such as beads, cubes, pegs, buttons, straws, and elastic bands

Structured number material: tens and units; notation cards

Coloured pencils, squared paper, flashcards for new words, scissors, glue

Two-pan balance

Objects for weight table including tins marked A, B, C, D, etc. and a piece of wood

Marbles, thread reels, chalk sticks, wooden cubes, etc.

Plastic bags   Sand, peas, sawdust   Egg-cup

Cardboard or plastic squares, circles, rectangles, triangles, pentagons, hexagons

The teaching notes for each page list the specific materials required and offer suggestions for alternative materials where appropriate.

The following items from the *Teacher's Materials Pack* will be useful for this workbook:

Notation cards 1 to 100	Card 5
Addition picture	Card 8
Number line to 100	Cards 10, 11, 12, 13
Money dominoes	Cards 21, 22, 23
Shopping cards	Cards 24, (23), (13)
Money game	Card 25
Shape game	Card 31
Shape cards	Cards 32, (26), (13)

Money to 20p   Pages 1 to 5

Content and development

Money to 10p was revised and consolidated in Stage 1, Workbook 1.

Children may have already had experience in money to 20p, for example in *Infant Mathematics: A development through activity*, Second Stage, where activities included finding the value of collections of coins, putting out coins for certain prices up to 20p, addition and subtraction activities to 20p, and giving back change from 15p and 20p.

This work is revised and consolidated in *Primary Mathematics*, Stage 1, Workbook 2. Emphasis is placed on finding the value of collections of coins and laying out amounts following an addition or subtraction activity. The introduction of the 20p coin provides new work and the final two pages of this money section deal with giving back change from the 20p coin.

Further work on money to 99p occurs in Pages 20 to 22 of this workbook.

Page 1   How much?   Money to 20p

Materials   1p, 2p, 5p and 10p coins if required

Before trying this page, the children should have worked on finding the totals of collections of coins ranging from 11p to 20p. Emphasis should be placed on amounts involving the 10p coin. For example:

To add up these coins the children could either 'count on', that is 10 and 5 (fifteen) and 2 (sixteen, seventeen) and 1 (eighteen), or they could be encouraged to count the 'units' first:

$$5p + 2p + 1p = 8p$$
$$10p + 8p = 18p$$

Amounts involving the 5p coin are also important, for example:

Page 1 deals with finding the values of collections of coins. Some children may need to put out coins on top of the coin pictures.
In questions 1 to 4, once the value of the coins has been found, the children are asked to find how much is left when a certain amount is spent.
In questions 5 to 7, once the value of the coins has been found, the children are asked to find how much more one child has than another. By this stage the children should know that the answer is found by subtraction.
On this page there is an emphasis on language as well as on finding the value of collections of coins. Children should be reminded to go over the dotted 'p' in each answer.

Introductory activities for Page 2

1 Putting out coins for amounts from 11p to 20p

The teacher may wish to separate this into two sections:
(a) putting out coins – 11p to 15p, (b) putting out coins – 16p to 20p

(a) An article priced in the range 11p to 15p could be selected from the class shop or from shopping cards and the children in the group asked to put out the appropriate coins. Emphasis should be placed on using the 10p coin first. For example:
$$12p = 10p + 2p$$
$$13p = 10p + 2p + 1p$$
Also, different ways of putting out, for example, 14p could be discussed.

    or

(b) An article priced in the range 16p to 20p could be selected from the class shop or from shopping cards. In putting out these amounts, the children should be encouraged to go to 15p first (that is 10p + 5p) and then to add on the necessary coins to reach, for example, 17p.

2 Class shop activities

The class shop could be set up with articles priced 11p to 20p and the children invited to buy and pay for one of the articles. Alternatively, they could be invited to choose two articles with a total cost of 20p or less, and to pay for these. Some consideration should be given to varying the type of shop set up in the classroom, for example newsagent, sweet shop, card shop, baker's shop, fruit shop, flower shop, kiosk.

3 Shopping cards

Cards could be made showing articles in the price range 11p to 20p and the child asked to put out the appropriate coins for each article.

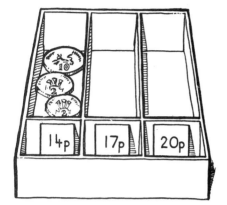

4 Sorting boxes   The children could be asked to put appropriate coins in each part.

Page 2	**Putting out coins**	Money to 20p

Materials   1p, 2p, 5p, and 10p coins

Questions 1 to 4 on this page deal with finding the cost of two articles in the price range 12p to 15p and putting out the appropriate coins.
Questions 5 to 8 deal with increasing the price of an article by 9p before putting out the appropriate coins, giving a price range of 16p to 19p.
In questions 1 to 4, some children, instead of putting out coins for the *total* amount, may put out coins for each amount separately. For example, in question 2, a child may put out

    and

This child would then have to collect the coins together and exchange them

for

In questions 1 to 8, the children are asked to *record the coins they have used in a table*. A demonstration by the teacher will be required before the children try this page.

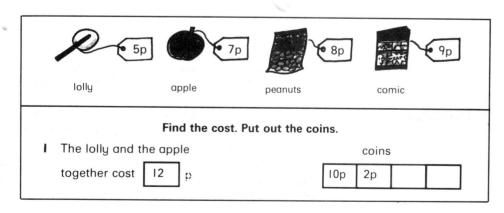

As a preliminary activity, the children may find it helpful to actually place the coins used on a strip of paper or cardboard:

They could then record their answer from this in the coins table on the workbook page. It should be emphasised that all four boxes in the coins table may not be needed, for example, 15p = 10p + 5p.

The children should be encouraged to use as few coins as possible.

In questions 5 to 8, the children are meant to score out the old price and write the new price on the price ticket below. They should then put out coins for this new price before recording their answer in the coins table in the workbook.

The idea of increasing the price of articles, for example, 'Make each 2p more', is one that was introduced in *Infant Mathematics: A development through activity*, First Stage and was also used in *Infant Mathematics: A development through activity*, Second Stage.

| **Page 3** | **The 20p coin** | Introducing the 20p coin |

Materials   1p, 2p, 5p, 10p, and 20p coins

The introduction of the 20p coin provides new work. Before trying this page, the children should have been shown various ways of putting out 20p. In particular, the teacher should have emphasised that:

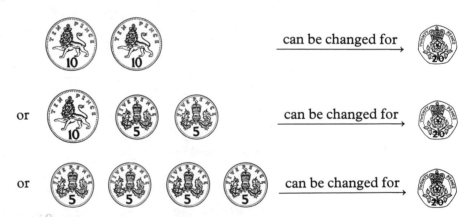

The shape and design of the 20p coin should also have been investigated. In Page 3, questions 1 to 4, the children should place coins on top of the outlines given and record their answers thus:

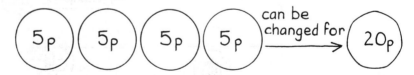

In questions 5 and 6, the children should put a 20p coin below the heading 'coin'. They can then record this by drawing round the 20p coin, by writing '20p', or by sticking on a gummed 20p coin. The cost of the two packets and the four packets can be found by repeated addition, that is 10p + 10p, and 5p + 5p + 5p + 5p.

Introductory activities for Pages 4 and 5

Although giving back change from two 10p coins may have been introduced previously, for example in *Infant Mathematics: A development through activity*, Second Stage, it is likely that some children were unable to cope with this topic at that time. Consequently, this work may be new for some children. Pages 4 and 5 are concerned with giving back change from a 20p coin.

1 Giving change from 20p

The teacher may wish to consider this topic for articles in the price range (a) 15p to 19p, (b) 10p to 14p, (c) 5p to 9p, (d) 1p to 4p.

(a) articles priced 15p to 19p

17p and *what* to make 20p?

'17p and 1p makes 18p'   '18p and 2p makes 20p'

(b) articles priced 10p to 14p

13p and *what* to make 20p?

'13p and 2p makes 15p'   '15p and 5p makes 20p'

In these examples the children should be encouraged to count on to 15p and then to 20p by putting out a 5p coin.

(c) articles priced 5p to 9p

7p and *what* to make 20p?

change

'7p and 1p makes 8p'   '8p and 2p makes 10p'   '10p and 10p makes 20p'

In these examples the children should be encouraged to count on to 10p and then to 20p by putting out a 10p coin.

(d) articles priced 1p to 4p

2p and *what* to make 20p?

| change |

'2p and 1p makes 3p' '3p and 2p makes 5p' '5p and 5p makes 10p' '10p and 10p makes 20p'

In these examples the children should be encouraged to count on to 5p, then to 10p by putting out a 5p coin, and then to 20p by putting out a 10p coin. Children who have difficulty in giving back change may find it easier to subtract 2p from 20p to find that the change is 18p. They would then put out coins for this amount. The intention in this unit is, however, to teach children to give back change *by counting on*, as a shopkeeper does. Examples (a) to (d) are progressively more difficult.

2 Class shop activities

The class shop should have articles priced from 1p to 19p. The children should be given a 20p coin and asked to select one article from the shop. The shopkeeper should give the change. The customer then becomes the shopkeeper and so on. Some supervision of this activity is desirable to ensure that the correct change is, in fact, given.

3 Shopping cards

Cards could be made showing articles in the price range 1p to 19p. A child could select a card and put out the change which would be received from 20p if this article were bought. The change and the card could be checked later. Some children could be asked to record each purchase, for example:
   pencil 11p
   change 9p.
They could be asked to write down the coins they put out as change, for example, ②p, ②p and ⑤p.

4 Sorting box

Price tags should be inserted as shown. The children should be asked to put in each part the change they would receive from 20p if they bought each of the articles. This could be checked and another set of price tags inserted. Some children could be asked to record each result, for example:
   price 14p
   change ①p, ⑤p.

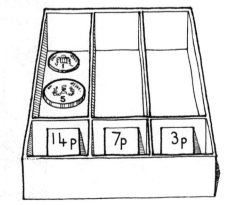

| Pages 4, 5 | Change from 20p | Change from 20p |

Materials 1p, 2p, 5p, 10p, and 20p coins

Page 4 deals with giving back change from a 20p coin for articles in the price range 10p to 19p.
Page 5 deals with giving back change from a 20p coin for articles in the price range 1p to 9p.
The children should place the appropriate coins on top of the outlines and record their answers thus:

Page 4, question 2

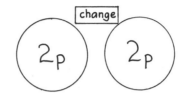

Number   Place value to 99   Pages 6 to 11

Content and development

It is assumed that the children will have some knowledge of the structure of numbers in the range ten to twenty before tackling this work. For example, they should know that the number eighteen is made up of one ten and eight units. This important concept is now extended throughout the range of two digit numbers up to 99.
Emphasis is placed on the use of concrete and structured number materials to show that units can be grouped in tens and units and, conversely, that tens and units can be expressed as a certain number of units.
Place value work on hundreds, tens, and units occurs in Stage 2.

Introductory activities for Pages 6 to 8

Place value – tens and units   Children who have coped successfully with Workbook 1 are already familiar with numbers up to 99. They can recognise, read, write, and order these numbers. Collections of objects in this range of numbers can also be counted. To grasp the concept of place value the children must appreciate the structure of these numbers and see that when a number like 34 is written, the '3' refers to the number of tens and the '4' refers to the number of units. The fundamental activity of 'bundling' into tens can help put across the concept of place value. The child counts out a heap of, say, 34 straws and then groups them into three bundles of ten and four single straws.

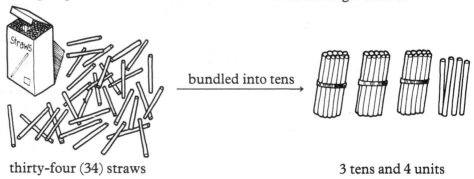

thirty-four (34) straws   bundled into tens   3 tens and 4 units

The use of structured apparatus allows the child to take this process one step further in that each 'bundle' of ten units can be *exchanged* for one ten.

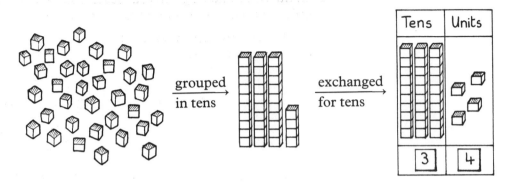

thirty-four (34) units   3 tens and 4 units

Most children will, of course, replace each group of ten units with one ten before grouping the next ten units.

The notation card is easily made from cardboard and need only be large enough to contain a number of tens and units. Looking ahead, however, to work on addition of tens and units, it might be wiser to make a card which would allow for the placing of two sets of tens and units.

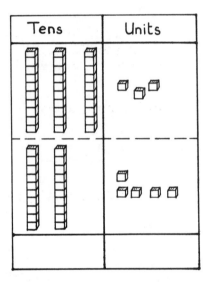

When such apparatus is introduced to the children, they will need time to 'play' and familiarise themselves with it so that they understand the equivalence of one ten and ten units.

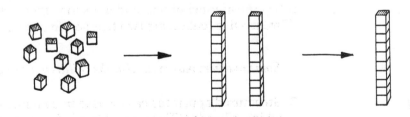

ten units   ten units matched   ten units replaced
against one ten   by one ten

Here are some activities which are designed to help in the teaching of place value.

1 Children should be given practice in counting out different numbers of objects and grouping or arranging these into tens. For example:

(a) **Put 28 counters in sets of 10 using loops of string.**

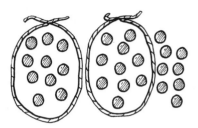

(b) **Put 32 marbles in sets of 10 using jars or trays or tubs.**

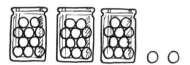

(c) **Thread 36 beads in sets of 10.**

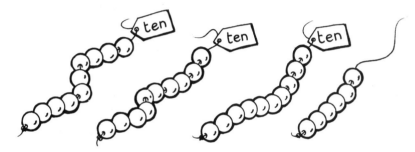

(d) **Pile up 31 counters in sets of 10.**

(e) **Put 25 interlocking plastic cubes into sets of 10.**

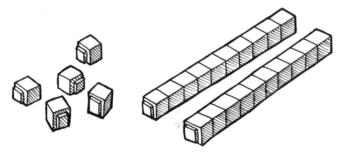

After the grouping has been carried out by the children they should be asked to say the number of tens and units they then have, for example, 'Twenty-five (cubes) are two tens and five units'.

Some teachers may now wish the children to try Page 6 of the workbook.

2 Structured apparatus can be used in conjunction with a notation card which is headed 'Tens' and 'Units'. As stated previously, it is important that the children should understand that ten ones can be exchanged for one ten. The number of unit cubes counted out by the children should probably be in the range 20 to 39, since it is tedious to count out large numbers of cubes and there is more possibility of casual error.

3 Using structured apparatus it is possible to play a game which will give the children practice in exchanging ones for tens. A die is thrown, the score represented with unit cubes, and as the game proceeds a ten is exchanged for every ten unit cubes which become available.

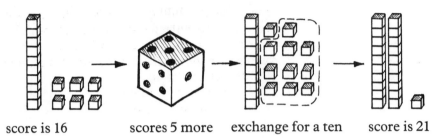

score is 16   scores 5 more   exchange for a ten   score is 21

The winner would be the first person to reach a total of 50.

4 The teacher could prepare a set of cards like these:

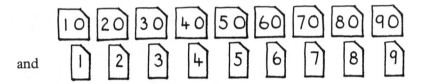

These could be used to show, for example, $20 + 3 = 23$ in the normal notational form, by using 20 and 3 and placing them thus: 23

Such a set of cards is available in the *Teacher's Materials Pack*, Card 5.

5 Using the sets of cards described above, a game can be played which gives further practice in constructing numbers and ordering them. The cards are spread, face down, in two sets as shown. Each player in turn chooses one card from each set. The child who has the largest number after one round wins the game. The others might be asked to show their numbers and could then place them in ascending or descending order. The rules could be changed so that the winner is the person who has chosen the lowest number. Another variation might be that the winner is the person whose number is nearest to 50, say, or some other preselected number.

| **Page 6** | **Tens and units** | **Place value to 99** |

Materials   straws and elastic bands

The children are asked to count out different numbers of straws and to put these into bundles of ten. Questions 1 and 2 revise place value with numbers less than 20.

| **Page 7** | **Tens and units** | **Place value to 99** |

Materials   tens, units, and a notation card

Questions 1 to 3 on this page should be answered by using Tillich or some other structured apparatus which allows for the exchange of ten units for one ten. It is hoped that question 3 can be completed without the materials, but the teacher should have discussed the answers to question 2 in order to establish the pattern:

32 = 3 tens and 2 units

28 = 2 tens and 8 units

| **Page 8** | **Tens and units** | **Place value to 99** |

Materials   coloured pencils; tens, units, and a notation card if required

It is hoped that practical materials will not be required for this page, although they may still be needed by some children.

Question 1 includes recording as, for example, 30+4 as well as 3 tens and 4 units. The dartboard and its significance in terms of tens and units may have to be explained to the children before they do question 2. Also, for questions 3 and 4, it will have to be pointed out that each lorry contains six tens and nine ones but only the correct number of boxes has to be coloured. As an extra question, the teacher could ask what number, in each case, is shown by boxes which have not been coloured.

Introductory activities for Pages 9, 10, 11

Up until now, the place value process has only involved counting out objects and arranging these into groups of ten, but it is also important that the child, when presented with, say, 3 tens and 5 units, should realise that there are 35 units altogether. For example,

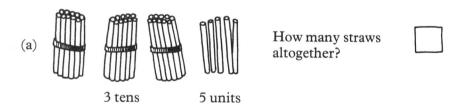

(a)   3 tens   5 units   How many straws altogether?

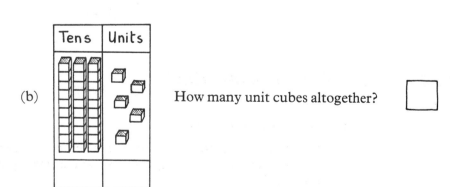

(b)   How many unit cubes altogether?

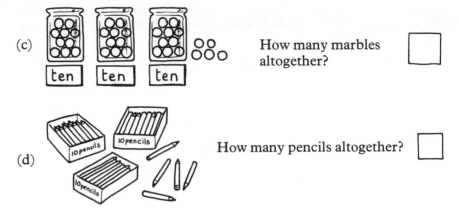

(c)   How many marbles altogether?

(d)   How many pencils altogether?

In each case, the child should be encouraged to count the tens, 'ten, twenty, thirty', and then count on the units 'thirty-one, thirty-two, thirty-three, thirty-four, thirty-five'.

It may be necessary, however, for some children to 'unwrap' the tens and recount the whole collection of single items. With structured apparatus they may have to exchange the tens for units to convince themselves that there are 35 units.

| **Page 9** | **Tens and units** | **Place value to 99** |

Materials   straws (in bundles of ten)

Questions 1 and 2 deal with numbers up to 20. In question 1 the children should be encouraged to count on from ten, saying 'ten, eleven, twelve, thirteen, fourteen'.

It may also be worthwhile, initially, to untie the ten and count from the start 'one, two, three . . .'.

The rest of the page provides similar examples with larger numbers and, although the materials are available for the children to look at and handle, it is hoped that 'untying' the tens and counting from one will not be necessary. They should be encouraged to count 'ten, twenty, thirty', etc.

| **Page 10** | **Tens and units** | **Place value to 99** |

Materials   tens, units, and a notation card

The exercises here are similar to those on Page 9 except that structured apparatus is used.

| **Page 11** | **Tens and units** | **Place value to 99** |

Materials   coloured pencils

This page contains miscellaneous examples based on the exercises on Pages 9 and 10. By this time children (except for those still having real difficulties) should not require actual materials.

In question 5, the teacher may need to explain that on the left half of the dartboard each dart represents a score of ten, while on the right half each dart indicates a score of one.

Number	Addition of tens and units	**Pages 12 to 19** **Cards 21, 23, 25, 27, 29** **31, 33, 35, 37, 39**

Content and development

In Workbook 1 the basic addition facts to 20 were revised. This section of Workbook 2 extends the work on addition to the techniques of adding tens and units to tens and units, with answers less than 100. The work is closely linked to the previous work on place value (Pages 6 to 11) where structured materials were used.

Addition of tens and units giving answers greater than 100 is introduced at Stage 2.

The development of the work is as follows:
1 adding tens to tens, e.g. $30 + 40$
2 adding without exchange
   units to tens and units, e.g. $23 + 4$
   tens and units to tens and units, e.g. $31 + 42$
3 adding with exchange
   units to tens and units, e.g. $28 + 7$
   tens and units to tens and units, e.g. $55 + 17$
4 adding three single digit numbers, e.g. $7 + 8 + 9$
   adding three two digit numbers, e.g. $26 + 31 + 25$.
It is recommended that teachers follow this sequential development, although some may prefer to do the two pages on addition of units to tens and units (Pages 13 and 15) before the two pages of work on addition of tens and units to tens and units (Pages 14 and 16).

There are ten cards associated with this unit. Five of the cards deal with further practice examples and the other five are puzzles involving addition.

Page 12	**Adding tens**	**Addition of tens**

Materials tens and a notation card

Workbook 1 revised the basic addition facts – the addition of units to units. This page gives practice in the addition of tens to tens before the children move on to learn the technique of adding tens and units to tens and units. Although materials are not essential, teachers are advised initially to see that children are able to use the 'longs' for addition of tens in the same way as they used 'cubes' for addition of units.

At this stage the children have not yet learned the technique of adding units first and then adding tens. To find the answer to $20 + 40$ a child would probably say 'forty and twenty makes sixty' or '4 tens and 2 tens makes 6 tens' and write the answer 60.

The differing formats of the questions should also be discussed with the children before asking them to complete the page.

Introductory activities for Pages 13 to 16

This new work might be introduced to a group of children. Each child will require structured materials and a notation card. Because the work is restricted to totals within 99, each child in the group would require a maximum of 9 tens (longs) and 18 units (cubes). The notation card would be similar to that used for the work on place value.

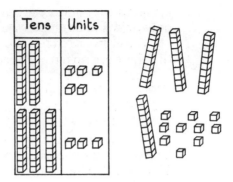

The work of each of these pages follows a similar pattern. Before asking the children to tackle any of the pages it is most important that the teacher carries out some practical work with the children to introduce the new idea contained on each page.

The work for each page could be approached as follows:

1 The new idea on the page is introduced by the teacher, who presents an addition problem. Materials are then used to find the answer, which is subsequently recorded.

2 The children do similar examples, using materials to find the answer and recording the answer *after* they have used the materials.

3 The teacher shows how the written technique evolves from the use of the materials by recording each part of the answer *as the materials are used*.

4 The children do further examples (using materials only if necessary) using the technique which has been taught. Some children may need to use the materials for some time before they fully understand the technique.

The notes for each page give details of this teaching approach.

Page 13	**Adding units to tens and units**	Addition to 99 No carrying

Materials tens, units, and a notation card

At this stage in the development of addition the children should be familiar with the basic addition facts, that is $8+1$, $6+7$, and so on, but do not have a method of adding, say, $23+4$ or $17+8$.

This page introduces the technique of adding a single digit number and a two digit number using structured materials and the notation card.

The teacher should first discuss how to add, say, $43+6$:

1 Put out 43   2 Put out 6 under 43   3 Add units together   4 Record answer

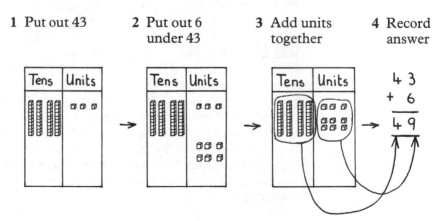

The children should then do a few examples in a similar way. The teacher may decide that questions 1, 2, and 3 may be done at this stage. Because of

the simplicity of the examples (the units always add to a total of 9 or less) the only points to be emphasised are:

(i) the units are added and recorded

(ii) there are no tens to be added on, so the number of tens remains the same and is recorded.

The idea of questions 4, 5, and 6 is important and should be discussed with the children. A child who knows that $4+2=6$ should appreciate that $14+2=16, 24+2=26, 34+2=36$ and so on. A larger version of the number line shown in the workbook would be a useful teaching aid. It could be fixed on the classroom wall. A number line of this type is included in the *Teacher's Materials Pack* for Stage 1, Cards 10 to 13. Cards of varying sizes would have to be made to match the number line.

  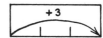 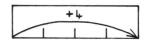

Further oral work could be based on similar patterns.

Page 14   **Adding tens and units**   Addition to 99   No carrying

Materials   tens, units, and a notation card

This page introduces the technique of adding a two digit number to another two digit number with *no* exchange from the units to the tens (no carrying). Using materials, the teacher would first discuss how to add, say, $42+15$.

1 Put out 42   **2** Put out 15 under the 42   **3** Add units together

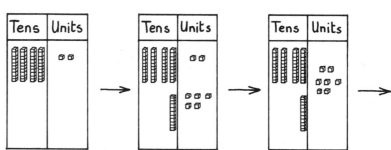

4 Add tens together   **5** Record answer

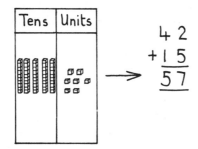

The children should then do a few examples in a similar way. The answer should be found using the materials and only then recorded.

The next stage in teaching would be to relate the written technique to the use of materials by recording each part of the answer as it is found when using the materials:

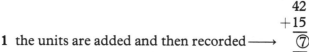

1 the units are added and then recorded ⟶

$$\begin{array}{r} 42 \\ +15 \\ \hline \text{⑤}7 \end{array}$$

2   the tens are added and then recorded ⟶

At this stage it is immaterial whether the units or tens are added first and this could be discussed, but the children should be guided to add the units first. It is hoped that most children would be able to do question 3 without the use of materials. Problems are introduced in questions 4 and 5. Some children may need an explanation as to where to set down their working so that their answers will appear between the two red lines.

Page 15	Adding units to tens and units	Addition to 99 With carrying

Materials   tens, units, and a notation card

This page is similar to Page 13 in that it deals with the addition of a single digit number and a two digit number. However, this time there *is* an exchange from units to tens (carrying). As before, the teacher would use materials to demonstrate how to add, say, 45+9:

1 Put out 45   2 Put out 9 under 45   3 Add units together

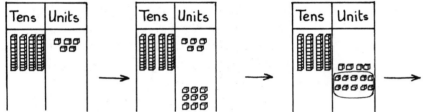

4 Exchange 10 units   5 Add tens together   6 Record answer
    for 1 ten

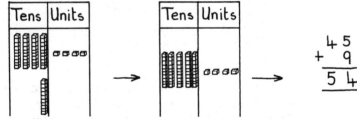

$$\begin{array}{r} 4\;5 \\ +\;\;9 \\ \hline 5\;4 \end{array}$$

The children should then do some examples (possibly questions 1 and 2) in a similar way, only recording the answer once they had found it using the materials.

Once again the teacher should show how the written technique is related to the use of material. For example with 45+9:

1 Add the units and exchange ten units for one ten. Record the 4 in the units column of the answer.

      $\begin{array}{r} 45 \\ +9 \\ \hline 4 \\ \tiny 1 \end{array}$ '9 and 5 are 14. Write down the 4 units in the units column and carry 1 ten'.

2 Carry the ten to the tens column. Add the tens. Record the 5 in the tens column of the answer.

      $\begin{array}{r} 45 \\ +9 \\ \hline 54 \\ \tiny 1 \end{array}$ '1 ten and 4 tens are 5 tens. Write down the 5 in the tens column. The answer is 54'.

The children should now do question 3, using the materials only if necessary. Again questions 4, 5, and 6 are important. A child who knows the basic fact $7+5 = 12$ should appreciate the pattern: $7+5 = 12, 17+5 = 22, 27+5 = 32, 37+5 = 42$, and so on.

| Page 16 | Adding tens and units | Addition to 99 With carrying |

Materials   tens, units, and a notation card

This page is similar to Page 14 in that it deals with the addition of a two digit number to a two digit number but this time *with* an exchange from units to tens (carrying).

Again the teacher should introduce the idea by discussing with the children how to add, say, $24+37$:

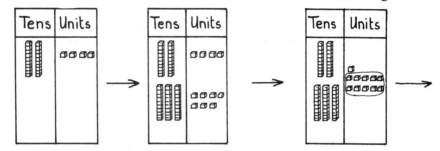

1 Put out 24   **2** Put out 37 below 24   **3** Add units together

4 Exchange 10 units for 1 ten   **5** Add tens together   **6** Record answer

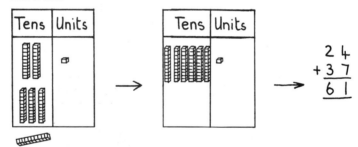

The children could then do questions 1 and 2 to practise this new step. They should use the materials to find the answer and then record it.

The way in which the written technique relates to the use of materials should then be shown to the children. For example, using $24+37$ again:

1 Add the units and exchange ten units for one ten. Record the 1 in the units column of the answer.

$$\begin{array}{r} 24 \\ +37 \\ \hline 1 \\ \hline {\scriptstyle 1} \end{array}$$

'7 and 4 are 11. Write down the 1 unit in the units column and carry 1 ten'.

2 Carry the ten to the tens column. Add the tens. Record the 6 in the tens column of the answer.

$$\begin{array}{r} 24 \\ +37 \\ \hline 61 \\ \hline {\scriptstyle 1} \end{array}$$

'1 ten and 3 tens are 4 tens. 4 tens and 2 tens are 6 tens. Write down the 6 in the tens column. The answer is 61'.

Questions 3, 4, and 5 provide further practice and it is hoped that most children would be able to do these without the use of materials. It is likely that some children will require further examples of this type.

Page 17   Adding two numbers   Addition to 99 Miscellaneous

Materials   tens, units, and a notation card if required

Having been introduced to the technique of adding tens and units in the previous four pages, this page is a revision page presenting examples in a variety of formats. It should act as a useful check as to how well a child has grasped the idea of addition.

Some children may find it difficult to answer the last part of question 4 unless they write down 29 and 38 vertically before adding. There is space for this on the right.

Page 18   Adding three numbers   Addition Associative law

Materials   none

The children have already had experience of adding three single digit numbers in Workbook 1, Pages 4 and 21. These examples were of the type

$$7+1+8 \qquad \text{or} \qquad 5+5+3$$
$$= \quad 8+8 \qquad\qquad = \quad 10+3$$
$$= \quad 16 \qquad\qquad\quad = \quad 13$$

in which the answer was found using basic addition facts only.
This page introduces examples of the type

$$7+9+8$$
$$= \quad 16+8$$
$$= \quad 24$$

in which the children have to know the technique of adding a two digit number and a single digit number (Pages 13 and 15). An important feature of the page is that it acquaints the children with the associative nature of addition – no matter which pair of numbers is added first, the answer remains the same:

$$\overbrace{6+8}+4 \qquad 6+\overbrace{8+4} \qquad \overbrace{6\quad+\quad4}$$
$$= \quad 14+4 \qquad = 6+12 \qquad = \quad 10+8$$
$$= \quad 18 \qquad\quad = 18 \qquad\qquad = \quad 18$$

Question 1 and some other similar examples should be discussed with the children to establish this fact. The children can then complete the rest of the page.

Some children find the number composition of ten easy to remember and use this fact when adding lists of numbers. Thus, a child might find the answer to $7+9+3$ by looking for a pair of numbers which add to ten and then saying $7+3=10$, $10+9=19$. In questions 2, 3, and 4, the children have to mark the way they find easiest. The various ways of finding answers could form the basis of a discussion. It should be noted that most of the examples have totals less than 20. Teachers should give the children some extra practice in examples with totals greater than 20, such as $9+7+6$, $8+8+7$.

Page 19   Adding three numbers   Addition of 3 numbers
Totals to 99

Materials   tens and units if required

Once the children are proficient in adding any three single digit numbers, they can use this knowledge to add three two digit numbers. This page gives

practice in this. Most children should not need materials for this and should
be encouraged to add both 'up' and 'down' in order to check their answer.
In questions 2, 3, and 4, the children should choose the appropriate numbers,
set them down vertically in the space provided and then carry out the
addition. Question 5 might prove difficult for some children in that a number
of tens and a number of units have to be added mentally. More able children
could be given practice in adding four or even five two digit numbers,
remembering that the total has to be within 99.

Number cards 21, 23, 25, 27, 29, 31, 33, 35, 37, 39 — Addition of tens and units

Cards 21, 23, 25, 27, and 29 provide further practice in addition of tens and
units. Cards 31, 33, 35, 37, and 39 are slightly more difficult and deal with
addition puzzles. The five cards in each set are of comparable difficulty and
may be done in any order. This will allow several children to use the cards
simultaneously.

Number cards 21, 23, 25, 27, 29 — Adding tens and units

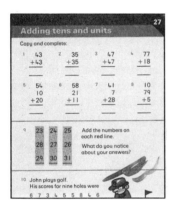

Each card gives practice in the addition of tens and units and follows the
same pattern. Questions 1 to 4 give practice in the addition of two 2 digit
numbers. Questions 5 to 8 give practice in the addition of three 2 digit or
single digit numbers. This is followed by questions in which the children
have to interpret the wording before choosing which numbers to add. Each
card ends with a word problem.
The cards introduce no new work but teachers should note that some
children may need to be reminded of the meaning of such words as 'sum',
'total', etc.

Number cards 31, 33, 35, 37, 39 — Addition puzzles

These cards contain various ideas such as 'missing numbers', addition
puzzles, odd and even numbers, and some number pattern work.

Cards 31, 33 — Missing numbers

Materials none

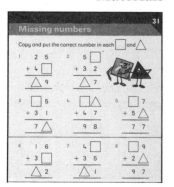

In these two cards the children have to find the missing numbers for □ and
△. In each example, the answer for □ is different to the answer for △.
Questions 1 to 5 involve addition with no 'carrying' while questions 6 to 8
involve addition with 'carrying' and are more difficult. Question 9 is rather
more open-ended. It may be that some children try only questions 1 to 5
while others may try the whole card. In either case some preliminary
explanation and demonstration by the teacher will probably be necessary.

Card 35   Even and odd

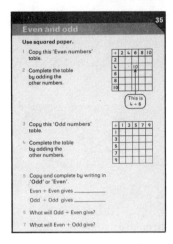

Materials   squared paper

This is the first *written* work involving even and odd numbers. Since the children have not yet 'divided by 2', *even numbers* should meantime be defined as a sequence of numbers starting at 2 and increasing by 2 each time, that is 2, 4, 6, 8, 10, 12, etc. Similarly *odd numbers* should meantime be defined as a sequence of numbers starting at 1 and increasing by 2 each time, that is 1, 3, 5, 7, 9, 11, etc. Because of this definition, the range of numbers under consideration on this card has been limited to 1 to 20. This idea will have to be taught to the children before they try the card.

Question 5 should be completed by referring back to the tables in questions 2 and 4. Questions 6 and 7 should be completed by considering specific examples of the addition of odd and even numbers and by noticing what type of number is obtained in the answer. For example, for question 6 the children could write down: $3+6 = 9$; $1+4 = 5$; $5+8 = 13$; $7+10 = 17$ and so on, and notice that the answer obtained each time is 'odd'.

More able children might find it interesting to think of *even* numbers as being represented by sets of 'paired off' counters or dots, for example:

Odd numbers might be represented as sets of 'paired off' counters or dots with an extra *one*, for example:

This means that when an *even* number of dots is added to an *odd* number of dots there is always an unpaired dot, so the number is *odd*:

$$\underset{\text{even}}{\text{⦚⦚⦚}} \quad + \quad \underset{\text{odd}}{\text{⦚⦚∙}} \quad \longrightarrow \quad \underset{\text{odd}}{\text{⦚⦚⦚⦚⦚∙}}$$

Card 37   Six numbers in order

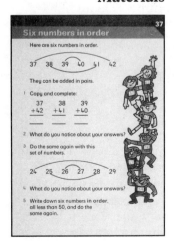

Materials   none

In this card the children add pairs of numbers and are then asked *what they notice about their answers*. This is a very important mathematical activity. In question 1, the numbers have been so chosen that the additions involve no 'carrying', while in question 3 the numbers have been chosen so that the additions do involve 'carrying'. In question 5, it is most important that the children write down six numbers *in order*, all less than 50, for example, 32, 33, 34, 35, 36, 37. The numbers have to be less than 50 so that the total of any two numbers is less than 100, since the children have only done examples of tens and units to 99.

Card 39   Pairs of numbers

Materials   none

The purpose of this card is to provide some slightly more open-ended questions on the addition of tens and units.

In questions 3, 4, and 5, the word 'pair' may be new to some children.

In question 7, the children should notice that the numbers being added have their digits reversed. In question 8 they should notice that the answers have the same tens digit as the units digit. For example:

$$\begin{array}{r} 54 \\ +45 \\ \hline 99 \end{array}$$

Additional activities for addition of tens and units

1 Some suggestions for extra worksheets are given below. These could be adapted to make workcards.

(a) To give extra practice in addition of tens.

> Complete:
> 1. $30+10=20+\square$ 2. $10+40=\square+30$
> 3. $70+20=50+\square$ 4. $20+\square=30+60$
> 5. $\square+40=20+60$ 6. $\square+60=10+70$
>
> 7. $27+10=30+\square$ 8. $42+20=60+\square$
> 9. $55+30=80+\square$ 10. $19+40=50+\square$
> 11. $13+20=10+\square$ 12. $49+40=60+\square$
>
> 13. $37+10=\square+7$ 14. $59+20=\square+9$
> 15. $74+20=\square+4$ 16. $23+40=\square+3$

(b) To give practice in adding single digit numbers.

> Complete:
> 1. $7+7+7=$ 2. $9+9+9=$
> 3. $7+8+9=$ 4. $9+7+6=$
> 5. $8+5+8=$ 6. $6+7+5=$
>
> 7. $\begin{array}{r}4\\7\\+6\\\hline\end{array}$ 8. $\begin{array}{r}8\\6\\+6\\\hline\end{array}$ 9. $\begin{array}{r}7\\7\\+8\\\hline\end{array}$ 10. $\begin{array}{r}5\\6\\2\\+9\\\hline\end{array}$
>
> 11. $1+2+3+4+5+6=$
> 12. $7+6+5+4=$
> 13. $1+3+5+7+9=$
> 14. $2+4+6+8=$

(c) To give practice in making word problems.

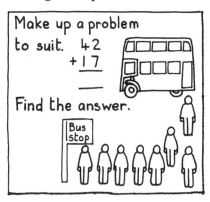

> Make up a problem
> to suit. $\begin{array}{r}42\\+17\\\hline\end{array}$
>
> Find the answer.
>
> Bus stop

(d) This type of worksheet deals with 'chain' additions. The answer to the first addition becomes the top number of the next addition and so on. A child who has completed each addition correctly should finish with the final answer given.

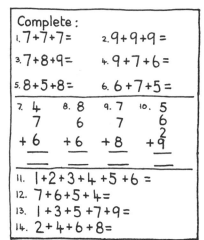

> Complete:
> 1. $\begin{array}{r}15\\+8\\\hline 23\end{array}$ $\begin{array}{r}23\\+19\\\hline\end{array}$ $\begin{array}{r}\\+26\\\hline\end{array}$ $\begin{array}{r}\\+12\\\hline 80\end{array}$
>
> 2. $\begin{array}{r}27\\+9\\\hline\end{array}$ $\begin{array}{r}\\+18\\\hline\end{array}$ $\begin{array}{r}\\+7\\\hline\end{array}$ $\begin{array}{r}\\+14\\\hline 75\end{array}$
>
> 3. $\begin{array}{r}23\\+11\\\hline\end{array}$ $\begin{array}{r}\\+27\\\hline\end{array}$ $\begin{array}{r}\\+5\\\hline\end{array}$ $\begin{array}{r}\\+33\\\hline 99\end{array}$

2 The *Teacher's Materials Pack* contains two items which can be used for addition of tens and units:

A number line to 100 (Cards 10, 11, 12, 13)
This should be placed on the classroom wall. Suggestions for its use are given in the *Teacher's Materials Pack* notes.

Addition picture (Card 8)
Children have to make a picture by correctly completing several additions.

Money to 99p   Pages 20 to 22

Content and development

Money to 20p, including the introduction of the 20p coin, was revised and consolidated in Pages 10 to 14 of this workbook. This topic is now extended to include finding the value to 49p of collections of coins and laying out amounts to 49p, both of which incorporate the use of the 20p coin.
The 50p coin is then introduced. Finding the value to 99p of collections of coins and laying out amounts to 99p concludes this section on money.
Addition and subtraction of money to 99p occurs in Stage 1, Workbook 3.

Introductory activities for Page 20

Money to 49p This topic falls into two parts, finding the value of collections of coins to 49p, and laying out coins for amounts to 49p.

1 Value of collections of coins to 49p

(a) The teacher should give the children a collection of coins to count orally.

The children should be encouraged to start with the 20p coin, then to add the 10p, then the 5p, and then the 2p, to find the total of 37p. Several examples like this should be done with totals 49p or less, with the teacher asking the children to count out the amounts orally.

(b) Money could be put in envelopes or bags or tubs and each child asked to find out how much money he or she has been given. Each child should be asked to put out the coins in order, largest value first, before counting orally to find the amount.

(c) Money could be put in each partition of a sorting box and the children asked how much is in each part. They should put the coins in order first.
Some children should be encouraged to keep a written record of each of these activities, for example ⟮20p⟯ ⟮10p⟯ ⟮10p⟯ ⟮2p⟯ → 42p.

Teachers may now wish the children to try the top part of Page 20 of the workbook.

2 Laying out coins for amounts to 49p

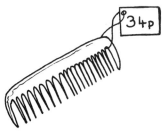

(a) An article could be selected from the class shop or from shopping cards and the money for this article put out.
The children should be reminded that 34 = 3 tens and 4 units.
As well as putting out

children should also, as an alternative, put out

Various examples like this should be done. Children should be encouraged to use as few coins as possible each time.

(b) Children could now buy one article from the class shop, in the price range 20p to 49p, and hand over the money for this article.

(c) Shopping cards similar to those supplied in the *Teacher's Materials Pack* (Cards 24, 23, and 13) could be used. The children have to put out coins to buy the article.

(d) The children could work in pairs. One child asks another for '37p, please' and the other child checks the transaction. The roles are then reversed.

(e) A sorting box could have price tags as shown. The children have to put appropriate coins in each part.

(f) Envelopes or tubs could be provided with an amount marked on them. The child has to put the correct amount in the envelope or tub.

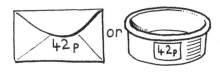

Page 20   **Coins**   Money to 49p

Materials   1p, 2p, 5p, 10p, and 20p coins

In the top part of the page the children have to total the coins shown. Some children may wish to put out coins on top of the coin pictures and then find the total value of the real or token coins.

In the bottom part of the page the children have to put out coins for amounts in the range 20p to 49p. In questions 7 to 14, the children should put out the required coins and *then* record the coins they have used in the given boxes. The method of recording on the page will have to be explained. As a preliminary step, children may find it helpful to have a strip of paper or cardboard on which the coins used can actually be put:

They would then record their answer from this on to the coins table in the workbook page.

It should be emphasised that all five boxes in the coins table are not always needed, as is shown above. Children should be encouraged to use as few coins as possible, for example

| 20p | 20p | 5p | 2p | | for 47p |

rather than

| 10p | 10p | 10p | 10p | 5p | 1p | 1p |

where extra boxes would have to be drawn.

Introductory activities for Page 21

1 Introducing the 50p coin

(a) The shape and design of the 50p coin could be investigated by coin rubbings.

(b) The teacher should show the children that

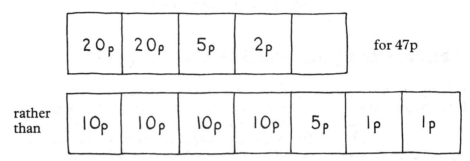

can be changed for

(c) Various other ways of putting out 50p should be considered, for example, 20p, 20p, 10p.

2 Using the 50p coin

(a) The children should now be asked to find the value of a collection of coins in the range 51p to 99p, for example:

They should be encouraged to count the 'tens' first, '50p, 20p, (70p) and 10p is 80p', and then the other coins, 3p, to give a total of 83p. Several examples like this should be given.

(b) Other activities using envelopes, tubs or sorting boxes to hold collections of coins could now be carried out. Details of these activities are given on pages 98, 99 of these *Teacher's Notes* in 'Value of collections of coins to 49p'. These can easily be adapted for 'Value of collections of coins to 99p'.

Page 21   **The 50p coin**   Introducing the 50p coin

Materials   10p, 20p, and 50p coins
1p, 2p, 5p coins if required

In the top part of the page the children have to put out coins to the value of 50p. The children should place the coins on top of the given outlines and record their answers thus:

      can be changed for

Alternatively they could stick gummed paper coins on top of the outlines. In the bottom part of the page the children have to total the coins shown. Some children may wish to put out coins on top of the coin pictures and then add the real or token coins.

Introductory activities for Page 22

Laying out amounts from 51p to 99p

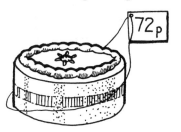

(a) Children should be encouraged to use the 50p coin and then other coins to make up the required amount, using as few coins as possible. Various examples of this kind should be done with teacher supervision.

(b) Activities using the class shop, shopping cards, sorting boxes, envelopes or tubs, as outlined on page 99 of these *Teacher's Notes* in 'Laying out amounts to 49p' can easily be adapted to 'Laying out amounts to 99p'. *These are very necessary preliminary activities for Page 22.*

Page 22	**Putting out coins**	Money to 99p

Materials   1p, 2p, 5p, 10p, 20p, and 50p coins

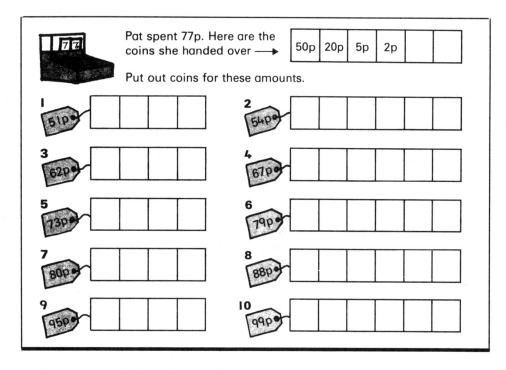

In the top part of this page the children have to put out coins for ticket prices in the range 51p to 99p. They should be encouraged to use the 50p coin and then other coins to make up the required amount, using as few coins as possible. The method of recording is similar to that for Page 20 of this workbook and, as before, the children may find it helpful to put out their coins on a strip of paper or cardboard and then to record the coins in the table in the workbook. It should again be emphasised that all four (or six) boxes in the coins table are not always needed.

The bottom part of the page is essentially a revision of putting out coins in the range 21p to 99p. A slight variation is introduced in that prices have to be increased by either 10p or 20p before the amounts are laid out. The method of recording the answers is similar to that of questions 1 to 10.

Additional activities for money to 99p

1 Coin cards   Coin stamps (or gummed paper coins) could be used to make coin cards. The children have to write down the total value of the coins.

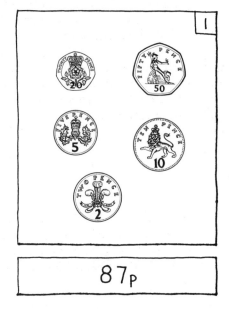

For less able children, answer strips, which have to be correctly matched to a coin card, could be supplied.

2 Purse cards   (a)

What **3** coins are in each purse?

1. 35p   2. 53p

3. 62p   4. 80p

Similar cards could be made up for 27p, 31p, 45p, 57p, 65p, 70p, 72p, 75p, 90p, 32p, 21p, 71p, and so on.

(b) A variation of this would be:
'What 4 coins are in the bank?'
Other suitable amounts are 37p, 43p, 32p, 58p, 66p, 82p, 85p, 77p, 91p, 95p, 74p, 81p, 47p, and so on.

3 Shopping cards   Shopping cards, similar to those supplied in the *Teacher's Materials Pack* (Cards 24, 23, 13), could be used with prices in the range 21p to 99p. The children have to put out money to buy the article shown.

4 Money game   (Card 25 of the *Teacher's Materials Pack*)

This game for 2, 3 or 4 children requires a track as shown, a die, counters, and a box of 5p, 10p, 20p, and 50p coins. Each child throws the die in turn and moves his or her counter forward. If the counter lands on a 20p, the player takes a 20p coin from the box. The winner of the game is the first person to collect one of each of the coins 5p, 10p, 20p, and 50p (or the first person to collect, for example, 95p exactly or any other amount decided before the game starts).

Another version of this game is for each child to have a different shopping card with a value in the range 25p to 95p. (The card should have a units digit of 0 or 5.) The children move their counters round the track as before, but this time the winner is the first child to collect sufficient coins to pay for his or her article exactly.

5 Money dominoes   (Cards 21, 22, 23 of the *Teacher's Materials Pack*)

Instead of 'dots' as in the usual dominoes, pictures of coins are matched to values of money or to other coin pictures of an equal value. Emphasis is given to the 20p and 50p coins. The game is played in a similar way to 'dominoes'.

Area	Comparison of areas	Pages 23 to 26

Content and development

Area is introduced here as an amount of surface and surface areas are compared by physically placing one surface on top of another. The children colour surfaces which helps to develop the pupil's concept of area. Activities are included to promote language development by use of such phrases as 'greater surface', 'smaller surface', 'greater area' and 'smaller area'.

The work concludes by comparing the areas of three surfaces and there is associated language work covering the 'greatest' and the 'smallest' surface or area.

Further work on area occurs in Stage 1, Workbook 4, where arbitrary standards of area which can be used to quantify area are considered. This enables the pupil to give a numerical answer to how much greater or smaller one area is than another.

Introductory activities for Pages 23 to 25

1 Pupils may have difficulty with the concept of surface. A demonstration which might be used is to spill some water on a table top. The pool of water has a surface which covers some of the table. A little more water added to the pool makes the pool spread so the surface becomes greater. Another suggestion is to spread ink or paint on blotting paper. The notion of the amount of table, paper, etc. which is covered may help with the understanding of area.

2 Pupils should be given pairs of objects and asked to find which has the greater (or smaller) surface, for example, a postcard and a birthday card, a Christmas card and a workcard, a magazine and a newspaper. The

comparison should be made by placing one object on top of the other to find which has more and which has less surface. Recording of the results may be carried out in a number of ways:

(a) Flashcards   (i) In this example the pupil is asked to label the object with the greater area.

(ii) Here the label identifies the object with the smaller area.

(iii) Both objects are labelled to show the larger and the smaller areas.

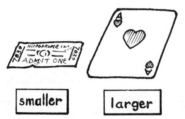

It is suggested that initially only one card is used. 'Greater' is usually easier than 'smaller'. The pupil should be able to talk about the findings, for example, 'The table mat has a greater surface', 'The counter has a smaller surface', 'The ticket has the smaller surface and the card the larger', 'The playing card has a larger surface than the ticket'.

(b) 'Story' arrows

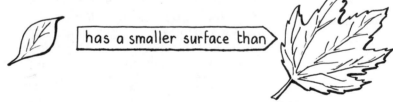

Another arrow might state 'has a greater surface than'. The arrows should be written during discussion with the group of pupils so that they are confident in making up stories when working on their own. The pupil should be able to make up sentences like 'This leaf has a smaller surface than that leaf.'

(c) A background card   Here a pair of objects are placed side by side in the appropriate column. The card should be large enough for the pupil to show about three comparisons.

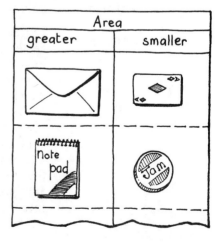

Page 23   Comparing surfaces   Surfaces   Comparison

Materials   coloured pencils

Pupils should be prepared for the vocabulary on this page by the teacher making and using the flashcards [surface], [greater] and [smaller]. Names of shapes should be revised and the flashcards [circle], [square], [triangle] and [hexagon] would be useful.

In questions 4 and 5, the pupil does not only colour the required shape but also has to write its name. Some pupils may have difficulty naming the tilted square in the last example.

If a pupil doubts the answer to any question, for example, in question 5 where it is more difficult to discriminate between the pairs, it is suggested that one shape is traced, or cut out, and placed on top of the other.

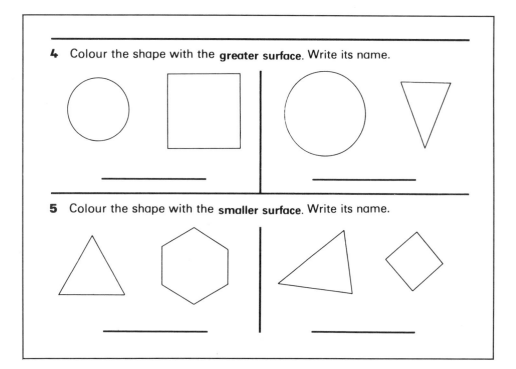

Pages 24 and 25   Comparing areas   Introduction of word area

Materials   coloured pencils

Pupils should by now be familiar with the concept of surface. They should realise that objects made of all sorts of materials – wood, paper, cloth, card – have surfaces. The amount of surface which an object has is called its area. For most pupils this will just mean a change of terms: 'area' instead of 'surface'.

At this stage most examples are being thought of as two dimensional, so it is useful to keep this in mind when choosing extra pairs of objects for comparison.

The last example in question 3 of Page 25 involves equal areas. Pupils may find the response 'no' difficult here.

It is suggested that responses for questions 4 and 5 of Page 25 are collated into wall charts, with, for example, the title 'Things with a smaller area than the blackboard'.

This will encourage pupils to find an object different from those chosen by their classmates so that their own particular object can be listed.

Additional activity

Pupils enjoy this oral game. The teacher asks a pupil to give the name of an object with a very small area. On the first occasion the teacher may wish to give an example and say something like 'finger nail'. Pupils, either in turn or chosen at random, have to suggest an object which has an area just a little larger such as a thumb nail. In this way a sequence could be built up: a finger nail, a thumb nail, a stamp, my rubber, a ticket, a card, a hand print, an envelope, . . . the playground, the town, Scotland, Great Britain, Europe, the world.

The game can also be played by beginning with an object with a large area, for example, the games field, and each pupil has to suggest an object with an area which is just a little smaller.

| Page 26 | Greatest and smallest | Area Ordering |

Materials coloured pencils

The superlative terms 'greatest' and 'smallest' are used on this page. Pupils should be introduced to these words, perhaps with flashcards, at the time when three obviously different areas are being considered, for example page of a book, postcard, and stamp. Before doing this page, the children should be given sets of shapes, three at a time, and asked to compare them to find the one with the greatest area and the one with the smallest area. Although three shapes are involved, it is probably easier for the pupil to first compare two by placing one on top of the other, and then to compare one of these with the third shape.

In question 1, the children have to identify only the shape with the greatest area and, in question 2, the one with the smallest area.

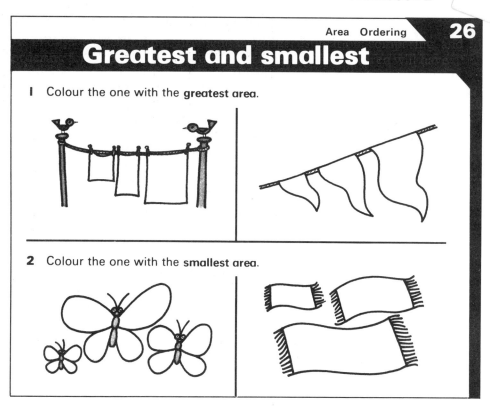

Greatest and smallest

1   Colour the one with the **greatest area**.

2   Colour the one with the **smallest area**.

Additional activities

1 A game   This game is for more able children and can be tackled by one individual or by two pupils working together. It requires three circles of different area, for example, 1p, 2p, and 10p coins and a strip with three compartments like this:

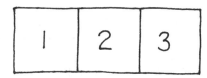

The three coins are placed in a pile on position 1 with the largest coin at the bottom and the smallest on top. The object is to move all three coins to position 3 to make a pile in their present order. Only one coin is moved at a time. A coin cannot be placed on top of one with a smaller area. It will be interesting to see how many moves are required to achieve this. A successful sequence of moves might be these: 1p coin to 3, 2p coin to 2, 1p to 2, 10p coin to 3, 1p to 1, 2p to 3, 1p to 3.

2 A competition   Pupils could be asked to bring in the smallest (or largest) leaf they can find. The areas of these can then be compared by laying one on top of the other. Difficulties may arise due to the different shapes of leaves. This could lead to interesting discussion and further activities.

Weight	**Pages 27 to 32** **Cards 22, 24, 26, 28, 30**

Content and development

As in other aspects of measurement, language, estimation, comparing, and ordering form an initial introductory structure. Most children will have some early experience of weight activities. Such activities appear in *Infant Mathematics: A development through activity.*

One cannot assume that the child's ability to use phrases like 'weighs more than', 'balances', 'is the heaviest' necessarily indicates complete understanding of the concepts associated with weight. It is for this reason that the first part of this unit is designed to provide real experiences of weighing activities using the see-saw model initially, then the two-pan balance. These experiences involve comparisons and orderings and on many occasions estimations precede the use of apparatus. It is hoped that appropriate language will be developed as a natural consequence.

A particular object can be compared with another object, and can take its place in a specific ordering by weight. But what is the weight of the object? The answer is found by weighing, using arbitrary standards such as marbles, cubes, etc. This is intended to lead the children towards a realisation of the need for a conventional standard such as the kilogram, which is introduced in Stage 2.

Children should use a variety of arbitrary standards and should discuss which is the most suitable for weighing a particular object. They should also find from their weighing experiences that 'exact' balances are seldom obtained with an arbitrary standard and a two-pan balance. This emphasises the inexact nature of measurement, and responses such as 'The blackboard duster weighs *about* fourteen marbles' are to be encouraged.

Throughout the unit a variety of ways of recording the results of activities are introduced, such as sentence completion, tables, and arrow diagrams where the arrow represents a stated relationship.

Page 27	**Heavier and lighter**	Weight Language

Materials   none

The principle of the see-saw can be used to develop the early concepts and the associated language of weighing. The two relationships 'is heavier than' and 'is lighter than' can be established using a full sized or model see-saw. There is a natural extension to the two-pan balance. Teacher demonstration on both models, and discussion of the variety of comparative weighing language, for example 'is heavier than', 'is lighter than', 'is *about* the same weight as', should precede asking the children to do this page.

Page 28	**Heaviest and lightest**	Weight Language

Materials   two-pan balance, prepared tins A, B, C with noticeable differences in weight when handled

One of the fundamental concepts in mathematics is that of ordering. The simplest ordering relationship has already been experienced by the children when comparing two objects by weight. Ordering by weight becomes more difficult when three, then four objects are introduced.

The examples on this page extend the language to include the superlatives 'heaviest' and 'lightest'.

Estimating the weight relationship between two objects when one is held in each hand is an important experience. When the weight differences are large, as they should be initially for tins A, B, and C, the decision for most children is not a difficult one. In any event, these decisions should be checked using a two-pan balance.

Additional sets of objects should be provided, where the weight differences are small enough to make it difficult to decide about the relative weights using hands only. The use of a two-pan balance for checking is more justified in these circumstances. An alternative way of recording weight relationships among objects is to use paper or cardboard arrows to link the actual objects. Each arrow is annotated as shown.

Page 29	**Balancing**	Weight Arbitrary standards

Materials   two-pan balance, marbles, a variety of objects for weighing

In questions 1 and 2, the child is asked to find the weight of a jotter and other chosen objects using marbles as units of weight. The important relationship is that the object 'weighs about' a number of marbles. Consider a situation where an object is being weighed in marbles.

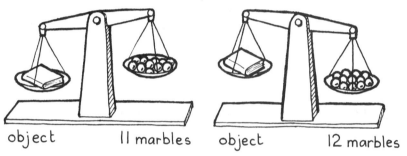

Here we can say that the object is heavier than eleven marbles and lighter than twelve marbles. The important relationship here is that the object 'weighs about eleven marbles' or 'weighs about twelve marbles'. This idea is common to all weighing activities although not specifically recorded in this way on the pages.

The block graph at the foot of the page is for interpretation only. However, some children could draw their own block graphs using the results of the first activity or of a different activity using other arbitrary standards.

Page 30	**Estimating and weighing**	Weight Arbitrary standards

Materials   two-pan balance, marbles, plasticine, piece of wood, a variety of objects for weighing

Following the work on Page 29, the child is asked to estimate the weight, in marbles, of different objects, and then to check these estimates by weighing. Estimation is a difficult skill; it should not be expected that all children will have this skill developed to the same level.

The second activity with wood and plasticine which have to be balanced by adding marbles to one pan, is well within the capabilities of most children. What is more difficult is the language and the concepts of 'How many marbles heavier?' and 'How many marbles lighter?'. The teacher should spend some time explaining this activity.

To consolidate the work in Pages 29 and 30, another arbitrary standard such as a thread reel, wooden cube or acorn, could be chosen to replace the marble.

Page 31   Weighing   Weight   Arbitrary standards

Materials   two-pan balance, marbles, thread reels, chalk sticks, wooden cubes, suitable objects for weighing in these arbitrary standards

Previously, children have been weighing objects using one arbitrary standard. Here the activity is based on weighing a single object with a variety of arbitrary standards. This shows that different answers are obtained for the weight of a particular object depending on which arbitrary standard is used. Again the standards given could be replaced by other suitable arbitrary standards.
For questions 3 and 4, it should be pointed out to the children that the name of the object should be written in the large box.
It may be best to discuss question 5 with the children before they attempt to give a written explanation.

Page 32   Arrows   Weight   Arbitrary standards

Materials   two-pan balance, plastic bags, sand, peas, sawdust, egg-cups, an object to be weighed

Here eggcupfuls of sand, peas, and sawdust are used as arbitrary standards. These filling materials are chosen because there is a noticeable weight difference between them. If the teacher finds it necessary to substitute a different material for one of those listed above, this weight difference should be maintained.
The children may require some help with the concept that if an object weighs, say, four eggcupfuls of sand and twelve of sawdust, then one eggcupful of sand is heavier than one eggcupful of sawdust. Actual weighings on a balance may be required here to make this clear: an eggcupful of sand could be weighed against an eggcupful of sawdust.
The teacher could use the activity on Page 31 to reinforce this concept.

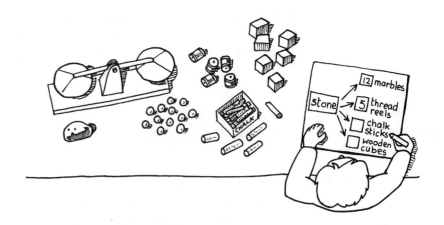

How many marbles weigh the same as 5 thread reels?
Which is heavier, a marble or a thread reel?

Weight cards
22, 24, 26, 28, 30

This batch of five cards is designed to provide further practice examples and activities for those children who have completed the unit.
None of the cards is intended to be any more difficult than the others, so they may be allocated in any order.

Card 22   Estimating

Materials   two-pan balance, objects labelled A, B, C, D, etc. for weighing

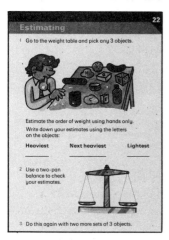

This card gives the children further practice in estimating the order by weight using hands only. The activity is concerned with sets of three objects. For some children this may be extended to four objects.
The two-pan balance is used to check the estimates.

Card 24   Order of weight

Materials   none

This card gives further examples of ordering, using arrows as the method of recording. The teacher should point out that the diagram shows that the brick weighs more than the tin and that it weighs more than the ball, i.e. emphasis should be placed on the direction of the arrowhead.

Card 26   A marble graph

Materials   none

This gives a block graph to be interpreted. It is similar to the one on Page 29 of the workbook. Some children may require help in reading this card.

Card 28   Balancing the stone

Materials   none

This card presents a situation similar to that on Pages 31 and 32 of the workbook, where one object is weighed using different arbitrary units.

Card 30   Weighing

Materials   none

This card provides pictures of various objects which balance each other. The questions can be used to test understanding of weight relationships. This card is designed for more able children some of whom may require further practice in this type of work. The teacher may wish to create additional cards structured in a similar way. Here are some examples:

Card 1

Look at these pictures. They show objects which **balance**.

1   Which is **heavier** a box or a cone?

2   The box is balanced by 12 marbles. How many marbles will **balance** a cone?

3   Which is **lighter** a book or a box?

4   How many marbles will **balance** a book?

5   Put the cone, box and book into order by weight starting with the **heaviest**.

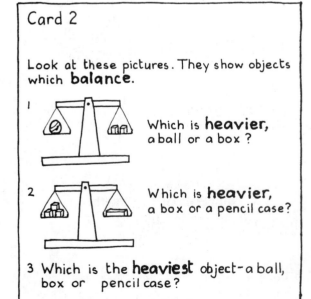

Card 2

Look at these pictures. They show objects which **balance**.

1   Which is **heavier**, a ball or a box?

2   Which is **heavier**, a box or a pencil case?

3   Which is the **heaviest** object – a ball, box or pencil case?

4   Which is the **lightest** object?

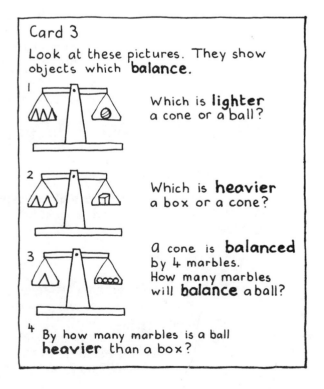

Card 3

Look at these pictures. They show objects which **balance**.

1   Which is **lighter** a cone or a ball?

2   Which is **heavier** a box or a cone?

3   A cone is **balanced** by 4 marbles. How many marbles will **balance** a ball?

4   By how many marbles is a ball **heavier** than a box?

Shape   Flat shapes   Pages 33 to 39

Content and development

This section deals with four shapes which the children will probably have met before – circle, triangle, square, rectangle. The children handle and sort several examples of each type of shape. Two 'new' shapes are also introduced – pentagon and hexagon.

The aim is that the children learn to recognise and name shapes just by looking at them or by counting their corners and edges. The word 'edge' is used rather than 'side' as it is more appropriate to the paper shapes used. No attempt is made to discuss equal edges and angles at this stage. Further work with these six types of flat shape appears in Workbook 3. An ability to recognise and name such shapes is required for all the shape work which follows, including the work on symmetry and tiling which appears in Stage 2.

Introductory activities for Pages 33 to 36

Some practical activities using cardboard or plastic shapes should be done before the children tackle the workbook pages. These could take the form of teacher demonstrations to a group or to the whole class, along with activities for individuals and groups to do on their own. Some suggestions are given below. Teachers might choose to use some of them or to approach the work in their own way.

1 The teacher could use a set of large cardboard shapes, consisting of different sized circles,

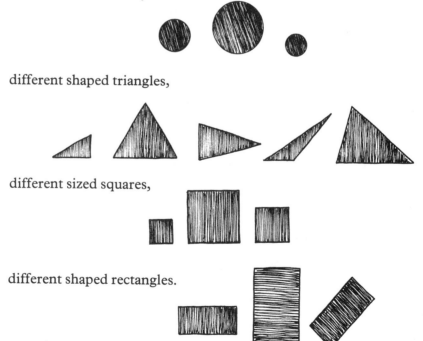

different shaped triangles,

different sized squares,

different shaped rectangles.

These shapes could be held up, one at a time or at random, and the children asked to name them. The teacher could show the children how to 'count round' the edges and corners of a shape to show that it has, for example, three straight edges and so must be a triangle. The name of the shape might be written on one side so that it can be turned round to confirm the answer.

Squares and rectangles all have four corners and four straight edges. At this early stage a square can be distinguished from other rectangles by just turning it round.

square 'looks the same'   rectangle 'looks different'

2 The large cardboard shapes could be used by the teacher to build up 'shape pictures', where the children choose which shape should fit on various parts of the picture. 'Sticky fixers' or 'Blu-Tac' will hold shapes in place if required.

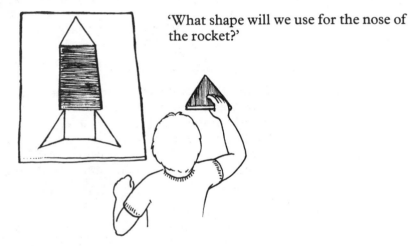

'What shape will we use for the nose of the rocket?'

3 A group of children could use the set of large cardboard shapes or a set of smaller plastic ones to sort into sets:

... and so on.

4 A group of children might 'name' a large collection of flat shapes or everyday objects with very little thickness, using name cards.

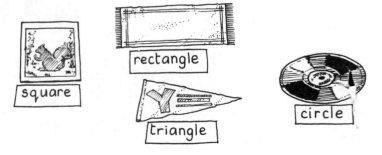

5 Pupils could also use name cards to name shapes in the classroom.

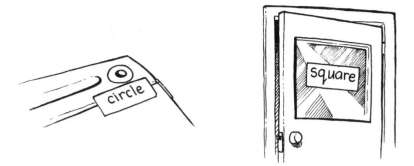

6 Gummed paper shapes could be used by children to make pictures and the names of the shapes added afterwards.

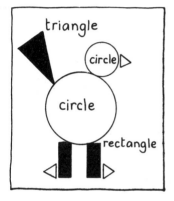
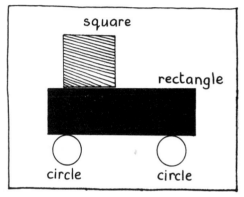

7 A wall chart of shapes and names could be made with new shapes added as required. This would help those with spelling difficulties when tackling the workbook pages.

8 Before attempting the middle section of Page 36 the teacher may wish to do some revision which relates flat shapes to the faces of three dimensional shapes. The children could use name cards for the flat faces of these shapes.

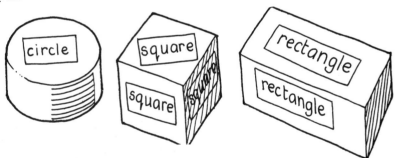

They could also draw round three dimensional shapes to make flat shapes which are cut out, named, and used for a wallchart.

Materials   set of shapes cut from Workbook 2, Page 34, scissors, glue

This page deals with sorting triangles and squares from the set of paper shapes on Page 34. The children should have had previous experience of recognising, sorting and naming such shapes, perhaps through some of the introductory activities given above. They should, in particular, have met different types of triangle and not just equilateral ones. The teacher should also have counted the corners and edges of shapes along with the children, introducing the idea of a straight edge by contrasting the circle, which has one curved edge, with the other shapes. The children should be guided to notice the connection between the number of straight edges and corners:

Triangle – 3 straight edges and 3 corners
Square   – 4 straight edges and 4 corners
Rectangle – 4 straight edges and 4 corners.

When doing question 1 on Page 33 the children could mark each triangle which they find on Page 34 with a cross before listing the letters of the set of triangles. It will be easier for the children to cut out the shapes if they remove the whole of Page 34 first and then cut in from the edges. Some children may need help in cutting, although great accuracy is not required for the activity of question 3 to be worthwhile. The aim of question 3 is that the children should recognise triangles of very different types, perhaps by counting edges, and should have the opportunity of handling them, turning them around and fitting them into frames as shown below.

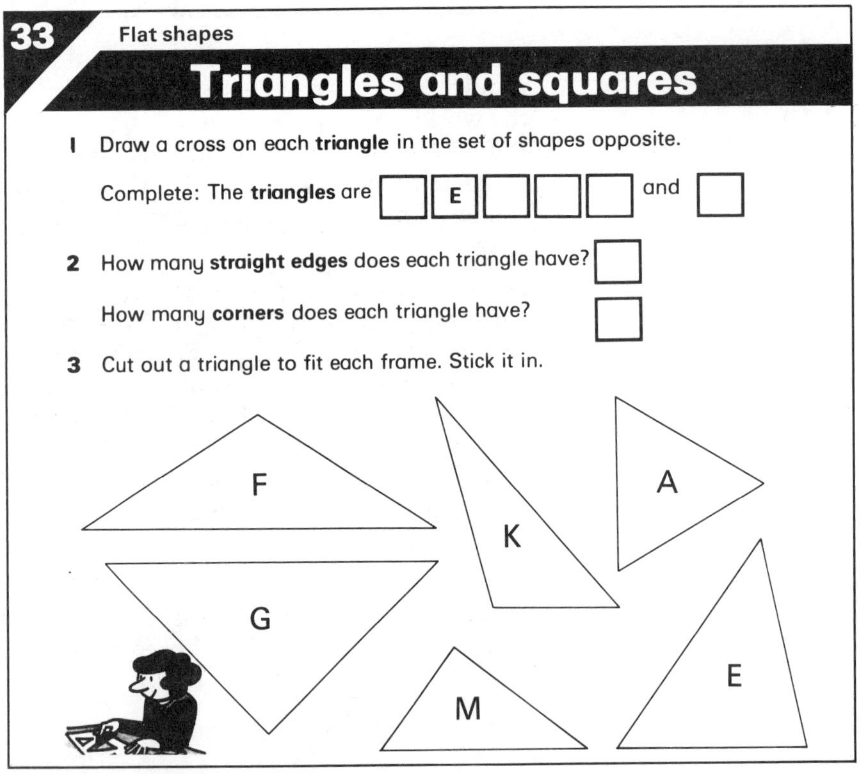

---

33   Flat shapes

Triangles and squares

1   Draw a cross on each **triangle** in the set of shapes opposite.

    Complete: The **triangles** are ☐ ☐E☐ ☐ ☐ ☐ and ☐

2   How many **straight edges** does each triangle have? ☐

    How many **corners** does each triangle have? ☐

3   Cut out a triangle to fit each frame. Stick it in.

    F   K   A
    G   E
        M

The bottom section of the page deals with the three squares L, J, and B. The children should count four corners and four straight edges for each one. At this stage a square can be distinguished from other rectangles by just turning it round (see introductory activity 1 on page 114 of these *Teacher's Notes*).

Squares and rectangles

No attempt has been made at this stage to make children aware of the sophisticated relationship between squares and rectangles – namely that all squares are special rectangles which have all their sides equal in length. In order to avoid the difficulty that this might cause with young children, the following could be used until the children are old enough to appreciate the meaning of the word 'rectangle':

'square' for

'oblong' for

However, this is *not* the approach used in *Primary Mathematics: A development through activity* where instead we use the terms

'square' for

'rectangle' for

until the full 'truth' can be revealed at a later stage.

| **Page 36** | **Rectangles** | **Flat shapes** |

Materials remaining shapes from Workbook 2, Page 34, scissors, glue

The top section of the page uses the remaining rectangles H, C, and D from the set of shapes on Page 34. This part can be handled in a similar way to Page 33.

Questions 3 and 4 give practice in writing the names 'circle', 'triangle', 'square' and 'rectangle'. Any child who uses 'rectangle' to describe the record cover might be told 'Yes, it is a rectangle, but it's even more special than that – it's a square'. Question 4 is difficult as it depends on the dots being joined correctly and in the right order. Particular difficulties are the 'long' line from 1 to 2, the lines joining 4 to 5 and 6 to 7 which cross a previous line, and the line joining 7 and 8 which also passes through 1. The finished effect should look like this:

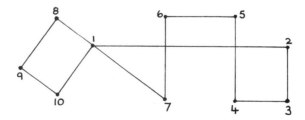

Introductory activities for Pages 37 and 38

Page 37 introduces two new shapes, the pentagon and the hexagon. These can be introduced by the teacher using cardboard or plastic shapes. It is important that the children see a variety of types and not just regular pentagons and hexagons. The teacher, along with the children, should count the corners and straight edges of these shapes.

Pentagons: five corners and five straight edges

Hexagons: six corners and six straight edges

Some of the introductory activities on pages 113 to 115 of these *Teacher's Notes* could be repeated for sets of shapes including circles, triangles, squares, rectangles, pentagons, and hexagons. The two new shapes should be added to any wallcharts of shapes and names. There are unlikely to be many examples of hexagons and pentagons in the classroom environment but it would be worthwhile discussing examples of these shapes in the outside world: hexagons in honeycomb cells, paving slabs, metal nuts, etc.

Page 37	Pentagons and hexagons	Flat shapes

Materials   none

This page gives practice in recognising pentagons and hexagons from cartoons of 'real life' objects. The children should be encouraged to concentrate on the red shapes only and to count edges or corners, to decide whether each one is a pentagon or hexagon.

Page 38	Colouring shapes	Flat shapes

Materials   coloured pencils or crayons

This page provides further work in the recognition of the six shapes circle, triangle, square, rectangle, pentagon, and hexagon. It might be used with all of the children or as revision in two ways:
(i) to give further practice to less able children
(ii) to occupy quicker children until others in the group catch up.
In any case, it is work which could be done at odd moments over a period of time.

Page 39	Revision	Flat shapes

Materials   none

This page provides further revision in recognition of the six shapes. The use of arrows in the top half of the page can be rather messy. Different colours could be used for the arrows to make the finished result easier to decipher. The table in question 2 is a systematic way of recording the previous work where corners and straight edges were counted. Some children will have difficulty with the circle which has no straight edges.

Additional activities

1 The children could contribute to a scrapbook of shapes cut from packets, magazines, etc.

2 The children could bring in objects with very little thickness which could be used to make a collection of squares, rectangles, etc. Such a collection could be mixed up and then sorted out again into sets by a group of children using name cards to place beside the shapes.

3 There are several simple shape games which would be suitable. For example:

(a) Shape dominoes

A set of dominoes like these can be made, using the six shapes from this section of work.

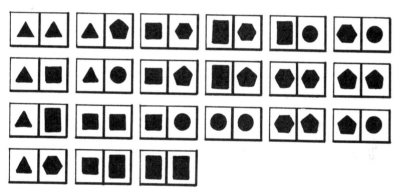

(b) A shape track game

The children throw an ordinary die to move around the track. Each time they land on a shape they can pick up a plastic shape of the same kind from the 'bank'. The first person to collect six different types of shape wins. A simpler game similar to this appears in the *Teacher's Materials Pack* for *Infant Mathematics: A development through activity*, Stage 1.

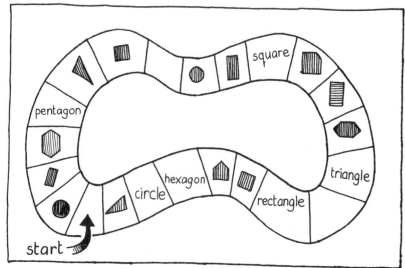

(c) Make a picture   Two or more children could be given worksheets with different shape pictures made up of the same number of shapes. They throw a special die with shape names written on it or turn over a card from a pack of shape name cards. They can colour in part of their picture to match the shape name on the card.

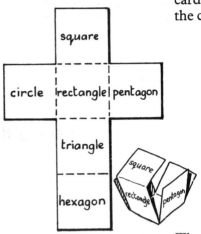

The first person to colour a picture completely wins.

(d) Shape paths game   The players pick shape cards like these to make moves on the board.

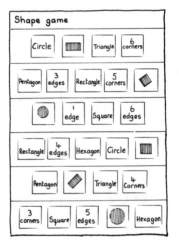

A game of this type appears in the *Teacher's Materials Pack* (Card 31).

(e) Match   A set of cards with shapes drawn on them and a set with shape names are dealt face down. Each player in turn turns over one card of each type to try to get a matching pair. If the cards do form a pair the player keeps them, if not they are turned over again for the next player's turn. The person who collects most pairs wins. Shape cards appear in the *Teacher's Materials Pack* (Cards, 32, 26, 13).

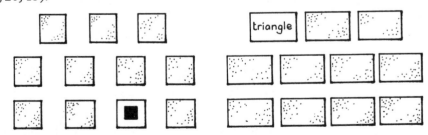

(f) Shape jigsaws   These can be made by cutting out large coloured cardboard shapes and then cutting them up into a *few* large pieces. These are then put in an envelope. The child assembles the pieces to make the shape asked for on the envelope.

Stage 1   Workbook 3

Stage 1   Workbook 3

Stage 1   Workbook 3

Introduction

As explained in the introduction to Stage 1, the workbook is arranged in such a way as to allow different sections of the work to be tackled at the same time by different groups within the class. It is not intended that the children work through the workbook in the order in which the pages are printed, nor is it necessary or even desirable for every child to do all the work on every page. The more able children can be guided quite quickly through the practice work but care should be taken to prevent the less able spending excessive time on one particular piece of work and so never reaching the valuable work on length, volume, and shape.

The number work, which should be tackled in sequence, can be split conveniently into four sections:

Pages 1 to 11 and	Subtraction within 99; addition and
Workcards 41 to 50	subtraction of money to 99p
Pages 12 to 15	Block graphs
Pages 16 to 20	Fractions – halves and quarters
Pages 21 to 25	Concept of multiplication

After any of these sections the children could be asked to do the corresponding parts of volume or shape. The length section includes work on half and quarter metres and teachers may wish to delay this until the section on fractions in the number work is being done. The work with half metres could be done after halves have been introduced and the work with quarter metres could be linked to the work with quarters.

The overall approach to the workbook will also be affected by the availability of materials. In particular it is likely that group working will be necessary when using the structured base ten material in the number work section, metre sticks in the length section, and nailboards in the shape section.

Teachers are again reminded that, in general, preliminary teaching is necessary before the workbook pages and workcards are attempted.

Contents

Materials

Counting materials such as counters, beads, buttons, cubes, and straws
Structured number material: tens and units
Notation cards
Number line to 100
Plastic, cardboard or real coins (1p, 2p, 5p, 10p, 20p, 50p)
Squared paper
Coloured pencils
Paper circles, squares, and rectangles suitable for folding
About twelve unmarked metre sticks or cardboard strips
Strips of cardboard about $1\frac{1}{4}$ m, 1 m, $\frac{3}{4}$ m, and $\frac{1}{4}$ m long
Mug, cup, teapot, egg-cup, paper cup, jar, carton, bottle, bowl, spoon,
    teaspoon, matchbox
Lentils, sand, peas, sawdust
Flashcards for new words
Six to ten nine-pin nailboards
String, scissors, sticky paper, glue, chalk, roll of paper
The teaching notes for each page list the specific material required and offer
suggestions for alternative materials where appropriate.
The following items from the *Teacher's Materials Pack* will be useful for this
workbook:

Addition picture   Card 8
Subtraction picture   Card 9
Number line to 100   Cards 10, 11, 12, 13

Number	**Subtraction within 99** **Money to 99p**	**Pages 1 to 11 and** **Cards 41, 43, 45, 47, 49**

Content and development

In Workbook 1 subtraction within 10 and then 20 was revised. In that section
children were expected to memorise facts such as

$14-4=10$		$14-\ 8=6$	
$14-5=\ \ 9$		$14-\ 9=5$	
$14-6=\ \ 8$		$14-10=4$	
$14-7=\ \ 7$			

where the answer is either a single digit or 10. Other subtractions such as
$17-3=14$ and $17-14=3$ were left to be done when children were familiar
with place value and were not intended to be memorised.
The first page of this section revises this earlier work and the remainder of
the section deals with the development of two digit subtraction. The
development is as follows:
1 Revision of basic facts
2 Subtracting tens
3 Subtraction without decomposition
   (i) units from tens and units
   (ii) tens and units from tens and units
4 Decomposition, showing the exchange of one ten for ten units

5 Subtraction using decomposition
   (i) units from tens and units
   (ii) tens and units from tens and units.
The unit contains problems involving addition and subtraction and money.
The extension to three digit subtraction occurs in Stage 2.

Introductory activities for Page 1

Some less able pupils may require practical activities to help them with this revision work. These activities could be chosen from the selection offered on pages 29 to 31 of these *Teacher's Notes*.

Page 1	Subtraction	Number Revision

Materials   cubes, counters, etc. if necessary

This page revises the subtraction facts which appeared in Workbook 1. There are arrow diagrams, simple word problems, and miscellaneous examples showing both horizontal and vertical recording. Most children should be able to recall these facts but less able pupils may need to use materials to find the answers.

Introductory activities for Page 2

Before starting the work of this page the children should try putting out and removing 'tens':

Put out 6 tens   Take away 2 tens

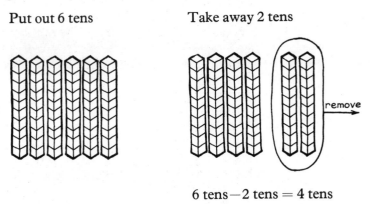

6 tens — 2 tens = 4 tens

This type of work could also be done using straws. The children should count out bundles of ten straws and put an elastic band round them.

Put out 6 tens

Take away 2 tens

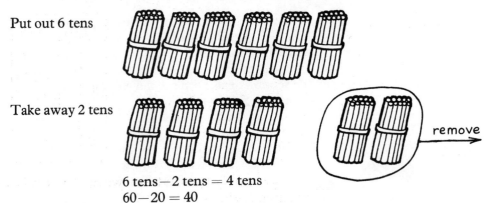

remove

6 tens — 2 tens = 4 tens
60 — 20 = 40

In this practical work the intention is to show children that the subtraction of tens is similar to that of units. The word 'tens' has to be said, and in final recording, six tens should be written as '60', etc.

Page 2	Subtracting tens	Subtracting tens

Materials tens and a notation card if required

Question 1 on this page highlights the use of the word 'tens'. Structured apparatus may be used in the way indicated in the introductory activities if this is necessary. Questions 2 and 3 use the numerical notation in both vertical setting and arrow diagrams. Question 4 deals with sequences, and a number line might be useful for some preparatory work in counting up and down in tens, for example

$$20, 40, 60, 80 \qquad\qquad 70, 60, 50, 40$$

The last example on the page is a simple word problem. Some teachers may wish to give more examples of this type, for example

'Harry had 80 nails.
He used 20 nails.
How many nails had he left?'

Introductory activities for Page 3

Page 3 involves subtraction of units from tens and units. Children should have the opportunity of working with structured material placed on a notation card. The notation card should be the same as that used for work on place value and for addition of tens and units.
Since the 'take away' aspect of subtraction is being considered, it is only necessary to lay out material to represent the larger number. The amount of material representing the smaller number is then removed. For example:

Put out 16 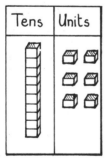   Take away 3 units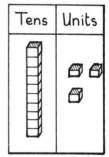

The 3 units are removed.

The answer is left on the notation card.

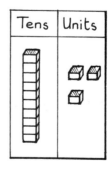

$$\begin{array}{r} 16 \\ -3 \\ \hline 13 \end{array}$$

The written form could be shown on the blackboard beside a sketch of the notation card.

Materials   tens, units, a notation card, and a number line

In question 1, the children should find the results using structured material and simply record these results in the appropriate places.

In question 2, the children should be encouraged to find the results without using materials.

As an introduction to question 3 it would be helpful to do some number line work. A number line is supplied in the *Teacher's Materials Pack*, Cards 10 to 13. The number line is used here to extend the memorised single digit subtraction fact to other related facts, for example $7-3 = 4$, $17-3 = 14$, $27-3 = 24$, $37-3 = 34$.

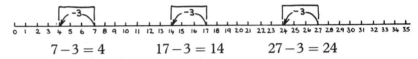

$$7-3 = 4 \qquad 17-3 = 14 \qquad 27-3 = 24$$

In this case a 'subtract 3' card is used to show the 'jump back' of 3. One would hope that as the card is moved along the number line to each new decade, a child would come to see that if 3 is subtracted from a number with 7 in the units column, the answer is always the same number of tens and 4 units.

Question 3 uses a number line and the idea of pattern to extend the basic subtraction facts to further decades, although the third example in this question does not start with the single digit subtraction fact. Some children may have to be reminded of $8-5$ before going on to $18-5$. Further oral work could be done using the class number line.

Introductory activities for Page 4

Subtraction of tens and units should be done using materials, the children working with structured apparatus to find the answers. A possible presentation for
$$\begin{array}{r} 37 \\ -22 \\ \hline \\ \end{array}$$
would be:

'Put out 37.

Take away 2 units.

Take away 2 tens.'

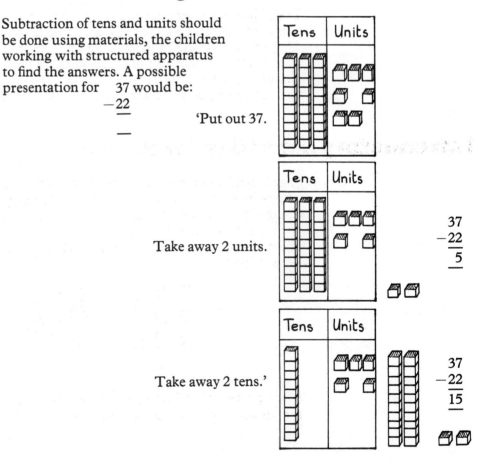

$$\begin{array}{r} 37 \\ -22 \\ \hline 5 \\ \end{array}$$

$$\begin{array}{r} 37 \\ -22 \\ \hline 15 \\ \end{array}$$

At first the children should use the structured apparatus to do the subtraction and should simply fill in the written answer by looking at the material which is left. It is very important that the teacher should choose a suitable time to relate the written calculation on paper to what happens when the children use the materials. The language used should exactly match the various stages when using materials. The aim is to move gradually to mental calculation recorded on paper without using apparatus. One possible form of language for this is as follows:

$$\begin{array}{r} 37 \\ -22 \\ \hline \\ \hline \end{array}$$ '37 take away 22.

$$\begin{array}{r} 37 \\ -22 \\ \hline 5 \end{array}$$ 7 units take away 2 units leaves 5 units.

$$\begin{array}{r} 37 \\ -22 \\ \hline 15 \end{array}$$ 3 tens take away 2 tens leaves 1 ten.

The answer is 15.'

Teachers should choose a language to suit themselves, their class and their school, so long as it matches the use of the materials. Some teachers may prefer to say, '2 units from 7 units is 5 units' and '2 tens from 3 tens is 1 ten'.

Page 4	**Subtracting tens and units**	Subtraction Without exchanging

Materials   tens, units, and a notation card

The children are expected to have had the opportunity of working with the structured apparatus as suggested in the introductory activities for Page 4. They should use this apparatus to answer the problems in question 1. It is hoped that the children will gradually make less use of the materials when tackling question 2. The teacher should relate the language to be used for the calculation on paper to what was done when using the materials.

Introductory activities for Page 5

Page 5 involves exchanging a ten for ten units. In Workbook 2, when dealing with place value, children experienced 'changing'. Sixteen units were changed to give one ten and six units. The reverse idea was also used, namely one ten and six units were changed to give sixteen units.

When doing addition, children should have put out nine cubes and then seven cubes:

In the process of addition ten units were exchanged for one ten to give one ten and six units.

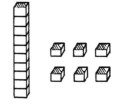

We now want to emphasise the exchanging in the reverse direction. The children should be shown how to use the materials on a notation card to get the result. For example:

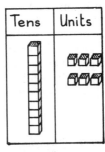

'Put out 1 ten and 6 units.   Change the ten for 10 units.

How many units altogether? 16 units.'

Other exchanges should be done with larger numbers, but only one ten should be exchanged for units each time.

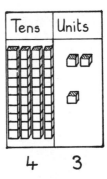

4   3

'Put out 43.

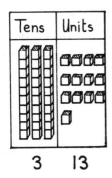

3   13

Change a ten.'

Four tens and three units can be changed to three tens and thirteen units. Several examples should be worked through like this with the children using materials before tackling the workbook page.

Some teachers may wish, for variety, to use other materials to show the same process. Straws and elastic bands could be used.

'Put out 31.

Change a ten.

3 tens and 1 unit can be changed to 2 tens and 11 units.'

Cuisenaire rods, Unifix cubes, and other structured apparatus may be used. Examples involving the exchanging of a ten when the number has a units digit of 9 are probably best omitted here as decomposition will be unnecessary in actual subtraction examples. For example:

79
−2★ ←No matter what units digit is placed here decomposition of 79
⎯   will not be required.
⎯

| **Page 5** | **Exchanging** | Decomposition |

Materials tens, units, and a notation card

The children should use structured material as described in the introductory activities to do question 1. They should then record the result.

The bottom part of the page contains two arrow diagrams to check that the pupils have understood the exchanging. For this part of the page, materials should only be used by pupils who cannot do without them.

Introductory activities for Pages 6 to 8

The preceding work should have taught the principle of exchanging. This principle will now be applied to subtractions involving tens and units where the number of units to be subtracted is greater than the number of units available.

1 Single digit subtraction The following procedure and language could be used, but teachers could use their own preferred language so long as it matches what is being done with the materials. For example:

There are 32 people on a bus. 7 get off. How many are left?

$$\begin{array}{r} 32 \\ -7 \\ \hline \end{array}$$

Put out 32.

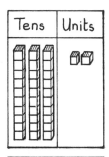

Subtract the units.
'2 units take away 7 units,
I cannot.'

Exchange a ten.

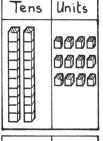

We now have 2 tens and 12 units.

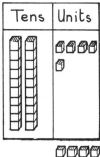

'12 units take away 7 units leaves 5 units.'
Subtract the tens.
'2 tens take away 0 tens leaves 2 tens.'

The answer is 25.

These are the 7 units which were removed.

The children would then record the result by writing in '25'.

$$\begin{array}{r} 32 \\ -7 \\ \hline 25 \end{array} \quad \text{or} \quad 32-7 = 25$$

The children should be talked through several examples like this to develop the language. When they have mastered this, they should progress to two digit subtraction, which can be dealt with in a similar way.

2 Two digit subtraction

Let us consider the problem

$$\begin{array}{r} 83 \\ -37 \\ \hline \end{array}$$

Put out 83.

Tens	Units
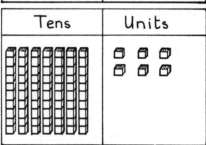	

Subtract the units.
'3 units take away 7 units, I cannot.'

Exchange a ten.

Tens	Units

We now have 7 tens and 13 units.

'13 units take away 7 units leaves 6 units.'

Tens	Units

Subtract the tens.
'7 tens take away 3 tens leaves 4 tens.'

Tens	Units

The answer is 46.

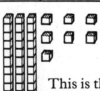

This is the 37 which was removed.

The answer is left on the notation card.

3 The written technique

The next step in the development is to show how the use of the structured apparatus leads to the written technique.

Subtracting the units:

'3 take away 7. I cannot.
I need more units.'

$$\begin{array}{r} 8\ 3 \\ -3\ 7 \\ \hline \end{array}$$

'Change a ten.
7 tens and 13 units.'

$$\begin{array}{r} \overset{7}{\cancel{8}}\overset{1}{3} \\ -3\ 7 \\ \hline \end{array}$$ or $$\begin{array}{r} \overset{7}{\cancel{8}}\overset{10}{3} \\ -3\ 7 \\ \hline \end{array}$$

'13 take away 7 leaves 6.'

$$\begin{array}{r} \overset{7}{\cancel{8}}\overset{1}{3} \\ -3\ 7 \\ \hline 6 \end{array}$$ or $$\begin{array}{r} \overset{7}{\cancel{8}}\overset{10}{3} \\ -3\ 7 \\ \hline 6 \end{array}$$ '7 from 10 is 3 and 3 is 6.'

Subtracting the tens:

'7 tens take away 3 tens leaves 4 tens.'

$$\begin{array}{r} \overset{7}{\cancel{8}}\ 3 \\ -3\ 7 \\ \hline 4\ 6 \end{array}$$ or $$\begin{array}{r} \overset{7}{\cancel{8}}\overset{10}{3} \\ -3\ 7 \\ \hline 4\ 6 \end{array}$$

Teachers should alter the details of what is said by pupils to suit their own class and school, provided the language matches what is happening with the material.

The method of decomposition was chosen by the authors because it can readily be explained to young children through the use of structured tens and units materials. Some schools may not wish to use this method of subtraction and may opt for one of the others. 'Equal additions' is one such method and is usually written with crutch figures as shown:

$$\begin{array}{r} 8\ \ ^1 3 \\ -3_1\ 7 \\ \hline 4\ \ 6 \end{array}$$

The examples in the workbooks can be used satisfactorily with children who do not use decomposition provided the diagrams of tens and units are ignored. The page on 'exchanging' would, of course, have to be omitted. While structured apparatus can be used to explain a method such as 'equal additions', its use is complicated for children of this age group.

Page 6   Subtracting units   Subtraction   With exchanging

Materials   tens, units, a notation card and a number line

The diagrams on this page simulate the work with structured apparatus. Question 1 should be done using the materials and the results recorded in the appropriate places. In question 2 children should gradually move from using the concrete materials to the more abstract written form. Some form of 'crutch figures' may be used. In these examples only units are being subtracted, but in each case a ten has to be decomposed.
As an introduction to question 3 it would be helpful to do some number line work. The number line is used to extend the memorised single digit subtraction fact to other related facts. For example:

$$14-7=7 \qquad 24-7=17 \qquad 34-7=27$$

A 'subtract 7' card is used to show the 'jump back' of 7.

After some practice it is hoped that children will be able to generalise that a jump back of 7 from any number with a units digit of 4, will always land on a number with a units digit of 7. They may also see that they land in the previous decade, so the tens digit is reduced by one.

Question 3 uses the number line as described above to extend the subtraction facts to succeeding decades. In parts 2 and 3 some children may have to be reminded of 15−8 before doing 25−8, and 11−4, 21−4 before doing 31−4. Further oral work could be done using the class number line.

Page 7	Subtracting tens and units	Subtraction With exchanging

Materials tens, units, and a notation card

The children are expected to have had the opportunity of working with the structured apparatus as suggested in the introductory activities. The diagrams at the top of this page simulate this working.

Question 1 should be done using the material and the results recorded in the appropriate places. In question 2, the children should gradually move from using the concrete materials to the more abstract written form. Some form of 'crutch figures' may be used. For example:

$$\begin{array}{r} {}^{3}\!\!\!\!\!\!{}^{1}\!\!\!\!\!\!4\,0 \\ -2\,3 \\ \hline \end{array}$$

Page 8	Subtraction	Subtraction Miscellaneous

Materials tens, units, and a notation card if required

This page contains miscellaneous examples on subtraction of tens and units, including problems, and could be used for revision.

Not all the examples require decomposition, so it is important that the children look carefully at the units column of each example before 'changing a ten'.

The word problems at the bottom of the page all involve subtraction. The children should use the coloured lines beside each example to position their written recording. For example:

There were 82 pupils at the school disco.   82
47 pupils were girls.   −47

How many boys were at the disco?   ——

Page 9	Addition and subtraction	Problems

Materials none

As the title suggests, this page contains both addition and subtraction problems. The first six questions relate to a record kept by a teacher of sales of crisps. A table is given showing the number of each variety of crisps sold to boys and girls. The totals should be completed by adding vertically.

Questions 1 to 6 do not exhaust all the possibilities for using the information in the table. Some teachers may wish to ask further questions involving this information. It is important that the pupils realise that they must set down working in the spaces provided for examples 3 to 8.

The bottom part of the page shows dart scores for Linda and Lorna. Totals have to be found first and then subtraction is required to find how many each girl needs to score 80.

Introductory activities for Pages 10 and 11

Both these pages deal with shopping activities involving addition and subtraction to 99p. It would be advantageous to have a 'class shop' which groups of children could use. Prices should be such that totals for two items are less than 99p.

One simple way to make up a class shop is to draw pictures on a large sheet of card and put price tags on the pictures. Another way is to stick pictures from catalogues and magazines on a large sheet of card. Each large card could represent a different shop, for example, sports shop, toy shop, shoe shop, sweet shop, clothes shop, ironmonger, restaurant, etc. If slots are cut in the card (shown as a dotted line in the diagram), price tickets can be inserted in the slots. This technique makes it easy to change prices without having to make a new shop. A more orthodox shop with toys or other objects on a counter, where children come up and buy, could also be used.

The children should be asked to buy two articles and find the total cost. Coins could be used to pay the 'shopkeeper' and the shopkeeper could give change where necessary. Each child should have the chance to be shopkeeper. Some revision may be necessary about giving change. In a real shop change would be given by counting on. For example, if 50p is given for an article costing 33p: '33p and 2p makes 35p, and 5p makes 40p, and 10p makes 50p'.

Page 10	Shopping	Money to 99p

Materials   coins, if required

Before attempting this page, the children should do lots of practical work, in which they work with coins.

The first example is partially completed to show the layout that is expected. For each purchase the prices are taken from the articles shown. Two different sets of objects are priced to give a variety of addition and subtraction problems.

The first six questions are all addition, finding the cost of two articles. Questions 7 to 11 all involve subtraction and in every case 'exchanging' is necessary. Question 11 gives the lead in to the next page where children are asked for 'change'.

Page 11	More shopping	Money to 99p

Materials   coins

The first five questions ask the children to find the cost of two articles. They then buy these articles and have to find the change they would receive from a given sum of money.

In each case they tender coins so that change is necessary. If something costs 37p, an amount of 40p or 50p should be tendered. To tender 60p made up of 50p + 10p or three 20ps would be unrealistic as one of the coins would be unnecessary each time.

In the last question the children have to find the cost of the two dearest articles.

Additional activities

A large toy shop price list could be used.
The workcards shown below are to be used in conjunction with this price list. Should teachers wish to use both sides of a card, the suggested even-numbered cards should be on the reverse side of the odd-numbered ones, that is card 2 on the reverse side of card 1, card 8 on the reverse side of card 7, etc.

The children could record their answers by putting a circle round a value, for example,

(20p) (10p) (5p) (2p)   for 37p.

Buy from the shop. 1	Buy from the shop 2	Buy from the shop 3	Buy from the shop 4
1. Copy and complete: boat costs ___ book costs ___ Total ___ 2. Put out coins for the total. 3. Write down the coins you put out.	1. Copy and complete: doll costs ___ book costs ___ Total ___ 2. Put out your change from 80p. 3. Write down the coins you put out.	1. Copy and complete: crayons cost ___ bat costs ___ Total ___ 2. Put out coins for the total. 3. Write down the coins you put out.	1. Copy and complete: game costs ___ boat costs ___ Total ___ 2. Put out your change from 90p. 3. Write down the coins you put out.
Buy from the shop 5	Buy from the shop 6	Buy from the shop 7	Buy from the shop 8
1. Copy and complete: bat costs ___ game costs ___ Total ___ 2. Put out coins for the total. 3. Write down the coins you put out.	1. Copy and complete: book costs ___ bat costs ___ Total ___ 2. Put out your change from 60p 3. Write down the coins you put out.	1. Copy and complete: crayons cost ___ boat costs ___ Total ___ 2. Put out coins for the total. 3 Write down the coins you put out.	1. Copy and complete: bat costs ___ boat costs ___ Total ___ 2. Put out your change from 80p. 3. Write down the coins you put out.
Buy from the shop 9	Buy from the shop 10	Buy from the shop 11	Buy from the shop 12
1. Copy and complete: doll costs ___ crayons cost ___ Total ___ 2. Put out coins for the total. 3. Write down the coins you put out.	1. Copy and complete: game costs ___ crayons cost. ___ Total ___ 2. Put out your change from 90p. 3 Write down the coins you put out.	1. Copy and complete: doll costs ___ boat costs ___ Total ___ 2. Put out coins for the total. 3. Write down the coins you put out.	1. Copy and complete: bat costs ___ doll costs ___ Total ___ 2. Put out your change from 90p. 3. Write down the coins you put out.

Number cards
41, 43, 45, 47, 49   Subtraction of tens and units

Materials   none

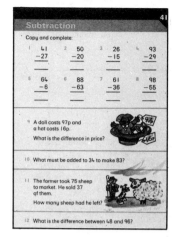

These cards are referenced from Page 11, after the children have done addition and subtraction of money to 99p. They provide extra practice examples and word problems about subtraction. As they are all similar in both content and level of difficulty, they may be done in any order.
A variety of language is used in the problems. 'Difference between', 'Difference in price', 'What must be added to?', 'How many left?', 'Subtract', 'How many more?' are examples of this. These phrases do not all appear on every card and some children may have to be reminded about some of them. The teacher should avoid telling the children that these examples are all 'subtractions' as some children will just look for the numbers and subtract without really reading the problem. The aim is for the children to understand what they read.
The sample card shown is typical of the layout of all the others in the set.

Number cards
42, 44, 46, 48, 50   Add or subtract

Materials   none

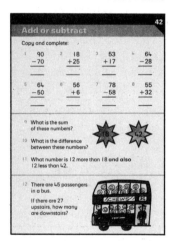

These five cards contain a selection of both addition and subtraction of tens and units. They could either provide further practice in this work as soon as Page 11 of the workbook has been completed, or could be used at a later date as revision cards.
The cards are of comparable difficulty and may be done in any order.
Each card follows the same pattern. Questions 1 to 8 are a miscellaneous selection covering additions and subtractions of tens only, additions with and without an exchange, and subtraction with and without decomposition. This is followed either by questions in which the children have to interpret the wording of the question before carrying out the appropriate addition or subtraction, or by a puzzle or pattern type question. Each card finishes with a word problem.
The children should be familiar with the language and type of examples used on these cards from work on the workbook pages. However, some children may find parts of these cards difficult.
The sample card shown is typical of the layout of the others in this batch.

Pictorial representation   Pages 12 to 15

Content and development

This section introduces the block graph, initially with a vertical display and then with a horizontal display.
In Workbook 1, objects or pictures of objects were arranged in columns (or rows) to construct a graph. In this workbook, each graph is built up by colouring squares. Centimetre squares are used but the square size does not matter. Each coloured square represents one object or one pupil and consequently the graph assumes a less pictorial appearance than the graphs constructed previously.

Throughout the work it is recommended that the children be given an opportunity to investigate topics of their own choice. They could carry out other surveys, collect their own data, and construct their own graphs. Some possible topics are included at the end of this section.

Pictorial representation is developed further in Stage 2 where the children are introduced to 'bar' or 'column' graphs.

| **Page 12** | **Breakfasts** | Graphs |

Materials none

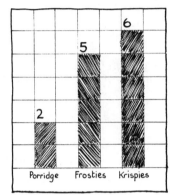

This page shows a completed block graph, arranged as a vertical display, which is followed by several interpretative questions. The teacher will have to explain the significance of the columns of coloured squares. It might be sufficient to point out that the two coloured squares above the 'Porridge' category show that two pupils in the class had eaten that particular cereal for breakfast that day.

To start with, the children might be asked to count the coloured squares for each cereal and to write the totals at the top of the columns. The information required to answer the questions is now available.

The children should now tackle the questions provided. When this is done, the teacher might encourage some general discussion about the graph. Questions like 'Would a graph for our class be the same as this?', 'Do you know any cereals not listed here?', 'Which cereal on the graph was more popular than any other?' might stimulate further interest. Indeed, it is recommended that the children make up a breakfast graph for their own class. This could be a large wall display graph, which could also include written comments from the children. Once the choice of cereals had been agreed, the data might be collected from a show of hands and the number for each cereal recorded on the blackboard.

| **Page 13** | **Colours** | Graphs |

Materials coloured pencils

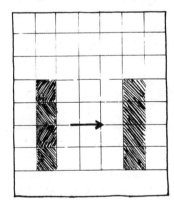

On this page there is a blank squared grid on which the children are to construct a block graph with vertical display. The topic here is 'favourite colours' and it would be appropriate if the children were to use the actual colours when colouring in the squares.

A few children may realise that instead of drawing and colouring one square at a time they can count up the total number of squares for each colour and then colour all the squares at once.

Question 3 is an attempt to elicit comments from the children with regard to the completed graph. Oral discussion would help the children to clarify their ideas and this should mean a better standard of written comment. The response will naturally vary from child to child and it may be worthwhile for the children to hear some of the other stories which have been written.

Again, it is suggested that the children should construct their own colours graph, after making up an agreed 'shortlist' of colours. Instead of a show of hands, it might be wiser to have the children write their preferred colour on a piece of paper. This avoids any 'bandwagon' effect and the votes, once collected, are opened and recorded in turn so that the shape of the graph is not complete until the last vote is opened.

| Pages 14 and 15 | Fruit, Games | Graphs |

Materials   coloured pencils for Page 15

These two pages are similar to Pages 12 and 13 except that now the graphs are in horizontal display. As suggested earlier, help from the teacher may still be necessary for some children. Discussion should be encouraged once the graph is completed, and the children might be asked further questions like 'How many more liked apples than bananas?', 'Which fruit was more popular than any other?', 'Would our class choose the same favourites?', 'Which other fruits do you like?'.

Again the children should have the opportunity to draw their own graphs for favourite fruit and favourite games.

Additional activities

There are many other activities which would be suitable for graphical work at this stage. The choice should be made by the teacher and will depend on factors like the interests of the children, the situation of the school, thematic studies covered, and the need for further practice. Here is a list of topics for consideration: favourite sweets, favourite TV programmes, favourite sports programmes, favourite ice-creams, favourite flat shapes, favourite solid shapes, favourite garden birds, favourite farm animals, favourite school day (Monday to Friday), favourite hobby. Also hair colours, eye colours, shoe colours, birthdays (Sunday to Saturday).

The teacher should discuss with the children which of these topics they would like to do. Further discussion would result in an agreed shortlist of about five or six items for each topic from which the children choose. The list could be written on the blackboard and the numbers for each item obtained by a show of hands.

It is often a useful idea to let the children group themselves into a formation which represents the data for the graph before drawing the graph itself.

Some of the graphs drawn should be large enough for display on the classroom wall. 2 cm or 5 cm squared paper is suitable for this purpose. Other graphs could be constructed on an individual or group basis using centimetre squared paper. The children should be asked to display some of the topics vertically and others horizontally.

Fractions – halves and quarters   Pages 16 to 20

Content and development

This unit provides activities which will help to develop the concept of one half and one quarter.

Some children may have been introduced to these concepts in earlier years, for example in *Infant Mathematics: A development through activity*. This unit should help to reinforce and extend these pupils' understanding.

Language introduced includes the words 'half', 'equal', 'part', 'halved', 'whole', 'quarter', and 'quartered'. The notation $\frac{1}{2}, \frac{2}{2}, \frac{1}{4}, \frac{2}{4}, \frac{3}{4}, \frac{4}{4}$ is introduced and this symbolic way of writing the words is explained to the children. Activities include folding and colouring parts of wholes.

In Stage 2 this fraction work is extended to include eighths, thirds, sixths, fifths, and tenths.

Introductory activities for Page 16

It is likely that the children have already met the expression 'one half' and possibly 'one quarter'. These are difficult concepts for a young child to grasp, so it is worthwhile giving further experience.

1 The children should be shown a wide range of objects which can be seen as a 'whole', for example, a cake, a biscuit, an apple, a picture, a shape. Each whole can be broken into parts:

Here the picture of a house is broken into parts.

The parts can be put together to make a whole.

These pieces can be put together to make a 'cake'.

2 Sometimes the parts are special ones. If one part fits exactly on top of another, the two parts are equal:

This tree is made up of two parts. These two parts are equal.

3 The children can place other equal parts together to make one whole, for example:

Three of these equal parts make a whole cake.

4 The children can be given a variety of shapes and asked to say how many parts make up each shape, for example:

5 The children should also be given experience of shapes which are composed of equal parts.

6 Paper shapes such as rectangles, squares, and circles could be folded to produce two parts. At first, folding should not be structured in any way and the children should make unequal parts. Then attention can be given to folding so that edges are aligned and two equal parts are produced. This prepares for the introduction of halves.

The shapes used in the first five activities described above could be plastic shapes, or cardboard ones made by the teacher. If the children have difficulty in recognising equal parts, paper copies can be cut up and the parts superimposed.

Flashcards for the key vocabulary could be made and used in these activities:

whole   equal   parts

Page 16   **Halves**   Fractions Halving

Materials paper shapes, coloured pencils

The children should know the words 'two', 'equal', 'half'. The word 'halved' should be introduced as 'What has happened when a whole has been made into two equal parts, into halves'.

Folding should either be introduced to the children before question 4 is tackled or help should be given with this question. The children should realise that to make equal parts they must try to match the edges very carefully when folding.

Labelling each part with 'one half' may also require guidance.

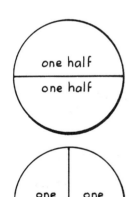

Other shapes which can be used for folding in half are the triangle (isosceles or equilateral), rectangle, square, regular pentagon, and regular hexagon. The children might see if they can fold a shape in a different way from their neighbour and yet still produce halves, for example, using a square the pupils can produce halves which are triangles or rectangles.

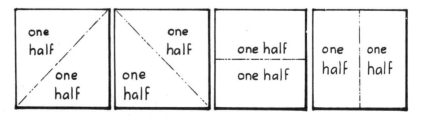

Some children may think that a horizontal fold line produces 'different' rectangles from a vertical fold line. Others will realise that they are the same. Rotation of the square should make this clear.

A display should be made of the folded shapes. This gives an opportunity to emphasise that two halves make one whole:

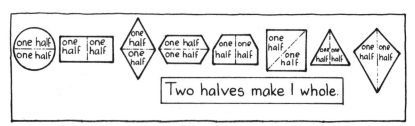

Introductory activities for Page 17

Page 17 concentrates on two ideas: visualising the whole from a given half and writing one half as $\frac{1}{2}$.

Visualising the whole

1 If pupils have difficulty in visualising the whole from the given half, the teacher could provide plastic or cardboard 'halves' so that the whole shape can be made, for example:

This can then be matched to the drawings to find the correct one.

2 A set of cards could be made for a matching game.

Initially the pupils can spread these face up and match the equal parts. This allows the children to become familiar with the cards before playing the game. The cards are then shuffled and placed face down in two rows. As in the pelmanism game, a pupil turns over a card from each row. If these match to make a whole shape he or she keeps these cards. If the halves do not make a whole shape, they are turned face down again and the next pupil has a turn. The player to collect most pairs of cards wins.

In this work with fractions, it is important that the pupil thinks of one half, not in a generalised way, but as one half of a particular whole – a circle, a house, a shape.

Writing one half as $\frac{1}{2}$

Notation of fractions should not be rushed. The children will realise from previous activities that to write 'one half' is time consuming. They should be shown how to use two numerals to write a fraction. In $\frac{1}{2}$, the 2 shows the number of equal parts that make up the whole and the 1 shows how many of these parts is being considered.

Page 17	Halves and wholes	Fractions Notation

Materials   coloured pencils

Questions 1 to 3 deal with visualising the whole from the given half. Once pupils have drawn their house in question 3 they should compare it with a neighbour's drawing. Question 4 deals with writing one half in fraction notation. The pupil is required to write $\frac{1}{2}$ neatly in the halves of each shape. The teacher may like to make up rectangular boards like these for pupils to use:

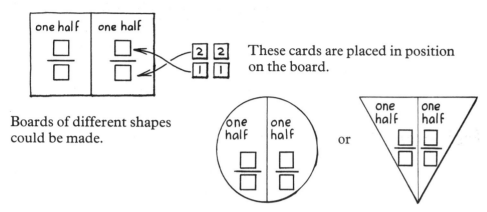

These cards are placed in position on the board.

Boards of different shapes could be made.

or

Introductory activities for Page 18

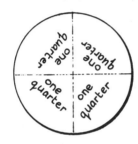

1 The children should fold different shapes. They will probably need help to fold the paper circle into quarters. The placing of the words 'one quarter' on each part will also need guidance.
   Other shapes which could be quartered include the square and the rectangle. These can be folded in different ways, for example:

squares   and rectangles

2 The phrases 'one quarter' and 'quartered' should be taught and might be used on wallcharts.

One quarter is coloured.

The apple has been quartered

3 The notation $\frac{1}{4}$ should be introduced. The children apply their knowledge of how to write one half as $\frac{1}{2}$ to a new situation. Here one of four equal parts is being referred to, so the pupil might suggest that $\frac{1}{4}$ is used.

Page 18	**Quarters**	Fractions Quartering

Materials   paper circles (about 10 cm in diameter), coloured pencils

In this page the children divide a shape into quarters and learn to read the words 'one quarter' and 'quartered'. There is also practice in recognising a shape which has been divided into quarters and in quartering shapes. Question 4 is intended to give the children experience in finding how many parts shapes have been divided into and if these parts are equal. If the shape has four equal parts, it has been 'quartered'. This word may be new to some children.

For the notation $\frac{1}{4}$, the teacher should revise the way in which one half was written in a short way and so establish which numerals are used and where each is written to show one quarter.

For the examples in question 5, the children should draw lines to show four parts and should make the parts as equal as possible.

Additional activity

A set of snap cards could be made, some cards showing diagrams with halves or quarters shaded and some with the notation $\frac{1}{2}$ or $\frac{1}{4}$. These could be matched by an individual pupil or used for a game of pelmanism or snap with two or three pupils.

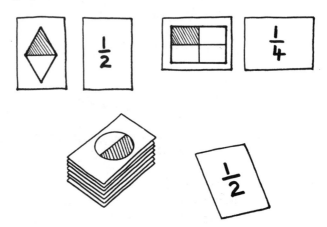

| Page 19 | Colouring quarters | Fractions   Quarters |

Materials   coloured pencils

Before trying this page, the children should have the opportunity to develop oral language involving quarters. The teacher could take a shape which has been divided into quarters, for example a circle made up of four equal parts. This could be used to find that:

  (i) four quarters make up the whole shape

 (ii) each piece is one quarter

(iii) two pieces are referred to as two quarters

(iv) three pieces are called three quarters.

In examples 2, 3, and 4 on this page, different colours can be used for each quarter, for example:

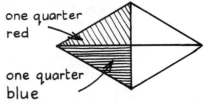

one quarter red

one quarter blue

| Page 20 | Halves and quarters | Fractions   Notation |

Materials   coloured pencils, string, scissors, sticky paper

This page introduces children to the notation $\frac{2}{4}, \frac{3}{4}, \frac{4}{4}$.

The notation $\frac{1}{2}$ for one half and $\frac{1}{4}$ for one quarter should be revised. The children should be asked to explain what each number in $\frac{1}{2}$ and $\frac{1}{4}$ represents. They could then be asked how they think three quarters would be written using numbers. Two quarters and then four quarters can also be discussed and recorded as $\frac{2}{4}$ and $\frac{4}{4}$.

The top section of Page 20 gives the written phrase, the notation, and two illustrations for $\frac{1}{4}$, $\frac{2}{4}$, $\frac{3}{4}$, and $\frac{4}{4}$.

In question 1, the children shade diagrams to match the fraction notations. Question 2 gives the children practice in writing the fraction notations for

given diagrams. For a diagram like this 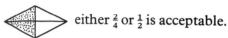 either $\frac{2}{4}$ or $\frac{1}{2}$ is acceptable.

In question 3, an attempt is being made to extend the type of 'whole' the children are using. When using shapes, they are halving and quartering areas. It is useful to give examples of lengths such as pieces of string, ribbon, and tape, which can be folded and sometimes cut into halves and quarters. Labels can be made for the string using gummed paper like this:

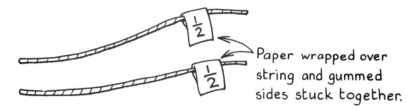

Paper wrapped over string and gummed sides stuck together.

Many children, when first presented with a length of string, point to the middle as 'half'. It is important that the children realise that half a piece of string is a length and not a point.

Additional activities

1   Halving a lump of plasticine or a volume of water would present a challenging problem for bright pupils.
2   The cards used for the snap game suggested at the end of the notes for Page 18 could be supplemented to cover fractions such as $\frac{2}{2}$, $\frac{2}{4}$, $\frac{3}{4}$, $\frac{4}{4}$.
3   Cards or worksheets could be made for additional practice:

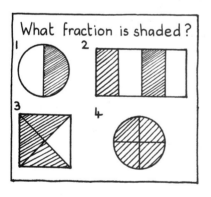

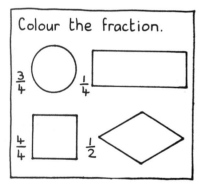

Number – multiplication

Content and development

This section revises and extends the kind of practical and visual approach to the concept of multiplication that is included in many courses for Infants. *Infant Mathematics: A development through activity* uses this kind of approach. The revision includes pictures of sets and written recording in the form □ sets of □.

The language of multiplication is extended and the symbol '×' introduced. Multiplication is then treated as the repeated addition of equal sets.

The section ends with the children laying out two equal sets of counters to obtain the facts of the '2 times table'.

The work is further developed (as far as the 5 times table) in Stage 1, Workbook 4.

Page 21	Equal sets	Multiplication The concept

Materials   counters, cubes, etc. if required

Practical work   Before children attempt the work on this page they should have the practical experience of laying out sets of objects, toy cars, counters, cubes, beads and so on, each set having the same number of objects. They should be encouraged to use the language of sets to describe what they have done.

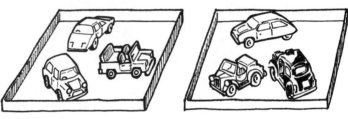

'2 sets of 3'

The children have to be able to answer questions like 'How many cars are in each set?' and 'How many sets of 3 are there?'.

Recording activities   Gummed paper shapes, stars, circles, etc. can be used by the children to make a visual record:

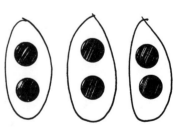

'3 sets of 2'

The teacher should show the children how to make simple drawings of, say, '3 vases each with 4 flowers'.

Written recording   In discussion, the teacher should highlight the different forms of written recording which the children will have to know for Page 21:
_____ sets of 3; 5 sets of _____; _____ sets of _____ .

Oral work   Oral work based on Page 21 might take the form of, 'How many fish in each bowl?', 'How many bowls of fish are there?' and so on.
With sufficient practical work, discussion, and oral questioning, the children should find this revision work in Page 21 fairly straightforward.

Multiplication – language and notation

The work on Pages 22 to 25 is most important since it deals with the extension of the language of multiplication, the introduction of the '×' symbol and the beginning of a systematic treatment of the '2 times' table. Particular care should be taken to present these ideas as lucidly as possible.

1 Extension of language   Practical work leads naturally to an extension of the language used in multiplication situations:

Put out 3 bundles with 5 straws in each.

   This gives '3 bundles of 5'.

Make 4 piles with 5 coins in each.

       This gives '4 piles of 5'.

Draw 3 dots in each of 4 sets.

       This gives '4 sets of 3' or '4 threes'.

2 The '×' symbol   All of these phrases, 'bundles of', 'piles of', 'sets of', can be replaced by 'times' which we symbolise by '×'.

So

is seen as 4 sets of 3 or 4 threes or 4 times 3 or 4 × 3.

This interpretation is not universally agreed. Some people interpret the operation symbol '×' as 'multiplied by', so 4 × 3 is read as '4 multiplied by 3' which would be illustrated as

which shows 3 sets of 4 or 3 fours.

With *young* children, we take the view that '3 sets of 4' or '3 fours' or '3 times 4' is better symbolised as 3×4 rather than as 4×3 which reverses the factors. In the next part of the development of multiplication, which is in Stage 1, Workbook 4, the important commutative law of multiplication is introduced by establishing in a variety of ways that the answer to 2×5 is the same as the answer to 5×2. Thus it is shown that $2 \times 5 = 5 \times 2$, similarly $4 \times 3 = 3 \times 4$, and so on.

To sum up: in Workbook 3 we are interpreting 3×4 as 3 sets of 4 or 3 fours or 3 times 4, so all the preliminary practical activities and the associated discussion and oral work should support this interpretation.

Introductory activities for Pages 22 and 23

1 The teacher (or a child) puts out a number of equal sets of objects:

The discussion might include:
'How many sets are there?'
'How many cubes in each set?'
'We could write 3 sets of 5.'
'Give another way of writing this.'
The teacher should ensure that all the forms that the children need to know for Pages 22 and 23 are included, that is 3 sets of 5, 3 fives, 3 times 5, 3×5.

2 The children could be given cards such as

| 3 sets of 5 | | 3 fives | | 3 times 5 | | 3 X 5 |

and asked to lay out appropriate materials such as cubes, buttons, or counters in trays or sorting boxes. The children can use gummed paper shapes, stars or circles to produce a visual record of this activity.

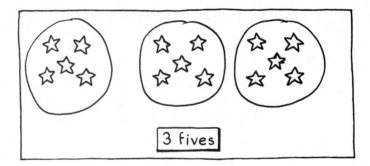

3 Cards made using 'picture stamps' or 'transfers' are convenient for this work.

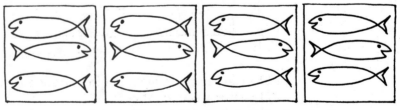

4 sets of 3 or 4 threes or 4 times 3 or 4×3

The cards should contain 2, 3, 4, 5, and 6 pictures of objects, and there should be six of each, which gives a set of thirty cards. Cards 25 and 26 of

Infant Mathematics: A development through activity, *Teacher's Materials Pack* for the Second Stage provide cards like these. The cards could also be made using dot patterns or gummed paper circles.

4 The children could be asked to lay out equal sets of counters and then to draw the sets. For example:

They should be encouraged to describe what they have done and to make a written record: 5 sets of 2, 5 twos, 5 times 2, 5×2.
This drawing activity and the making of a written record is needed for Pages 22 and 23.

Page 22	**Making equal sets**	Multiplication The '×' sign

Materials   counters, straws, coins, and cubes

This page will be difficult for some children if it is done only as a paper and pencil exercise. The children will benefit more from the work if they lay out materials and discuss what is required. The introductory activities described earlier should prepare children for this important work although the teacher will have to ensure that the children know what they have to 'fill in'.

Page 23	**Drawing equal sets**	Multiplication The '×' sign

Materials   counters, straws, cubes, etc. if required

This page depends on the particular interpretation of the '×' sign detailed in the introductory activities. The children should be reminded of this interpretation, perhaps by means of the example at the top of Page 23.

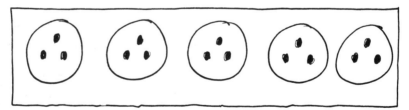

This illustrates 5×3

The teacher could highlight important meanings by asking
'How many sets are there?'
'How many dots in each set?'
'Can you say what this shows?'.
Some oral discussion of question 2 is advisable if children are to attempt the work with confidence. The teacher might also use the blackboard to

illustrate how to attempt the question. For example, for '4 × 3' the teacher might ask 'How many sets do we have to draw?', and then choose a child to draw the sets:

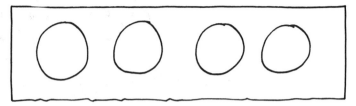

The teacher could then ask, 'How many dots should there be in each?' and ask another child to finish the job by putting in the dots.

Introductory activities for Pages 24 and 25

Multiplication as addition of equal sets

This work should show children that multiplication facts can be found by repeated addition:

3 sets of 4 or 3 fours

is equal to	4	+	4	+	4	
so 3 × 4	=	4	+	4	+	4 = 12

Later it will be more convenient to know multiplication facts such as 6 × 3 = 18 rather than having to repeatedly add 3+3+3+3+3+3. Here are some suggestions for practical activities.

1 Children could use objects such as counters, cubes, etc. to show

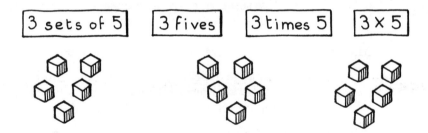

then should write 3 × 5 = 5+5+5 = 15.

2 The set of thirty cards described on page 146 of these *Teacher's Notes* could be used to speed up the laying out of equal sets. Laying out 3 sets of 5 or 3 fives or 3 times 5 is conveniently done by selecting three cards such as

This should be followed by recording 3 × 5 = 5+5+5 = 15.

3 Children should have the experience of drawing sets of dots or using gummed paper shapes. For example three sets of five dots

This should be followed by writing $3 \times 5 = 5+5+5 = 15$.

Page 24	Adding equal sets	Multiplication Repeated addition

Materials   counters

In question 1, the children will have to be shown the kind of written work that is expected of them. These examples on this page deal with multiplication as repeated addition of equal sets. Although the actual totals are not required, it would be worthwhile asking the children for the totals. Oral work based on an example such as

should include questions like
'How many sets are there?'
'How many dots in each set?'
'How many dots altogether?'.
This oral work should then be recorded as $5 \times 4 = 4+4+4+4+4$.
In question 2, the children are expected to put out counters for each example and then to complete the written record. The totals are found, initially, by repeated addition, but some children might be helped by the use of a number line.

After some work using counters, the ablest children may not need them to complete subsequent examples.

Page 25	Two equal sets	Multiplication The 2 times table

Materials   counters

Before children attempt this page the teacher should use other materials such as cubes to build up the 2 times table.

       $2 \times 1 = 2$

then $2 \times 2 = 4$

then $2 \times 3 = 6$
and so on.
The children will need explicit instructions about how to do question 1:
'Put one counter in each set. What do you have?'
'Two ones, that's two altogether. So two times one equals two.'
'Put out another counter in each set. What do you have now?'.
'Two twos, that's four altogether. So two times two equals four', and so on.

In question 2, the teacher could lead the children in this work by showing dot patterns for 2×1 to 2×5. The children should be told to draw the dots in each set in a paired pattern as far as possible. Thus:

shows $2 \times 7 = 14$.

Since the ultimate intention is for children to memorise the facts of the 2 times table, considerable oral work based on Page 25 is desirable. Earlier work on 'doubles' should help children to remember these facts.

Additional activities

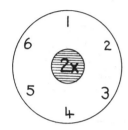

1 A large dial could be used for oral work with the children. The teacher points to a number, say 4, and then a child has to give the answer to 2×4. Later the dial could deal with all the numbers 1 to 10. There could be a team game where a score is kept for each team. The team gets a point for each correct answer.

2 A small group of two to four children could play a 'doubles' game on a board like this:

2	4	6	8	10
4	6	8	10	12
8	10	12	6	2
12	8	10	2	4

Coloured counters or cubes are needed so that each player has a different colour. An ordinary die or a set of thirty cards (five of each numeral 1 to 6) is used. The players take turns to throw the die (or to take a card from the shuffled pack which is blank side up).

or

The score, say 3, is doubled and the answer, 6, is covered on the board (if a 6 is still uncovered) with a counter or cube of that player's colour. The game is finished when all the numbers on the board are covered. The winner is the player who has covered most numbers.

Later on the children could play on a board containing all the facts of the 2 times table like this:

2	4	6	8	10
20	18	16	14	12
12	14	16	18	20
10	8	6	4	2

Two dice, each marked 0 to 5, or a set of thirty cards (three of each numeral 1 to 10) would be needed.

3 The sequence 2, 4, 6, 8, . . . 20 and also 20, 18, 16, 14, . . . 2 could be practised orally. The teacher could start off the sequence then ask a child for the next number 'up' or 'down'.

This could be played as a team game, where a point is scored for each correct answer.

Additional worksheets and cards for multiplication

Many children would benefit from doing extra work on this important topic. Here are suggestions for worksheets and cards which might be used.

1 Picture stamps, stars or simple drawings could be used to make a range of worksheets or wipeable cards.

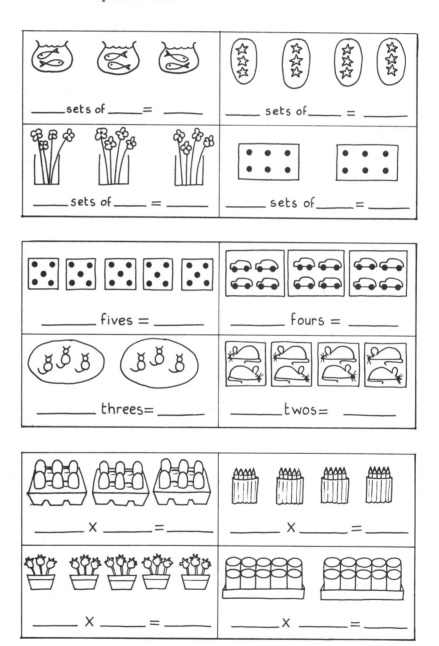

Draw 2 dots in each set. ◯ ◯ ◯ ◯

_____ sets of _____ = _____

Draw 3 eggs in each nest.

_____ sets of _____ = _____

Draw 2 straws in each glass.

_____ twos = _____

Draw 4 matches in each box.

_____ fours = _____

Draw 5 spots on each dog.

_____ x 5 = _____

Draw 3 fish in each tank.

_____ x 3 = _____

2 Cards could be made to suit the more able children.

1	2	3	4
Use 3 tubs. Put 4 buttons in each. Copy and complete ___ sets of___ = ___	Use counters. Put out 5 sets of 3. Copy and complete ___ sets of___ = ___	Make 2 strings of 10 beads. Copy and complete ___ tens = ___	Make 4 piles of 5 coins. Copy and complete ___ fives = ___

5	6	7	8
Put out cards to show 5 sets of 3. Copy and complete 5 x 3 = ___	Put out cards to show 3 sets of 6. Copy and complete. 3 x 6 = ___	Lay out counters to show 3 x 4. Draw what you have put out.	Use cubes to show 4 x 3. Draw this.

9	10	11	12
Draw sets of dots to show 6 x 3. Copy and complete 6 x 3 = ___	Draw sets of dots to show 5 x 6. Copy and complete 5 x 6 = ___	Draw 3 rings. ◯ Draw 5 marbles in each. Copy and complete 3 x 5 = ___	Draw 4 jars. Draw 3 flowers in each. Copy and complete 4 x 3 = ___

Length

Note: The notation for ½ m and ¼ m is used in this unit. It is therefore recommended that the unit on fractions, Pages 16 to 20, should be done before this unit.

Content and development

In this section the children are introduced to the metre and two of its fractional parts, the half and the quarter metre. The metre is the first conventional standard that the children have met.

Earlier, in Workbook 1, the work on length covered the language of length as used in simple comparisons of pairs of objects and the ordering of more than two objects. The idea of measurement was introduced using arbitrary standards such as rods, straws, cubits, and spans. The children will probably have begun to see the need for a conventional standard.

This section begins with an activity specifically designed to show that a conventional standard is necessary. This leads to the children using the metre as their first conventional standard for measuring lengths. After some experience in using metres the children are encouraged to estimate lengths. The skill of estimation is developed in order to secure the concept of the unit used, thus formalising the guessing which was part of the earlier work. Thereafter, measuring activities are carried out using half metres and quarter metres.

The metre is the only conventional standard measure to be introduced in Stage 1, the kilogram, litre, and square centimetre first appear in Stage 2.

Page 26	Measuring lengths	Length Need for a standard unit

Materials   about twelve unmarked metre sticks or cardboard strips one metre long

The work on this page is designed to emphasise the need for a conventional standard. Before the children tackle question 1 the teacher should work with the class or group to ensure that they know what is required.

The teacher should choose two children, one with large and one with small hands. They should measure the length of the teacher's desk using their own spans and should make a record of their results. For example, John measures the length of the desk to be 15 spans and Alice measures 18 spans. Discussion of the results should include the question, 'Do you know why the measurements are different?'.

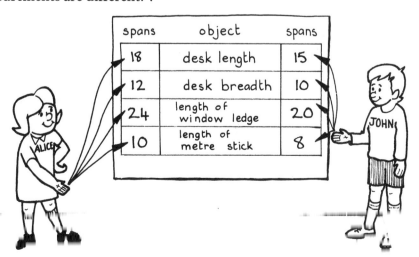

spans	object	spans
18	desk length	15
12	desk breadth	10
24	length of window ledge	20
10	length of metre stick	8

The children should realise that Alice has a *shorter* span than John. This conclusion should then be tested by direct comparison of their spans. The two children should be asked to measure other objects in the same way and their ensuing results collected on a chart drawn on the blackboard, similar to the one on the workbook page.

Discussion of these results should emphasise that if Alice needs *more* spans than John for a particular measurement, Alice has a *shorter* span than John. In question 1, the children work in pairs. The teacher may prefer to change the arbitrary standard for some pairs to a cubit or foot length to avoid repetition. The children will have to choose objects which can be suitably measured using cubits or feet.

In question 2, the children have to measure a single length (the length of the classroom) using three different standards. Again they work in pairs so that results can be compared. The metre stick should be *uncalibrated* and can be made from card if necessary. The teacher may well have referred to this uncalibrated length as a metre stick in Workbook 1. If not, the term metre stick should now be used. This 'arbitrary standard' will be adopted as the first conventional standard in the ensuing work.

It is important that some discussion of the results in question 2 takes place. Children may notice that the number of feet differs from child to child (as does the number of giant steps) and that the number of metres does not, but the full significance of this will only be brought out in discussion with the teacher. The children should be made aware of the advantages of the metre, a fixed unit of length, over the foot length, giant step, cubit, and span, all of which may vary from child to child.

Page 27   Measuring with metres   Length   The metre

Materials   metre stick, strip marked A, strip marked B (strip A should be $1\frac{1}{4}$ m long, strip B should be very close to 1 metre. These strips can be made from paper or card, ribbon, dowelling, etc.)

The work in this page and in Page 28 is concerned with measurement using the metre – the first conventional standard to be introduced to the children. Before the individual child begins question 1, the teacher should recall the use of metres on Page 26. The metre should be represented by an uncalibrated length at this stage and it is desirable that wooden metre sticks are used, although paper or card substitutes are possible. A diagram similar to the one on the workbook page can be drawn on the blackboard and one or two lengths filled in after measuring with the metre stick. The opportunity should be taken to emphasise that lengths are to be recorded as, for example, '*length* of my desk' and not merely 'desk'.

longer than a metre	about the same length as a metre	shorter than a metre

Some discussion will be necessary before the children tackle question 2. Indeed some children will need help in reading and understanding the instructions. In these cases the instructions are best handled orally so that the children can concentrate on the measuring tasks and the completion of the table. In previous work children have been encouraged to guess lengths before measuring them. Now they are introduced to the more formal term 'estimate'. One of the aims in the measurement programme is that each child should develop the ability to make reasonable estimates of lengths. Clearly this ability is dependent upon the child's conception of the metre. It is important to ensure that the child estimates, *then* measures each length *in turn* (rather than makes all the estimates and follows this with all the measurements) in order to develop the concept of a metre. It would be helpful in this context if a metre length, clearly labelled, were permanently on display in the classroom.

Similar tables have to be completed when the child first measures using half metres (Page 30) and also quarter metres (Page 31).

Page 28	Longer lengths	Length Using metres

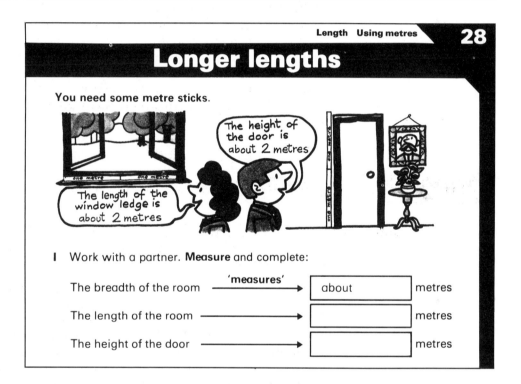

Materials   a supply of metre sticks

Work on Page 27 was concerned with lengths which were just under, about the same as, and just over one metre in order to develop the concept of a metre. Now the children are asked to measure (in question 1) the dimensions of the classroom and to express their measurements as 'about' a certain number of metres. In question 2 this activity is repeated but the children are asked to estimate each length before measuring. In question 1, it is hoped that a supply of metre sticks will be available which can be laid end to end along, for example, the breadth of the room and then counted. In question 2, it would be more reasonable to restrict the number of metre sticks available to two, which can be laid end to end alternately. If the school does not have a hall then the teacher should direct the children to some other part of the building or playground.

In the table of results the column headed 'Difference' may cause difficulty for some children. If a length is estimated to be 'about 3 metres' and the measurement is found to be, for example, 'just over 4 metres', then the 'difference' should be stated as '*about* 1 metre'. The need to use 'approximate' language should be pointed out.

The final question, question 3, restricts the children to a single metre stick when measuring lengths, this time in the corridor. A finger should be placed on the floor to mark the end of the metre stick when it is being moved forward to mark out the next metre. Some children may cope more easily if they are allowed to use two metre sticks.

In these measuring situations lengths which are parts of a metre will inevitably arise and should be dealt with using phrases such as '2 and a bit' metres or 'about 2' metres or 'nearly 2' metres or 'just over 2' metres. The illustration at the top of the workbook page could be discussed from this standpoint. It is important that the children come to appreciate the approximate nature of measurement and this use of 'approximate' language should be encouraged from the beginning.

Page 29	**Measuring with half metres**	Length The half metre

Materials   metre stick, roll of paper, scissors, strip marked C (similar to those on Page 27 but $\frac{3}{4}$ metre long)

Children gradually become less satisfied with the 'and a bit' situation in measurement. There is a need to make a more precise statement. On this page the children are introduced to the half metre.
In question 1, the child makes his or her own half metre strip. Although the instructions are clear it may be worthwhile discussing the procedure with a group of pupils. One or two children could be chosen to construct a 'metre stick showing half metres'. Cut off a metre length of coloured card or coloured gummed paper roll. Repeat using a second (and, if desired, a third) colour and cut into half metre strips. Stick the half metre strips and the metre strip together thus:

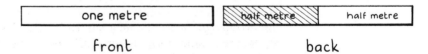

front   back

This metre stick could be used instead of individual metre and half metre strips in questions 2 and 3. If using metre sticks which have been purchased from an educational supplier, these should be calibrated in half metres only. Question 2 follows the pattern of question 2 on Page 27. This time fewer instructions are given on the assumption that the child's experience on Page 27 will help towards an understanding of what is required. Nevertheless some children will need to discuss the question with the teacher in order to clarify what is required. Again, each estimate should immediately be followed by the actual measurement before moving on to the next object for estimating then measuring.

In question 3, some of the objects to be measured may be more than one metre long. The child must realise that he or she should use a mixture of metre and half metre strips. Before the children tackle this question the teacher could discuss the illustration on the workbook page and ask a child to measure the classroom blackboard in a similar way. The teacher should also discuss the form of recording used and emphasise the use of the word 'about' in, for example, 'about two and a half metres'.

The metre and half metre strips should be retained for use with Page 30.

Page 30   Half metres   Length   Using half metres

Materials   the children's metre and half metre strips, chalk

In question 1, the children are shown 'the short way' to record. For example, two and a half metres is recorded as '$2\frac{1}{2}$ m'. Many teachers may prefer a group discussion of this form of recording before asking the children to attempt the question. Note the use of a lower case 'm' and the absence of a full stop. Questions 2 and 3 provide further practical work and more recording using metre and half metre strips. The questions asked introduce a competitive element, as children try to outdo one another in their hops, bunny jumps and so on. It is suggested that at any one time only a small group undertake this activity, which most children will find enjoyable.

As in the similar tables encountered previously, the children have to find the difference between each estimate and the corresponding measure. On this occasion some estimates and measures will involve half metres and this could cause greater difficulties for the children. If so, it might help if the child lays down strips for the estimate, and alongside these another set of strips for the measure, thus:

Nevertheless, the idea of 'difference' where half metres are involved may be beyond the capability of some children and they should simply omit this column in the table of results.

Page 31   Quarter metres   Length   The quarter metre

Materials   metre stick, roll of paper, scissors, strip marked D (similar to those for Page 27 but close to $\frac{1}{4}$ metre long)

On this page the children are introduced to the quarter metre. Again *each* child should make his or her own quarter metre strip. Before doing so it may be necessary to revise or even introduce the idea of 'quartering' an object. This will depend to some extent on whether the child has experience of one quarter from the number work on Pages 16 to 20. The teacher could discuss with the children how to cut a long piece of string into quarters, a short piece of string into quarters, a long thin 'sausage' of plasticine into quarters, etc. This should lead on to the children constructing their quarter metre strips in question 1. Again, it may be worthwhile for one or two children to make 'a metre stick showing quarters' using coloured card or gummed paper strip.

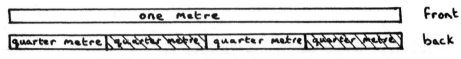

A variation on this idea which might prove useful would be:

Question 2 follows the approach taken for the metre (Page 27) and the half metre (Page 29) and the comments made there apply equally here.

In question 3, the fractional notation, $\frac{1}{4}$m, is introduced, and the children are asked to record, for example, two and a quarter metres the short way as '$2\frac{1}{4}$m'. Again, many teachers will wish to discuss this notation with the class or group before the children attempt the question.

In question 4, the children have to use the fractional notation in a practical situation. If desired, more practical work could be given. The children might be asked to measure out on the floor or in the corridor lengths specified as $1\frac{1}{4}$m, $2\frac{1}{4}$m, etc. By this means lengths involving the fractional notation '$\frac{3}{4}$m' can be avoided. However, the fraction $\frac{3}{4}$ is introduced on Page 20 in the work on number and, if desired, specified lengths could include $1\frac{3}{4}$m, etc. If it is felt that more work is necessary to reinforce the idea of $\frac{3}{4}$m, the teacher might proceed as follows:

(i) Lay three quarter metre strips alongside a half and a quarter metre strip.

(ii) Lay four quarter metre strips alongside a metre strip.

In discussion bring out the possibility of replacing $\frac{1}{2}$m by $\frac{2}{4}$m, 1 m by $\frac{4}{4}$m, and the $\frac{1}{2}$m and $\frac{1}{4}$m by $\frac{3}{4}$m.

Additional workcards

Cards could be prepared and used to supplement the work of Pages 29 to 31. Here is one such card.

> 1. Copy this heading.
>
>   <u>Shorter than a half metre.</u>
>
> 2. Make a list of objects in the classroom you <u>estimate</u> are shorter than a half metre.
>
> 3. Now use your half metre strip to check. Tick where you were correct.

Clearly, the 'heading' to be written in the child's jotter can be varied considerably. The objects could be 'shorter than', 'longer than', and 'about the same length as'. The lengths could be a half metre, a quarter metre, three quarters of a metre, and possibly even one and a half metres.

Volume
Cards 32, 34, 36, 38, 40
Pages 32 to 35

Content and development

Most children in their first two years at school will have attempted filling and pouring activities with water and sand, such as are found in *Infant Mathematics: A development through activity*. These activities will have involved language such as 'pour', 'fill', 'full', 'holds more'. Problems such as 'How many spoonfuls fill the tub?' will have provided an approach towards the use of non-standard measures.

This work is revised and extended in Cards 32, 34, 36, 38, and 40 and in workbook Pages 32 to 35.

In the main, the cards provide consolidation of the ideas and language covered in the first two infant years and are meant to be done before the workbook pages.

The workbook pages provide practical work with water, lentils or similar dry material, and develop the language associated with volume by use of phrases such as 'holds more', 'holds less', 'has a greater volume', 'has a smaller volume', 'holds most', 'holds least', 'has the greatest volume', 'has the smallest volume'.

This work is developed further in Stage 2, when arbitrary standards and later, standard measures, are considered.

Introductory activities for Cards 32, 34, 36, 38, 40

Before the children are asked to do the cards, the teacher should use containers, water, lentils, sand, sawdust, etc. to discuss with the children the kind of activities found in the cards.

Some children are slow to grasp the concept of volume and the teacher should set up activities and discussion which will show up any doubt or insecurity which the children may have. For example, a tall bottle is filled with water. This water is then poured into a wide bowl or basin. The bottle is then refilled with water and the child asked, 'Which has more water in it, the bottle or the basin?'. The child who understands the principle of conservation will know that there is the same amount of water in both containers. The child who has *not* grasped the concept may think that the bottle has more water, since there is a greater *depth* of water in it than in the basin. Any child who is in this latter category is not yet ready for the activities which are concerned with finding which of two containers holds more than the other.

Here are some examples of activities and discussion which should prepare children for Cards 32, 34, 36, 38, and 40.

1 'Do you think the mug or the cup would hold more water?'

'John, would you like to find out, by pouring, which holds more?'

2 'Betty, fill this jug with water.'
'Mary, find how many times you
can fill the glass from the jug.'
'Now, Tom, you fill the jug up
again and then find how many
times you can fill the *mug* from the
jug.'

3 'Bobby, take this egg-cup full of
water and pour it into the mug.'
'Now find how many eggcupfuls it
takes to fill the mug up to the
brim.'
'Jean, you find out how many
eggcupfuls it takes to fill the carton
to the brim.'
'Which one needed more
eggcupfuls to fill it?'

4 'Robert, take the spoon and the jar of lentils (sand, etc.) and find how many
spoonfuls it takes to fill the matchbox.'
'Peggy, it's your turn now. Find how many spoonfuls it takes to fill the
doll's teacup.'
'Which needed more spoonfuls to fill it, the matchbox or the doll's
teacup?'

The kind of activity and discussion outlined above should give the children
the confidence needed to tackle the workcards. The teacher should also make
sure that the children understand words like 'brim' which may be unfamiliar.
Some help may be required with reading words like 'eggcupfuls'. A set of
flashcards to highlight such words would be useful.

Card 32	Mug or cup?

Materials   mug, cup, water

This is a straightforward activity, but children should be encouraged to fill
and pour carefully and to try not to spill too much water when pouring from
the cup into the mug. The mug and cup should be such that it is clear from
the pouring activity that one holds more than the other.
In this and the other cards in this section, the children gain valuable practical
experience of filling and pouring with minimum spillage.
With regard to the concept of volume, they are learning in an informal way
that the mug, say, holds more than the cup. Teachers should not insist on
written statements such as 'I found that the mug holds more than the cup',
but if a child writes this without prompting this is fine. Many children will
probably write statements like 'The teapot filled the mug 4 times and it filled
the cup 7 times and a bit more'. Such statements are perfectly acceptable.

Card 34   The teapot

Materials   teapot, mug, cup, water

This activity relates to everyday experiences such as Mum pouring out the tea.

Card 36   Filling

Materials   egg-cup, paper cup with level line marked inside with indelible marker, water

This card provides experience in careful filling and counting, using an egg-cup as a measure. The activity is related to one which the child will probably encounter later, when, say, filling a graduated measuring jar up to a specific mark.

The children should be advised to note down the number of eggcupfuls needed to fill the cup to the brim, so that the number is not forgotten, before proceeding to the second activity of filling the cup up to the mark.

Card 38   Spoonfuls

Materials   egg-cup, teaspoon, matchbox, jar of lentils or similar material

This activity provides further practice in careful filling with as little spillage as possible, this time with a dry material instead of water.

The teacher should discuss with the children whether they should use heaped or level spoonfuls. Indeed, it would be interesting for the activity to be completed with level spoonfuls first and then with heaped spoonfuls. Alternatively, some children might use level and some heaped spoonfuls.

The children should be advised to write down the number of spoonfuls needed for the egg-cup, say, before going on to find how many are needed for the matchbox.

Written statements such as, 'I needed 3 heaped spoonfuls for the egg-cup and 4 heaped spoonfuls to fill the matchbox' are acceptable.

After completion of the activity and the written work, the teacher could discuss what had been done and go on to ask children what they think would happen if they filled the egg-cup, say, and then poured the contents into the matchbox. This could then be tried to see if the expected result actually happened.

Card 40	**The same amount**

Materials

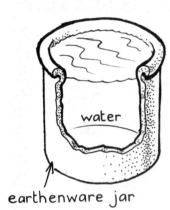

earthenware jar

A carton labelled 'A' and a box labelled 'B' each of which holds the *same amount* of lentils, a spoon, a supply of lentils (or sand, or sawdust)

This activity gives the children experience of containers of different *shape* which hold the same *volume* of material. This is an important idea. When the lentils are poured carefully from the filled carton into the box, it should be found that the box is also filled. The children should then be able to deduce that the same number of spoonfuls would be needed to fill either container.

Introductory activities for Pages 32 & 33

These two pages are concerned with:
1 Estimation to determine which of two containers holds more than the other.
2 Activities involving pouring from one container to another to determine which holds more.
3 Associated language – 'holds more', 'holds less', 'has a greater volume', 'has a smaller volume'.

It is important that children develop skill in estimation since this is associated with calculation and measurement in everyday life. It is through constant practical work that accuracy in estimation improves.

In these and the following pages the word 'volume' is used rather than 'capacity'. When used in context the word 'volume' is normally unambiguous. In later work the volume of water, or other material, which a container holds (its capacity) is usually measured in units based on the litre, whereas the volume of the material of which a container is made is measured in units based on the cubic metre, for example in cubic centimetres. In this course, when we talk of the volume of, say, an earthenware jar, we are referring to the volume of water it can hold and *not* to the volume of solid earthenware of which the jar is made.

Children have already had experience of pouring from one container to another, and Pages 32 and 33 are once again concerned with this kind of activity. New language is, however, introduced here, with phrases like 'holds less', 'has a greater volume', 'has a smaller volume'. The teacher should involve the children in some of this 'pouring' work and introduce the new language. The children should be given ample oral practice in the use of this new language. Special care should be taken to ensure that words which may be new to the children, for example, 'estimate' and 'volume' are thoroughly understood. Flashcards such as the following, would be useful.

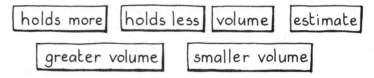

Here is an example of the kind of discussion which might take place:

Teacher: 'Ann, do you think the mug or the cup holds more water?'
Ann: 'The mug will hold more.'
Teacher: 'Find out by pouring, then.'
Ann: 'Well, I have filled the cup from the mug and the mug still has some water in it. The mug holds more than the cup.'
Teacher: 'What could you say about the cup?'
Ann: 'The cup does not hold as much as the mug.'
Teacher: 'That's right. We say that the cup holds *less* than the mug.'

Similar activity and dialogue could take place with other children. Repeated use should be made of words and phrases such as 'estimate', 'has a greater volume', 'has a smaller volume'.

Page 32	**Which holds more?**	Volume Language

Materials   jar, carton, mug, water, lentils (or sand, or sawdust)

In questions 1 and 2, the children are first asked to write down an estimate. An ability to make sensible estimates of volume develops with experience and practice. Children have to learn that more than one dimension is relevant here. It is not enough to look at the relative heights of two bottles since width is equally important.

Volume   Language   **32**

Which holds more?

Do Volume Cards, 32, 34, 36, 38, 40 **before doing this page.**

You need:

a jar   a carton   a mug   water   lentils

I   Which do you **think** holds **more**,

the jar or the carton? _____

Fill one of them.

Find out by pouring which

holds more.   _____

2   Which do you **think** holds **less**,

the jar or the mug?   _____

Fill one of them.

Find out by pouring which

holds **less**.   _____

After estimating, they have to pour from one container to another to determine which holds more. They should be interested to see if their estimate is correct or not.

It should be made clear to children that 'wrong' estimates are not a cause for shame or ridicule. Everyone becomes better with practice. It is often almost impossible to estimate with assurance, so a practical test is essential.

Teachers are left to decide whether water or a dry material like lentils should be used. It is desirable that the children have experience of working with both water and dry materials in the course of the work.

In questions 3 and 4, the children are expected to judge by looking at the pictures of the containers.

Page 33	Volume	Volume Language

Materials   mug, cup, carton, water, lentils (or sand, etc.)

This page follows the pattern of Page 32 but the phrases 'has a greater volume' and 'has a smaller volume' are used instead of 'holds more' and 'holds less'.

Introductory activities for Pages 34 and 35

The work on Pages 34 and 35 involves *three* containers. The teacher should discuss at some length how to find which holds *most* and which holds *least*, in this kind of situation:

We might fill A and pour its contents into B, thus finding that A holds more than B. We could then refill A and pour its contents into C, to find that A also holds more than C. We can then say that A holds *most*. We can now settle, by pouring, whether B holds more or less than C and so the problem is solved.

Again, suppose we fill A and pour into B to find that A holds more than B. We then refill A and pour into C to find this time that A holds *less* than C. It follows that C holds most and B holds least. Trials and discussions of this kind are a necessary preliminary to the work of Pages 34 and 35.

Children should also be given an opportunity to practise the new language. Flashcards like these would be helpful:

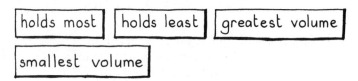

Page 34	**Which holds most?**	Volume Language

Materials   bottle, jar, cup, water (or lentils, etc.)

In questions 1 and 2, the children are again asked to make an estimate and then to find out in a practical way.

In questions 3 and 4, the children are expected to answer by just studying the pictures. Some children may benefit from oral discussion of the pictures with the teacher and/or other children before writing answers.

Page 35   **Greatest and smallest volume**   Volume   Language

Materials   jug, bowl, teapot, water

The work of this page is similar to that of Page 34 but the phrases 'has the greatest volume' and 'has the smallest volume' are used instead of 'holds most' and 'holds least'.

In the illustration for questions 3 and 4, the occupants are of comparable size to avoid any doubts or difficulties that children might have with perspective. For example, if a large balloon was further away from the observer than a small one, the large distant balloon could appear smaller than the nearer small balloon. In Page 35 it should be clear that balloon P is the largest, balloon R is next in size, and balloon Q is the smallest.

The picture of the balloons could lead to some interesting discussion covering some, or all, of the following ideas:

1 The containers this time are balloons. Instead of containing water or lentils they contain a light gas, or perhaps hot air. They rise up because the gas or hot air inside is *lighter* than the air outside.

2 Party balloons do not usually float upwards – certainly not if they are blown up by mouth.

3 Sometimes small rubber balloons like party balloons are filled with a light gas so that they float away high into the sky.

Additional activities

1 Working with bottles   The children should be encouraged to bring to school any odd-shaped bottles. These could be used as a focus for discussion of volume. There could be further attempts at estimating which had the greater, or greatest, volume, followed by pouring activities to determine if estimates were correct. Bottles are interesting in that although they may be quite different in shape, they may well have the same volume.

2 Using jugs   Some jugs are better than others when it comes to pouring without spilling. One or two such jugs could be used to give children further practice in careful pouring and filling.

3 Using funnels   Funnels are used in everyday life for many purposes. One or more funnels would make the business of pouring and filling more interesting and easier for children, especially when a container with a narrow opening such as a lemonade bottle has to be filled with water.

4 Using translucent containers   Plastic containers of this type are often used to hold such things as detergents and soft drinks. These containers provide a means of comparing, as the level of water in the translucent container can be seen and marked.

Shape　　　　　**Flat shapes**　　　　　**Pages 36 to 39**

Content and development

This section provides further experiences with the shapes introduced in Workbook 2. The names 'triangle', 'square', 'rectangle', 'pentagon', and 'hexagon' are revised using nailboards. These shapes are then drawn by joining dots. Finally, squares are folded and cut to form other shapes. No new shapes or properties are introduced in this section. The pages need not be done in the order in which they appear in the workbook.

Pages 36 and 37　Using a nailboard　　　Flat shapes

Materials　enough nine-pin nailboards for a group of children

A simple nine-pin board can be made by pasting a piece of squared paper to a piece of wood and hammering in nine nails. The nails should not be less than 2 cm apart. Nails about 3 cm apart give shapes of a more suitable size.
A corner of a larger geoboard could be used, although this is less satisfactory, particularly for less able children.

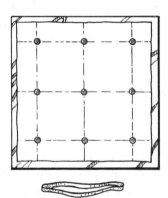 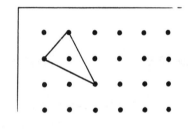

The children should be shown how to make shapes by stretching an elastic band around the nails. They should also be made aware of the connections between the number of corners which a shape has and the number of 'corner' nails which they are joining up. A triangle can be made by joining three 'corner' nails. Some children may be able to draw the shapes on Pages 36 and 37 straight away, but a nailboard is valuable as it allows them to make shapes and change them until the correct one is obtained *before* drawing.
In question 1 on Page 36, the children are asked to make six different triangles. There are eight completely different ones to choose from:

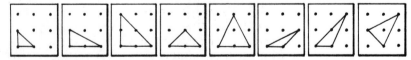

Some of the children may make the same (congruent) shapes in different positions. For example:

At this stage these might be accepted as different and the children
encouraged to *turn the board round* to look at such shapes.
In question 2 they should make three squares which are of a *different size*.
They will have most difficulty in finding this one:

Once again, they should be encouraged to *turn the board round* to see that it is
really a square.

For Page 37, question 1, they should make the shapes and
then count the number of edges to decide whether each
shape is a pentagon or hexagon. The middle shape is a little
unusual in that it looks as if it has a piece cut out of it. It still
has six straight edges and so is a hexagon.

For question 2, the children should make a pentagon and a hexagon *different*
from those in question 1. For example:

The children might be allowed to make any shape they like in question 3 and
not just shapes already known to them. Here are some shapes and names
which children have found:

Kite   Cheese   Boomerang

Page 38   Join the dots   Flat shapes

Materials   none

This page asks the children to join up dots to make shapes and then to name
the shapes. The teacher should encourage the children to guess what the
shape is before they draw it. If there are six dots, the shape has six corners
and so is a hexagon. Children are often familiar with dot pictures in comics.
Here they should use a ruler if possible. Accurate drawing is not of vital
importance as long as the shape is recognisable.

Page 39   Folding squares   Flat shapes

Materials   scissors, glue, and the two squares cut from the bottom of Page 39

The best way to cut out
square A is first to
remove it from the page
by cutting round it
roughly. It can then be
held more easily and be
neatly trimmed.

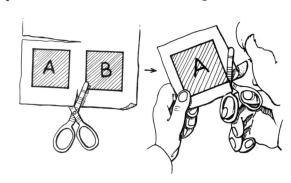

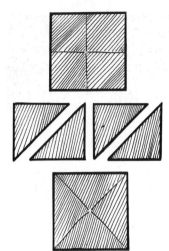

Many children will see instinctively how the square has to be folded to make four smaller squares. Those who find it more difficult could be encouraged to draw the squares first with a pencil before folding.

The four small triangles are much more difficult to spot, as they have been deliberately drawn on Page 39 in a way which does not exactly match their position in the large square. Some pupils will need help with this activity, and again drawing before folding might help.

The children might be encouraged to fit their four small squares on top of each other to see that they are indeed the same size before sticking them on to the page. The four triangles might be compared in a similar way.

Additional activities

1 Folding and cutting

More able children might follow up the folding and cutting activities of Page 39 with activities or worksheets like those shown below left.

2 Fitting shapes

The children could use a large cardboard or plastic hexagon as a template. Such shapes are available from educational suppliers.

The children could be given a set of shapes which includes identical shapes and asked to fit them together to make new shapes. The shapes would have to have compatible edge lengths. Suitable large, thick, plastic shapes are available commercially.

The following workcard would require four equilateral triangles, four squares, and one regular hexagon, all with the same edge lengths. These should be kept in a box labelled 'A'.

You need scissors, glue and a hexagon.

1. Draw round the hexagon to make a paper hexagon.

2. Fold and cut the paper hexagon to make:

6 triangles.

3. Stick the triangles in your exercise book.

You need scissors, glue and a hexagon.

1. Draw round the hexagon to make a paper hexagon.

2. Fold and cut the paper hexagon to make:

a rectangle and 2 triangles.

3. Stick them in your book.

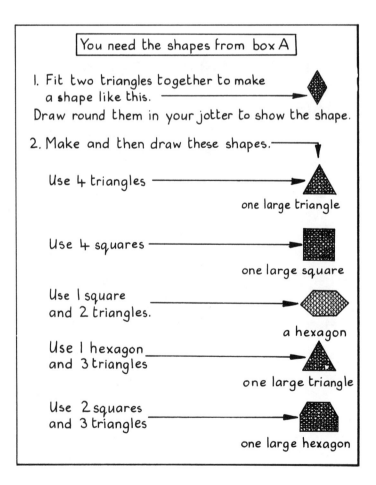

Stage 1 Workbook 4

Stage 1   Workbook 4

Introduction

This is the final workbook in Stage 1 and represents for the average child the completion of a session's work.

About half of the workbook is concerned with number work which can be split conveniently into these sections:

Pages 1 to 6	2 and 3 times tables
Pages 7 to 15	2 to 5 times tables
Workcards 51, 53, 55, 57, 59	Multiplication
Pages 16 to 19	Division: sharing aspect and the ÷ sign
Pages 20 to 23	Division: grouping aspect and the ÷ sign
Workcards 61, 63, 65, 67, 69	Number puzzles

After any of these sections children could be asked to attempt any of the other sections on time, area or shape.

Contents

Materials

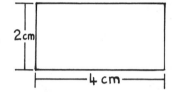

Counting materials such as counters, beads, buttons, cubes, pegs or straws
Coins – real, plastic or cardboard (1p, 2p, 5p, 10p, 20p, 50p)
Number lines, scissors, glue, cardboard or paper hoops
Clock or clockface with moveable hands
Coloured pens, pencils, crayons
Plastic or cardboard squares, triangles, circles, hexagons, rectangles
Envelopes, magazines, newspapers, postcards, playing cards
Three parcels labelled with names of children
Three identical empty jars
Sand, peas, marbles
Flat trays
Three mugs labelled with names of children
Wooden or plastic cubes (Cuisenaire or Tillich units would do)
Cuboids (matchboxes), dice, cylinders, cones, triangular prisms (Toblerone packets)
← Cardboard or plastic jigsaw pieces for a square

Dominoes or other small identical rectangles →

The teaching notes for each page list the specific materials required and offer suggestions for alternative materials where appropriate.
The following items from the *Teacher's Materials Pack* will be useful for this work:

Window card: 2 and 3 times tables	Card 4
Multiplication picture 1: 4 times table	Card 6
Multiplication picture 2: 5 times table	Card 7
Multiplication stories	Cards 14, 15, (16)
Multiplication chains	Cards (16), 17, 18
Cars: division by 2, 3, and 4	Card 19
Garages: division by 2, 3, and 4	Card 20
Clock	Card 26
Months of the year	Card 27
Cover the picture	Cards (29), 30

Number	2, 3, 4, and 5 times tables	Pages 1 to 15 Cards 51, 53, 55, 57, 59

Content and development

In this section the easier multiplication facts are grouped into their tables. The concept of multiplication was first met in Workbook 3 and is reinforced here as each table is developed. The facts are presented in a variety of ways and a link with money is made by providing examples of buying more than one of an article. The section ends with work on the commutative aspect of multiplication and a consequent introduction to some of the facts of tables above the 5 times table.
It is important to note that the language associated with a fact such as 3×4 in this section is either 'three times four' or 'three fours'. This form of stating the fact was introduced in Workbook 3 and is extended here. In Stage 2 the phrase 'multiplied by' will be introduced before the children attempt the

vertical form of multiplication of two and three digit numbers by a single digit number.

The 'zero facts', that is $2 \times 0, 3 \times 0, 4 \times 0, 5 \times 0$, are not explicitly stated in the tables but are dealt with in the *Teacher's Notes*. They are subsequently used in sequence examples such as 'Fill in the missing numbers: 10, 8, 6, □, □, 0' and also in examples of the type $(3 \times 0) + 4 = □$. Since these 'zero facts' can be difficult for some children, care should be taken when presenting them.

Introductory activities for Page 1

1 The concept of multiplication should be revised. The teacher should use a variety of materials (buttons, beads, cubes, counters, pencils, sticks, rods) with a group of children to show, for example, that:

2×3 (stated as 'two times three' or 'two threes') means $3 + 3$.

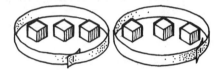

2×4 (stated as 'two times four' or 'two fours') means $4 + 4$.

2 It would be helpful to end the introductory activities with one using materials such as coloured cubes or Unifix cubes since this would lead more easily into the work of Page 1 where the diagrams represent materials of this type. For example:

2 fives  $2 \times 5 = 10$

The fact $2 \times 5 = 10$ should be stated as 'two times five is equal to ten' or 'two times five equals ten' or, possibly, 'two times five is ten'. The alternative form 'two fives are ten' may also be used, depending on personal preference. A variety of language is used throughout this section and the teacher should provide oral practice as appropriate.

Page 1	The 2 times table	2 times table

Materials none

This page first shows material arranged in the form of facts from the 2 times table. (The 2 times table was introduced in Workbook 3.) The children should have arranged material in this way in the introductory activities for this page. Two forms of recording are used, '2 fours' and '2×4'. When the ordered list of facts from the 2 times table has been completed, the children are asked to complete these facts when presented in a random order, in question 2. It is worth noting that the form $2 \times □ = 6$ occurs in question 2. This is an important form for later work on division. Some children may require assistance with this. It may help to verbalise this form as, for example, 'two whats are six'.

Question 3 contains two diagrams in which arrows must be inserted to show the answers. The first one is straightforward since the facts are presented in the form '2 × 6 $\xrightarrow{\text{"is equal to"}}$ 12', but the second diagram is in the reverse form, '16 $\xrightarrow{\text{"is 2 times"}}$ 8'. The children will require some explanation of this form before they tackle the questions.

An essential feature of the work on multiplication facts is the amount of oral work and the variety of experience that the teacher can give the children. After a workbook page in this section has been completed, the teacher should provide further practice, both oral and written. The children could also play games which make use of the facts. (Some suggestions about these activities are given later.) It is in this way that the multiplication facts become fixed in the memory and are consequently recalled easily.

Page 2	Missing numbers	2 times table

Materials   none

Facts from the 2 times table are presented in a variety of ways on this page. Question 1 contains some sequence examples in ascending and descending order. The children have to complete the sequences by inserting the appropriate fact (or 'station') of the 2 times table. The teacher should point out that the 'stations' of the 2 times table are presented here and, of course, that 2 is being added or subtracted each time. This structure is important as it is the essential feature of a multiplication table. It enables a child to move from a known multiplication fact to the next fact and so can assist in memorisation and expansion of the facts. Within the sequence examples the opportunity is taken to introduce the '0' or 'zero' fact, for example $2 \times 0 = 0$. Some children will find this a difficult idea to grasp and the teacher should try to present it in a number of ways, for example:

1 Using materials as in the introductory activities for Page 1 as follows:

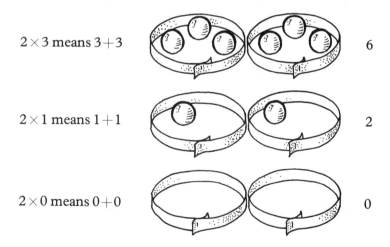

2×3 means $3+3$ 6

2×1 means $1+1$ 2

2×0 means $0+0$ 0

2 Presenting the ordered list of facts as follows:

$$2 \times 3 = 3+3 = 6$$
$$2 \times 2 = 2+2 = 4$$
$$2 \times 1 = 1+1 = 2$$
$$2 \times 0 = 0+0 = 0$$

The emphasis here is on the addition pattern and reinforces the work above.

3 Using the ordered list of facts to point out the structure as before but inserting the zero fact as follows:

$$2 \times 3 = 6 \quad | \quad \text{going}$$
$$2 \times 2 = 4 \quad | \quad \text{down}$$
$$2 \times 1 = 2 \quad \downarrow \quad \text{by 2}$$

Insert ⟶ $2 \times 0 = 0$

Here emphasis is on the multiplication pattern.

In question 2, the examples use dice with dots or numbers on their faces. In order to avoid confusion, the teacher should point out that the unshaded faces are the ones to be recorded.

In question 3, facts from the 2 times table in brackets are combined with addition or subtraction of a single digit number. Some children might find it useful to write the answer for the multiplication fact above the bracket before adding or subtracting the other number, for example:

$$\overset{14}{(2 \times 7)} - 9 = \square$$

The last two examples are in the form $(2 \times 3) + \square = 10$. The children may need help with this complementary addition aspect. Instructions might be given in this way:

'Insert the answer for the bracket.'

Question: 'Six and what equals ten?' (to recall the addition fact $6 + 4 = 10$.)

'Put your answer (4) in the box.'

Question 4 also uses brackets with subsequent addition of a number but this time there is a pattern in the presentation of the work. Some children might still find it useful to write the answer above the bracket.

Page 3	**The 3 times table**	3 times table

Materials   counters

Before this page is attempted the teacher should ask the children to lay out counters to show how the table is built up, for example, three sets of one can be laid out:

This gives $1 + 1 + 1$, leading to $3 \times 1 = 3$. Now one counter should be added to each set to give three lots of two:

This gives $2 + 2 + 2$, leading to $3 \times 2 = 6$.

This work should be extended until the teacher feels that the children can be set to work on the page.

In question 1, each line of the table should be laid out before the fact is recorded in the workbook. After the children have completed the table they will be able to use it to complete questions 2 and 3.

Question 2 presents the facts in the form $3 \times 4 = \square$ and should not be difficult to complete.

Question 3 presents the facts in the form $3 \times \square = 6$ and provides a more difficult task for children. This form is important as it occurs in later work on division. Once again the teacher should provide lots of oral and written practice and games to consolidate the learning of these table facts.

Page 4	**Arrows**	3 times table

Materials none

Practice in the 3 times table facts is provided using examples with different formats – arrows joining fact and product, other arrow diagrams, sequences, and table facts combined with addition or subtraction of a number. The 0 or zero is again used in a sequence, but this time in an ascending order type. Later, in question 5, the fact 3×0 is used. It may be helpful to show the following pattern again:

$3 \times 1 = 3$
$3 \times 2 = 6$ $(3 \times 0 = 0)$ Insert afterwards
$3 \times 3 = 9$
$3 \times 4 = 12$

and then to insert $3 \times 0 = 0$ at the top as indicated. Alternatively, three empty hoops could be put out to show that $3 \times 0 = 0 + 0 + 0 = 0$.

In questions 1 and 2, the presentations 'is equal to' and 'is 3 times' are used, as with the 2 times table on Page 1, that is

$$3 \times 6 \xrightarrow{\text{``is equal to''}} 18 \quad \text{and} \quad 15 \xrightarrow{\text{``is 3 times''}} 5$$

It may be necessary to remind the children how to deal with the second form. In question 3, the sequences use the facts or 'stations' of the 3 times table. The teacher should emphasise this. The children should realise that 3 is being added or subtracted each time. (This kind of presentation will be repeated for the 4 and 5 times tables in later pages.)

Questions 4 and 5 have facts from the 3 times table in brackets combined with addition or subtraction of a number. Again, the children may find it useful to write the answer for the bracket above it before adding or subtracting the other number. For example:

$$\begin{array}{c} 15 \\ (3 \times 5) + 2 = \square \end{array}$$

Additional activities for the 2 and 3 times tables

There are various activities and games which will allow children to practise and memorise facts from the tables, for example:

1 Clock game A modified clockface using the numbers 1 to 10 could be used, such as:

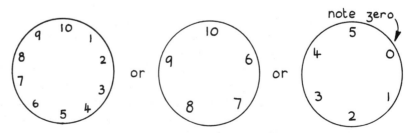

The 'clock(s)' could be drawn on the blackboard or on a large sheet of paper.

The table number should be inserted in the middle of the face. When a number on the dial is indicated, the child should respond by stating the table fact and its product thus:

Teacher points to 8.
Child responds (in words) 'Three times eight is twenty-four' or 'Three eights are twenty-four'.

As the children become more proficient, the responses are given more quickly. Indeed, with an able group, the response might be the product only, that is 'twenty-four'.

2 Flashcards   (i) Cards such as $\boxed{2 \times 3}$, $\boxed{3 \times 5}$ can be used to give oral or written practice as appropriate.
(ii) Simple number cards such as $\boxed{5}$, $\boxed{8}$ can be used, with instructions such as 'Give three times the number I hold up'.

3 Window cards   Card 4 of the *Teacher's Materials Pack* for Stage 1 provides additional work on the 2 and 3 times tables and it might be helpful to use this card before moving on to Pages 5 and 6 which deal with money and problems. This 'window card' can easily be made and has already been described in the *Teacher's Notes* for Workbook 1 regarding stories of 14 and 15 (see page 34).

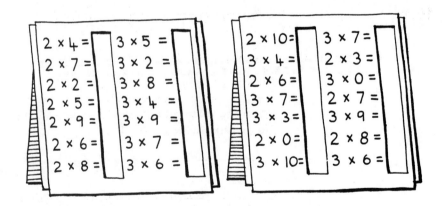

Paper is inserted between the folded halves of the card and the answers are written on it through the cut out slots. The paper can be removed after correction and another child can use the card by inserting a fresh piece of paper. A master card could be kept for correction purposes and this may speed up the use of the window card. This type of card is very useful for providing extra practice for individuals over a whole range of work. The dimensions of the card can be tailored to suit particular requirements.

Introductory activities for Page 5

Page 5 deals with the application of the facts in the 2 and 3 times tables to money examples. Work in the class shop would be a useful introduction to this page. The cost of articles (and the type) would need to be adjusted to suit this particular activity, for example, no cost should be more than 10p. The children should be instructed to buy 2 *or* 3 of an article each time. A few purchases should be made under the teacher's supervision before any of the following activities are undertaken:

1 The children could continue this work by making their own choice of article and choosing whether to buy two or three of it. The correct sum of money should then be handed over to the shopkeeper.

2 A more systematic approach could be adopted by making cards which instruct the children to make a particular purchase. For example:

| Buy 3 lollipops | | Buy 2 choc ices |

The money handed over would again have to be calculated by the purchaser so that the correct amount was tendered.

3 A development of **1** and **2** would be for the purchaser to tender an amount of money greater than the cost so that change was necessary. The children could be helped by the use of cards such as

Take 20p
Buy 3 chews

4 A child could be asked to select two cards such as

| Buy 3 sweets | | Buy 2 chocolates |

and then to work out how much money should be given to the shopkeeper for this double purchase. Each part could be dealt with separately, then the total money counted from the coins put out. Many variations on the above are possible, and the teacher could adjust the activities according to the needs and abilities of the children.

Page 5   Buying more than one   Money   2 and 3 times table

Materials   coins if required

Question 1 uses items costing up to 5p each and is a development of the practical work done beforehand. In the latter part of question 1, some children may need to note the separate costs above each item before inserting the total in the box:

9p   4p
3 lollipops and 2 sweets   13 p

Question 2 is similar but uses items costing more than 5p. There are no 'double' purchases here.

In questions 3, 4, and 5, it may be helpful for children to insert the cost of the articles on the page before they calculate the change:

Jane bought 3 apples.   18p
What change was there from 20p?   2 p

These three questions on change received are simple two-step problems which prepare the children for future, more difficult work on problems.

Page 6	**Problems**	2 and 3 times table

Materials none

The first part of this page deals with simple one-step problems such as:

> There are 6 apples in a pack.
> How many apples are there in 2 packs?   ☐

The latter part of the page deals with pictorial records of simple darts scores:

The score should be verbalised as 'two threes and a five'. It can then be recorded as $(2 \times 3) + 5$ and the total finally calculated. Some children may find this translation from speech to mathematical statement too difficult, and it should therefore be left until a later stage. All children should have their attention drawn to the position of the darts. They should be looking first for the sector in which two or more darts have stuck in order to start recording. (The more difficult form of $5 + (2 \times 3)$ will arise at a later stage in the development of the children's mathematical skills.)

Page 7	**The 4 times table**	4 times table

Materials counters

The development of this page is similar to that of Page 3. The children should be asked to lay out counters to show some facts from the 4 times table. When the teacher feels that the children could complete the table they should be asked to do so. If necessary, counters can be used to help build up the table.

The examples given in question 2 are of the form $4 \times 3 = \square$, that is, 'Four threes are what?'. In question 3 they are of the form $4 \times \square = 8$, that is 'Four whats are eight?'. The latter form is more difficult and is important as it is the form used in later work on division. The teacher should revise this aspect and include further oral work on the 4 times table.

Page 8	**Arrows**	4 times table

Materials none

Different types of diagrams containing arrows are used here. The format of question 1 is the same as question 1 of Page 4 for the 3 times table.
Question 2 has the format

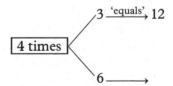

and may require some explanation. The zero fact 4×0 is introduced in question 2 and the children should be reminded of the earlier work on this aspect in the 2 and 3 times tables.

The forms of recording used in question 3 are like the verbalisation of the table facts, i.e. '4 fives are ☐', and '4 times ☐ is 40'. It may help if the children try these orally beforehand. The latter form can now be stated as 'Four times what is forty?' in contrast to the previous form 'Four whats are forty?' which was used in Page 7.

Question 4 is an entirely new presentation of the table facts and makes use of two number lines (of different scale) linked together. The upper line is from 0 to 10 and the lower line is from 0 to 36.

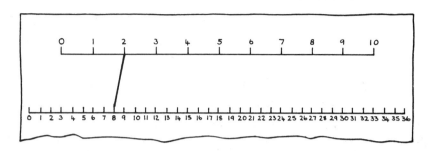

The upper line gives the numbers to be used and the lower line gives the product in the table. The link between them is the phrase '4 times', that is, 2 is joined to 8 because 4 times 2 is 8. The presentation used in the workbook is actually '2 is joined to 8 because $4 \times 2 = 8$'.

After children have completed question 4 it might be helpful to ask them the converse, 'Why is 8 joined to 2?' This should lead to the statement '8 is joined to 2 because 8 is 4 times 2.'

It might also be helpful to complete all the linkages in this work and the teacher could point out that the stations of the 4 times table can now be seen from 4×0 to 4×9. (There is not enough room for 4×10 to be shown but children should be asked for this missing fact.)

| **Page 9** | **Problems** | 4 times table |

Materials   none

The first five examples are all simple one-step problems of the form:
   'There are 7 sweets in a bag.
   How many are there in 4 bags?'
The teacher should work through some examples of this kind with the children so that they see that the answer to the problem is obtained by finding 4 times the particular number quoted. An understanding of the language used and the translation of this into a mathematical statement is critical to the successful solving of problems. A great deal of practice may be required by some children before they achieve this success. A variety of presentation is necessary and the skill is developed over a period of time throughout the stages of this material.

Question 6 presents sequences in ascending and descending order for children to complete, making use of the stations of the 4 times table. The counting up or down in fours that was done on the previous page will assist with this work.

Question 7 asks children either to add a single digit number to a table fact or to subtract a single digit number from a table fact, for example, $(4 \times 3) + 2 = \square$ or $(4 \times 5) - 3 = \square$. The children could be reminded of the earlier work of this kind on Pages 2 and 4, where they inserted the product above the fact before completing the example:

$$32$$
$$(4 \times 8) + 2 = \square$$

The presentation in question 8 is more difficult and has the form
(a) $(4 \times 9) + \square = 37$ or
(b) $(4 \times \square) + 5 = 25$.
In (a) the verbalisation, after noting the product above the bracket, could be, 'Thirty-six and what equals thirty-seven?'. The answer could be given as

'Thirty-six and one equals thirty-seven', thus completing the example:

$$36$$
$$(4 \times 9) + \boxed{1} = 37.$$

In (b) the verbalisation would need to be in stages:
'What and five equals twenty-five?'
Answer: 'Twenty and five equals twenty-five' – recorded as

$$20$$
$$(4 \times \square) + 5 = 25.$$

Then 'Four times what equals twenty?'
Answer: 'Four times five equals twenty' – recorded as

$$20$$
$$(4 \times \boxed{5}) + 5 = 25.$$

Alternatively, some children may try a number until they find the correct answer:

$$(4 \times \boxed{3}) + 5 = 17$$
$$(4 \times \boxed{4}) + 5 = 21$$
$$(4 \times \boxed{5}) + 5 = 25$$

Some children may find these examples too difficult and they should, therefore, omit them at this stage. Other opportunities to cover these ideas will occur later, with different tables, and the teacher could also help by judicious presentation of this idea when an occasion presents itself.

Page 10	The 5 times table	5 times table

Materials   counters or other objects

The development here is similar to that of Page 7 where the 4 times table was considered. This time the teacher might use the counters, or other materials, to demonstrate one or more of the facts from the 5 times table, rather than letting the children do it. However, this is for the teacher to decide. The children should then complete the table, if necessary using counters to help them.

Question 2 uses the form $5 \times 3 = \square$, while question 3 uses the form $5 \times \square = 30$. That is, question 2 asks, 'Five times three is what?' and question 3 asks 'Five times what is thirty?'.

It may be possible for the teacher to introduce the zero fact at this stage by inserting it at the top of the table when the children have completed it:

$$5 \times 0 = 0 + 0 + 0 + 0 + 0 = 0$$

A lot of oral practice on the 5 times table should now be given.

Page 11	Arrows	5 times table

Materials   none

The practice provided here is similar to that on Page 4. The examples are in several different formats – arrows joining fact and product in the form '5 × 8 $\xrightarrow{\text{"is equal to"}}$ 40' and '5 times 7 $\xrightarrow{\text{"gives"}}$ 35', other arrow diagrams, sequences, and table facts combined with addition or subtraction of a single digit number. The 0 or zero is used both in an ascending and a descending sequence.

Questions 1 and 2 provide another type of presentation in using the term 'gives'. The teacher should ensure that the children understand the form '5 times 7 —"gives"→ 35' and can complete the form

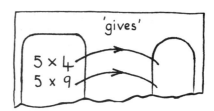

In question 3, all the numbers used in the sequences are stations of the 5 times table and the teacher should ensure that the children recognise this. Questions 4 and 5 on the page are similar to questions 7 and 8 on Page 9. The children should be reminded of the work there and could insert the product above the multiplication fact before completing the example:

$$\overset{20}{(5\times4)}-7=\square$$

The first two examples of question 5 should be verbalised as indicated for Page 9 question 8.

For examples of the type $(5\times\square)-2=28$ children may find the answer by trial and error:

$$(5\times\boxed{4})-2=18$$
$$(5\times\boxed{5})-2=23$$
$$(5\times\boxed{6})-2=28$$

Additional activities

1 The additional activities suggested for the 2 and 3 times tables on pages 175 and 176 of these *Teacher's Notes* could be used for the 4 and 5 times tables. These would give the necessary oral and written practice to help children memorise multiplication facts.

2 The *Teacher's Materials Pack* for Stage 1 provides cards for a variety of work on the 2 to 5 times tables as follows:
  (i) Card 4. Details of this card are supplied on page 176 of these *Teacher's Notes*. A similar card could be made for the 4 and 5 times tables.
  (ii) Card 6 provides a jigsaw type activity for the 4 times table. Card 7 provides a similar activity for the 5 times table.
  (iii) Cards 14 to 18 provide 'multiplication stories' and 'multiplication chains'.

3 Further practice can be gained using a multiplication grid on a worksheet or card which the children complete:

5x	9	3	7	5	1	6	8	0	2	10
	45									

This could be done for each of the tables.

4 A grid could be completed either by the class or by individuals. A large completed grid could be displayed on the classroom wall.

X	0	1	2	3	4	5	6	7	8	9	10
1	0	1	2	3	4	5	6	7	8	9	10
2	0	2	4	6	8	10	12	14	16	18	20
3	0	3	6	9	12	15	18	21	24	27	30
4	0	4	8	12	16	20	24	28	32	36	40
5	0	5	10	15	20	25	30	35	40	45	50

3 times 4 equals 12

Introductory activities for Page 12

Page 12 uses the facts in the 4 and 5 times tables in money examples, including 'Find the cost of . . .', change from 50p after 4 or 5 of an article are bought, and finding the total cost of a double purchase:

> 4 caramels cost   p
> 5 chocolates cost _____ p
>   Total cost _____

The class shop could again be used, as outlined for Page 5 of Workbook 4 (see page 177 of these *Teacher's Notes*). Suitable prices and articles would have to be chosen, for example, no price should be more than 10p. The children should buy four or five of the same article each time, under the teacher's supervision. They could then be left on their own to undertake some of the following activities:

1 The children choose the article and the number of that article to purchase. The correct money should be handed to the shopkeeper.
2 Cards could be used to instruct the children to make a particular purchase:

> Buy 4 oranges   Buy 5 pears

The correct money should be handed to the shopkeeper.
3 Change could be given after purchasing articles. A card such as

> Take 50p
> Buy 4 toffees

would be helpful.
4 The children could select two cards such as

> Buy 5 chews   Buy 4 cones

and work out the total cost for this double purchase. Variations of the above are also possible and the teacher could adjust the activities according to the needs and abilities of the children.

Page 12   Buying more than three   Money   4 and 5 times table

Materials   coins, if required

Question 1 is a straightforward calculation of the cost of four or five of the same article. The children should be able to deal with this work if they have used the class shop.

Questions 2 and 3 ask for change from 50p. The teacher should ensure that children insert the cost of the articles purchased under the 50p and in line with it, that is:

$$
\begin{array}{lr}
\text{James had} & 5\ 0p \\
\text{He bought 4 apples} & \underline{2\ 8p} \\
\text{His change was} & \underline{\quad p}
\end{array}
$$

Questions 4 to 7 are of the double purchase type and ask for the total cost, for example:

$$
\begin{array}{lr}
\text{4 apples cost} & p \\
\text{5 chews cost} & \underline{\quad} p \\
\text{Total cost} & \underline{\quad} p
\end{array}
$$

The children could be reminded of the class shop activity of this kind and instructed to enter each cost before the addition is completed.

Page 13   Checking-up   Miscellaneous examples

Materials   none

This page provides a variety of different examples so that the teacher can make some assessment of what has been done previously. The teacher should ensure that children understand what is to be done in each of questions 1 to 4. Questions 5 to 7 are interrelated and the teacher should emphasise this point to the children. It would be possible to leave this page until later when it could be used for checking-up purposes.

Introductory activities for Page 14

The commutative aspect of multiplication

Knowing that $4 \times 2 = 2 \times 4$ is as important for multiplication as knowing that $5+3 = 3+5$ is for addition. The teacher should introduce children to this aspect of multiplication by the use of a variety of concrete materials.

1 Unifix cubes or Cuisenaire rods could be used to show that 4 threes gives the same total as 3 fours

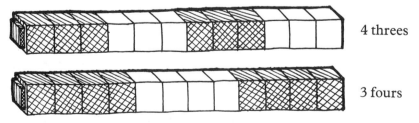

4 threes

3 fours

Hence $4 \times 3 = 3 \times 4$.
Many similar examples should be given: $2 \times 3, 3 \times 2; 5 \times 3, 3 \times 5;$ etc.

2 Counters could be used. For example, two lots of 12 counters could be put out as follows, separating the groups with straws:

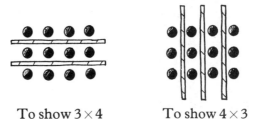

To show 3×4 To show 4×3

A pegboard and pegs could be used in a similar way.
When it is felt that the children understand this idea, Page 14 of the workbook can be attempted.

Page 14	Pairs	Commutative aspect

Materials   coloured pencils

A visual representation using strips of squares is first given for 5×2 and 2×5. The children are then asked to colour similar strips to show other relationships, for example $2 \times 4 = 4 \times 2$. The teacher should ensure that the children understand how many squares they have to colour at a time.
The lower part of the page has number lines in pairs to show, for example, that $4 \times 3 = 3 \times 4$. The teacher may have to remind the children of previous number line work before they attempt questions 3, 4, and 5.

Page 15	Problems	Commutative aspect

Materials   none

This page gives pictorial representations of the commutative aspect of multiplication. The relationships are now extended to include facts in tables beyond the 5 times table, for example, $4 \times 6 = 6 \times 4$.
The last question uses random facts and asks children to link them appropriately. This enables a relationship like $5 \times 9 = 9 \times 5$ to be seen and lets the children calculate $9 \times 5 = 45$. The teacher should go through one or two examples of this kind with the children before they tackle this page.
On completion of this work the teacher could draw the children's attention to real-life examples, such as milk bottles in a crate, window panes, children in teams, patterns. It is important to consolidate the facts presented in this work and teachers should ensure that regular systematic practice, either oral or written, is given. A few minutes each day would be of greater value than a lengthy period once a week. The following five workcards are available to assist with this consolidation.

Number cards 51, 53, 55, 57, 59	Multiplication

All the five workcards are of comparable difficulty. The examples present the facts previously encountered in a variety of ways and will enable the teacher to assess the children's ability and knowledge. Two or three problems follow

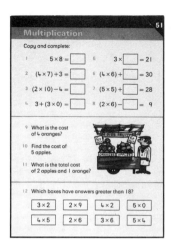

the examples. A card ends with the activity of linking random facts using (a) the commutative relationship, (b) equivalent product relationships such as $2 \times 9 = 3 \times 6$.

It must be stressed that the teacher should decide which pupils use the cards and how much of each card they should do. It is not envisaged that all pupils should do all of the cards nor indeed all of one card.

Division   Pages 16 to 23

Content and development

The aim of this unit is to provide children with practical activities which will enable them to secure the concepts of the operation of division.

By this stage most children will have some experience of the 2, 3, 4, and 5 times tables, and many will be able to recall a number of table facts. It is most important that teachers realise that the aim of the unit is not dependent on table awareness, and that the children's responses to the variety of division situations will be as a result of activity and the use of materials.

Many children have difficulty with the concepts and skills associated with the operation of division. The reason for this may be that the division operation has two aspects, (a) equal sharing (or partition), and (b) grouping (or quotition).

The unit is structured so that it deals with each aspect. Pages 16–19 cover equal sharing and Pages 20–23 cover grouping. Each of the two aspects is dealt with in three parts:

(i) use of materials   (ii) acquisition of appropriate language
(iii) recording in words and with the division symbol.

At this stage no formal work with remainders has been included. The division units in later stages of *Primary Mathematics: A development through activity* use the concept and associated language of equal sharing when developing the algorithm for division. Nevertheless, grouping is a most important mathematical concept closely related to equal sharing, hence its inclusion in this unit.

Introductory activities for Page 16

The teacher, whether working with the whole class or with groups, should initially demonstrate the nature of the sharing aspect of division using suitable models and appropriate language. For example, 'I have eight sweets to be shared equally between John and Mary. How many will each receive?' Eight sweets are put out and shared as shown.

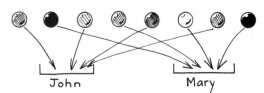

This type of situation can be set up several times, using cubes, counters or 1p coins. The children should share out the objects one at a time, and then count how many are in each share to find the answer. A set of cars and garages which can be used for sharing is included in the *Teacher's Materials Pack* for Stage 1, Cards 19 and 20.

Page 16	Equal sharing	Division Sharing

Materials   scissors and glue

Following the introductory activities described above, this page provides an activity in which the children cut out twelve fish and share them equally 'between' two, and then 'among' three and four 'fish tanks'. It is easier for children to cut out the twelve fish at the foot of the page as a block. They can then cut them more easily into twelve individual fish. At the final stage, the fish are glued into the four fish tanks. It is important to point out that the answer each time is found by counting the number of fish in *one* share.

Page 17	Equal sharing between 2	Division The ÷ sign

Materials   hoops and cubes

The hoops referred to above can be easily made from strips of paper or thin card stapled at the join.
The page is restricted to equal sharing activities between two. What is new is the introduction of a word statement and the ÷ sign. These give the appropriate language and a recording format for the result of the activity. For example:

$$\boxed{\text{14 shared equally between 2 gives 7 each}}$$

and

$$\boxed{14 \div 2 = 7}$$

As an introduction to the interpretation of the division symbol, the teacher may wish to demonstrate sharing using prepared cards such as:

$$\boxed{10 \div 2 =}$$

After the sharing activity the following is achieved:

and the card could then be completed thus

$$\boxed{10 \div 2 = 5}$$

It is important to note that the ÷ sign should be translated as 'shared equally between' and not as 'divided by' at this point.

Page 18   **Equal sharing among 3, 4, and 5**   Division   Sharing

Materials   hoops and cubes

The six activities on this page form an extension to the work in Page 17. Here the sharing is among 3, 4, and 5 hoops. It is suggested that change in language from 'between 2' and 'among more than two' is a consolidation of the informal language developed by the teacher at the introductory activities level.

Again emphasis should be placed on the language, and the translation of the ÷ sign as 'shared equally among'.

Many children will require further examples of the type on this page. The teacher could make worksheets or use the blackboard to provide examples like these:

> Use material to find
> $20 \div 5 =$ ___ $12 \div 4 =$ ___
> $9 \div 3 =$ ___ $18 \div 2 =$ ___
> etc.   etc.

Page 19   **Problems**   Division   Sharing

Materials   hoops and cubes

Questions 1 and 2 on this page provide illustrations of completed sharings. The children are asked to interpret each illustration quantitatively. Some preliminary teaching and discussion will be necessary. For example, the teacher could lay out material thus:

 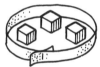 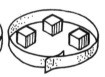

The teacher asks 'How many cubes altogether?', gets the answer and writes '12'. He or she then asks 'How many equal shares?', gets the answer and writes '12 ÷ 4'. The next question is 'How many cubes in each share?'. The answer is given and the teacher writes '12 ÷ 4 = 3'. After some discussion of this kind the children could be asked to do the page.

It is intended that questions 3, 4, and 5 are the subjects of language and recording interpretations. *The solutions to these questions should be found using materials.*

When question 5 has been completed correctly, some children may discover from the pattern that the product of the last two numbers gives the first number. That is:

$$18 \div 3 = 6 \quad \text{is associated with}$$
$$3 \times 6 = 18$$

Such pattern recognition should not be discouraged, but it is recommended that no formal statement should be made regarding the equivalence of these relationships at this point.

In order to extend and diversify the work contained on Pages 16–19, teachers are advised to create additional activities and worksheets based on the situations already described.

Introductory activities for Page 20

The teacher, whether working with the whole class or with a group, should demonstrate, using suitable models and appropriate language, the nature of the grouping aspect of division. For example, 'I have twelve pencils. How many boys can be given three pencils each?'. Twelve pencils are put out and grouped as shown:

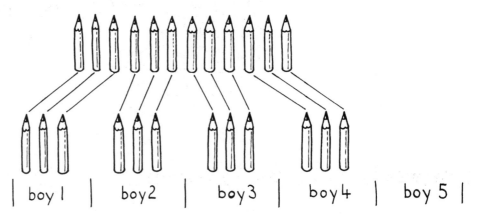

Four boys receive three pencils each.

The teacher should first work through several practical examples with the children, in which straws, counters, blocks, toys, 1p coins, etc. are put into groups. The children should then be asked to complete the page. It is important to point out that each time the answer is found by counting the *number of groups* and not the number of objects in each group.

Page 20	Grouping	Division Grouping

Materials   none

On this page the children are given practice in forming groups of two and groups of three. It is suggested that the objects are ringed and the groups then counted.
For example, in question 3, the letters would be ringed as shown:

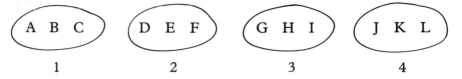

It is important that the children realise that the answer '4' is found by counting the number of groups of three and *not* by counting the number in each group.

Page 21	Grouping	Division Grouping

Materials   cubes

The first three questions are an extension of the activities of Page 20 to groups of four and five objects.
The remaining questions require the manipulation of materials – twenty cubes are grouped in twos, fours, fives, and tens. It is suggested that the

twenty cubes are collected as a set and that the groups are formed and moved to a clear area of the desk. The groups should then be counted.

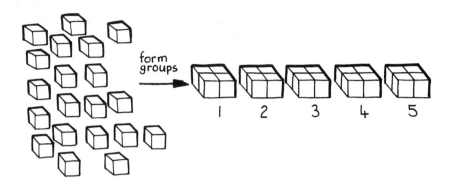

Page 22   **More grouping**   Division   The ÷ sign

Materials   cubes

The three situations in this page have already been experienced by the children. What is new is the formalisation of language and recording. For example:

> 15 grouped in 3s gives 5 groups

> 15 ÷ 3 = 5

As an introduction to the interpretation of the division symbol, the teacher may wish to demonstrate further grouping using prepared cards, for example:

> 12 ÷ 3 =

The grouping activity gives the following result:

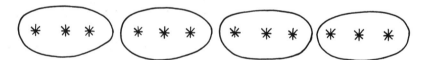

and the card could then be completed thus:

> 12 ÷ 3 = 4

Again, care should be taken regarding the ÷ sign. The phrase 'divided by' should not be used. On this page it is important to translate the ÷ sign as 'grouped in'.

Page 23   **Problems**   Division   Grouping

Materials   hoops and cubes

The first three questions on this page continue with the consolidation of language and recording. However the grouping of discrete objects is replaced by a grouping on a number line.
It should be noted that no arrows are placed on the 'jump lines'. It could be

argued that the problem, 'How many groups of 2 are there?' can be effectively described by this diagram.

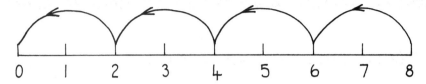

Not only that, but it has a strong relationship with 'How many 2s are there in 8' as a repeated subtraction model. However, since this repeated subtraction interpretation is not the subject of this unit, either method, i.e. moving from 0 to 8 in jumps of 2, or moving from 8 to 0 in jumps of 2 is equally acceptable.

Questions 4 and 5 are problems to be solved with materials. Materials may also be used for question 6 and the children could choose to group *or* share to find the answer.

Teachers are advised to create additional activities and worksheets based on the grouping situations on Pages 20 to 23.

Number Cards
61, 63, 65, 67, 69 Number puzzles

Materials   two dice for Card 67

The five cards contain extension material for average and above average children, mostly on addition and subtraction. The work includes sequence of numbers, money examples, number problems, and revision of language such as 'How many more?', 'difference between' and 'total'. The cards can be tackled in any order.

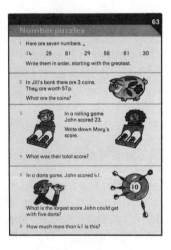

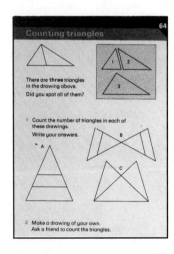

Two typical cards are shown above. It is expected that the children selected by the teacher to try these cards will require little or no guidance in their completion. The purpose of the cards is to provide enrichment material for average and above average children and to encourage these children to read with understanding.

Time

Content and development

This section continues the development of the work on time started in Workbook 1. It begins by revising 'o'clock' and 'half past' clockface times and the idea of 'just before' and 'just after' these times. 'A quarter past' and 'a quarter to' are introduced. The idea of a sequence of times is dealt with by asking the children to put times in their correct order. This portion of work concludes with revision of the months of the year, which is included in many courses for Infants. Such work is introduced in *Infant Mathematics: A development through activity*. In Stage 2 the work on time is developed further to deal with telling the time to five minute intervals.

Introductory activities for Pages 24 to 28

'A quarter past' and 'a quarter to' times

Clockface work is an ongoing experience for children both in and out of school. Actual times will normally be mentioned as part of their daily routine. For example 'time to get up', 'time to leave for school', the times of television programmes and so on, will involve clockface times such as 'half past seven', 'nearly 9 o'clock', etc.

Here are some ideas for activity and discussion.
1 A large real clock or a plastic clock with gears could be used to show the movement of the hands round the dial. A demonstration clockface is provided on Card 26 of the Stage 1 *Teacher's Materials Pack*.
  (a) The hands move round in the direction indicated by the numbers 1, 2, 3, 4, . . . 12.
  (b) The long minute hand moves from 12 right round to 12 in one hour, while the short hour hand moves only from one number to the next.
  (c) When the long minute hand points to 12 it is an 'o'clock' time. Half way round it points to 6 to show a 'half past' time. For 'a quarter past' it points to 3 and for 'a quarter to' it points to 9.

The children could fold a paper circle to halve it, then halve it again, so that the fold lines show the 3, 6, 9, 12 positions.
  (d) The short hour hand indicates which 'o'clock' it is 'past' or coming 'to'.

'past' 7 o'clock   'to' 8 o'clock

Some teachers may wish to highlight how each hand moves by dealing with them separately. The demonstration of one full turn of the minute hand should emphasise the words and phrases which the children will need to know, such as 'just after', 'just before', 'just past', 'a quarter past', and 'a quarter to'. Particular attention should be paid to 'just before' and 'just after' half past times.

Similar care will be needed in considering how the hour hand moves from one specific o'clock time to the next. The position of the hour hand is of fundamental importance in reading 'a quarter past' and 'a quarter to' times.

2 The children should be involved in a lot of oral work dealing with both telling the time and setting the hands to show a time. The teacher could tell a story such as 'Little Red Riding-Hood' using a lot of different times. As each time is mentioned the children could set a clock to show that time.

3 The oral work should include other time language such as 'morning', 'afternoon', 'evening', 'night', 'noon' (midday), 'midnight'. This should bring in the fact that there are two cycles of 12 hours (the hour hand goes round the dial twice) in a whole day of 24 hours.

4 It is important that telling the time should be related to familiar events in a child's day. Drawings could be made or pictures used for a classroom display associating events with times.

5 The way the hands move round the clockface indicates the sequence of time. Ideas such as one hour before, one hour after, one hour earlier and one hour later should be dealt with
  (i) for 'o'clock' times
 (ii) for 'half past' times
(iii) for 'a quarter past' and 'a quarter to' for those children who can cope with this idea.
The recurring cycle 'o'clock, a quarter past, half past, a quarter to, o'clock' should be highlighted.

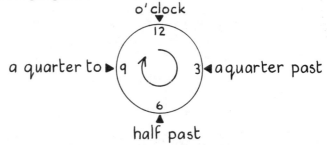

This is necessary preparation for the ordering work on Page 28.

6 A set of flashcards and matching clockface cards dealing with the kind of times used on Pages 24 to 28 would be useful for the oral sessions. These cards, or selections from them, would give children worthwhile matching and ordering activities.

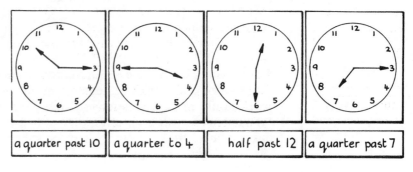

Page 24	**Revision**	Time Hours and half hours

Materials   none

The introductory activities outlined above should provide an adequate preparation for the revision work on this page.

In question 1 the children have to write the time shown on each clockface. The cartoon pictures are intended to make the work more interesting. The teacher could use the pictures to ask questions such as 'What is the girl doing at half past one?', 'When was she playing badminton?'. These questions could be part of a discussion after children have completed the page.

The ablest children could be asked to write the story of a girl's day shown by the times and the pictures.

Question 2 is written work on 'just before' and 'just after' certain o'clock and half past times. Part 1 in the introductory activities recommends careful demonstration and discussion of this difficult but useful clockface work. Telling the time in this way is fairly common. The phrase 'just past' is often used instead of 'just after' and 'coming up to' or 'almost' instead of 'just before'.

Page 25	**A quarter past**	Time A quarter past

Materials   none

a quarter past 2

The teacher could check if a child is able to attempt this work by asking him or her to match a range of 'a quarter past' cards to clockface cards from the set of flashcards suggested in part 6 of the introductory activities.

Questions 2 and 3 make specific reference to the minute and hour hands. This rather formal language may be difficult for some children who naturally speak about the 'long' and 'short' hands.

The teacher could deal orally with the 'a quarter past 6' and 'a quarter past 9' seen in question 1.

The cartoon pictures in question 4 allow questions such as 'What is John doing at a quarter past ten?' and 'At what time is John cycling?'. The ablest children could be asked to write the story of John's day shown by the times and the pictures. This could include the words 'morning', 'afternoon', and perhaps 'evening'.

Page 26	**A quarter to**	Time A quarter to

Materials   none

a quarter to 11

This page is similar to Page 25. The introductory activities should provide an adequate preparation. The teacher could check if a child is able to attempt this work by selecting appropriate 'a quarter to' cards for the child to match from the set of cards suggested in part 6 of the introductory activities.

The teacher could deal orally with the other time shown in question 1 which is not used in questions 2 and 3.

In questions 5 and 6 the children have to write words or even sentences. Some prior oral work would help children with their written answers. Oral work could include questions such as 'What does Pam do in the morning?', 'What does she do in the evening?'.

| **Page 27** | **Reading the time** | Time   Miscellaneous |

Materials   none

This page deals with a mixture of 'a quarter past' and 'a quarter to' times. The introductory activities, especially the matching work recommended in part 6, should provide adequate preparation.

In question 1, the cartoon pictures should make the work more interesting and provide a source of worthwhile questions.

Questions 2 and 3 revise the work on '1 hour before', '1 hour after', '1 hour earlier' and '1 hour later'. Oral work, perhaps using the flashcards

and a demonstration clock, would be helpful to most children. The children should participate in this oral work by setting the clock to a specified time and then choosing the flashcards, say,

for another child to reset the clock. The times should cover the full range of 'o'clock', 'half past', 'a quarter past', and 'a quarter to' times.

| **Page 28** | **Ordering times** | Time   Sequences |

Materials   none

In this page the children have to read, then write, the times shown on sets of three clocks. Each set of three times has then to be written in order starting with the earliest. This will have to be explained and the children told to look very carefully at the position of the hour hand. Parts 5 and 6 of the introductory activities are particularly important as a preparation for this work. Children should be given a lot of practice in arranging sets of three or more cards in this same order.

Additional activities for Pages 24 to 28

A clockface stamp or template could be used to prepare work for the children.
1 Worksheets or wipeable cards could be made to give more examples like those in Page 24 question 2, Pages 25 and 26 questions 1, 2, and 3, Page 27 questions 2 and 3, and Page 28.

2 Worksheets could be made to lend some variety to the work.

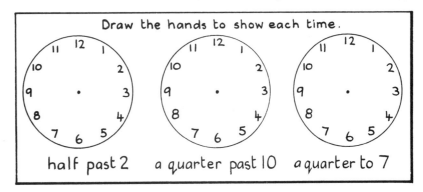

3 The children could be given a clock/clockface whose hands can be set and cards like these for matching.

The teacher should make a quick visual check. Cards would then be swopped and the procedure repeated.

Introductory activities for Page 29

Learning the names of the months and their correct order is an ongoing activity throughout the year. The recurring cycle of the months and the changing pattern of the seasons are fairly sophisticated ideas which take a long time to develop in most children.

1 At the start of each new month a poster could be put on the classroom wall and used to display events which happen during that month.

2 A prepared chart could be up-dated each morning.

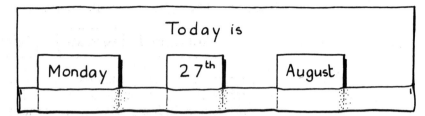

3 A chart of birthdays could be kept.

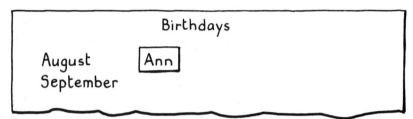

4 There is at least one commercially available wall poster which has a panoramic, continuous but changing scene extending over one entire year. Card 27 of the *Teacher's Materials Pack* for Stage 1 provides a set of twelve month cards which can be used by children to show a cartoon scene which is continuous over the twelve months.

The fact that the scene for December joins on to the scene for January means that the cards can be placed to show a continuous panoramic scene starting with any month. The twelve cards may also be placed in a 'circle' to highlight the recurring annual cycle.

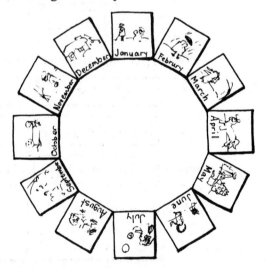

The cards could be laid out so that some of them are in the wrong places and the children asked to arrange them correctly.
Some cards could be removed or turned over and the children asked to name the missing month(s).

5 It may help some children to memorise the names of the months if they are associated with the seasons. This could be done using flashcards or pictures (some calendars are a good source).

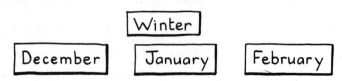

The groups of three months for each season can then be put in order by seasons. The children should eventually be able to start with any season.

Autumn		Winter		Spring		Summer

6 In oral work and discussion with the children, important events, particularly those required on Page 29, should be associated with the month and included in any poster of the month.

Guy Fawkes
November

7 After a good deal of practice involving the above introductory activities, some children could use flashcards in a team game. A pair of flashcards are laid out and one team selects a month card. The other team has to place the correct card to win a point.

This month   Next month
August

Other pairs of cards could also be used:

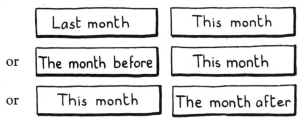

Last month   This month

or   The month before   This month

or   This month   The month after

Eventually the ablest children could use the sets of three related cards.

Last month   This month   Next month

or   The month before   This month   The month after

8 A classroom chart of months could be changed each month.

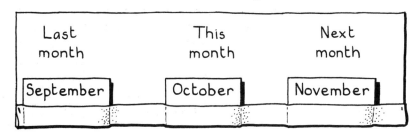

Last month	This month	Next month
September	October	November

Page 29	The months	Time Months of the year

Materials   none

This page, in which the children have to write the names of the months, may have to be left until later in the year. The introductory activities suggested above should ultimately prepare most children for this work. The teacher should point out that all the months are shown in their correct order (stress the direction indicated by the arrows) at the top of the page.

Question 1 requires discussion and the cartoons should help with this.

In question 2, the teacher should ensure that the children know that January is the first month of the year.

Additional activities for Page 29

Most children will need a lot of written practice. Worksheets or cards could be made containing similar problems to those in questions 2, 3, and 4 on Page 29.

> January is the first month.
>
> Name the second month _____
>
> the fifth month _____
>
> the eighth month _____

and so on

> Name the month <u>before</u> March _____
>
> <u>before</u> July _____

and so on

> Name the month <u>after</u> January _____
>
> <u>after</u> May _____

and so on

Last month	This month	Next month
	February	
	April	

and so on

The month before	Month	The month after
	October	
	June	

and so on

Area   **Arbitrary units**   **Pages 30 to 34**

Content and development

This section first revises the work in Stage 1, Workbook 2, by considering
  (i) area as an amount of surface
 (ii) the comparison of two areas to find which has the larger or smaller area
(iii) comparison to find the largest or smallest area.
Different units of area are then considered to find which are best for measuring surface and which are of an appropriate size for the specific surface to be measured.
Areas of given shapes are recorded as a number of units.
Shapes are drawn to given requirements, for example, a shape with an area of seven squares. Comparison of shapes is then carried out in numerical rather than merely qualitative terms, for example, 'This shape has a larger area than that one, it is four squares more in area'.

Page 30   **Revision**   Area   Language

Materials   paper, scissors, coloured pencils, some small objects such as rubbers, plastic animal shapes, coins, stamps, biscuits, sweets

The examples on this page revise area as an amount of surface. Shapes are cut out or drawn and comparisons are made to find the greater/smaller area and later the greatest/smallest area.
For question 1, the children could cut out any type of shape they like, for example, a house, a shape with straight edges, with curved edges, with corners or without. The children could compare the areas of their cut-out shapes by placing them on top of each other.
It is suggested that the children either stick their three shapes on a sheet of paper or make a group display on a length of frieze paper. The cut-out shapes should be labelled, perhaps like this:

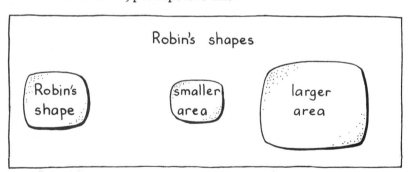

In question 2, the children can again make a drawing of any shape they wish as long as it has a greater area than the given one. Some pupils may find it easier to cut out a larger area from gummed coloured paper and stick it on the page.
In question 3, the children should be encouraged to lay out three or four objects on the page. Having made sure there is enough space, each object can then be drawn around and labelled. Less able pupils may like to stick on pictures rather than draw.
Any doubt about which drawing has the greatest (or smallest) area can usually be solved by placing the appropriate object on top of the outlines to compare the areas.

Materials   pennies, squares, triangles, counters; sets of identical shapes such as circles, hexagons, rectangles; sets of larger units, e.g. jotters, envelopes, sheets of paper, magazines, newspaper pages; objects to measure, e.g. envelope, postcard, workcard, book, table top, desk top

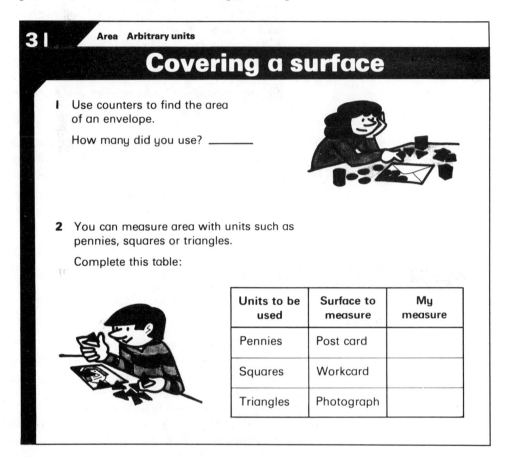

Up until now, the children have compared the areas of shapes by placing them on top of each other or by making a perceptual decision. Through the examples on this page they will be introduced to the idea of finding an area as a number of units.

The children will need instruction in how to use units to cover an object in order to measure its area. The units should be placed as close together as possible. Decisions have to be made about units at the edges – 'Should I count this one?'. Pupils should realise that the measures are not exact and answers are 'about' the recorded number.

On this page the children use a variety of units, and the teacher can ask which are easier to use and which seem to give a better, or more accurate, measure. The children should be able to say that counters and pennies are not as good as squares and triangles. Units which fit together without spaces are better for measuring the amount of surface.

It is suggested that the teacher introduces this work to a group of pupils by using a unit to find the area of the surface of, say, an envelope. This should be done before the children tackle questions 1 and 2 on the page. In question 3, materials should be available so that the children have a choice of units for measuring the given surfaces. For example, for the book, units could be playing cards or cardboard rectangles; for the table top, units could be jotters or sheets of A4 paper; for the desk top, units could be envelopes, postcards or workcards; for the floor, units could be newspaper sheets or quarter-metre square tiles.

All answers should be considered as 'about' a number of units. The teacher should demonstrate and discuss with the children how a suitable 'unit of area' may be chosen to measure a specific area.

Additional exercises could be done using other surfaces such as a rug, the floor of the library corner, a workcard, an open magazine.

| **Page 32** | **Estimating areas** | Area   Arbitrary units |

Materials   sets of cards, pennies, squares, triangles, a workbook, a magazine

Two key issues are tackled on this page:

(i) making an estimate before measuring is a useful procedure

(ii) many units can be used to measure area but some are better than others.

The word 'estimate' may present difficulty for some children. A flashcard used for teaching and then display is useful. The children should find out that estimation helps them to plan the measuring task, in terms of what unit to use, how many units are required, etc. Before the children are asked to estimate an area, they should have had experience of measuring a surface with the given unit.

In question 1, the children find the area of a workcard with a set of identical cards such as playing cards, numeral cards or picture cards. Question 2 can then be tackled by making a comparison between the new surfaces to be measured and the known one: 'Has the workbook a larger or a smaller surface than the workcard? If it is larger, will more or less units be needed to cover it?'. If the children consider the new surface in this way, their estimate should be a sensible one.

The children should try to improve their ability to estimate but should not feel they are wrong if the estimate does not match the answer obtained by measuring. In questions 1 and 2, answers for 'My measures' are expressed as a specific number of cards but the children should realise that the number required is an approximate one.

For questions 3, 4 and 5 on Page 32, the child has to place the units (pennies, then squares, then triangles) on the given rectangle. Plastic or cardboard coins may be used. The child will probably find the area is about 15 pennies. If 2 cm squares are used the child will again find that about 15 are used. Any size of square may be used, but if they are smaller than 2 cm, rather a large number is required, for example, sixty centimetre squares. Any type of triangle may be used, but right-angled isosceles or equilateral are probably easiest for the child to fit together. The answer here is likely to be very approximate and this will help the child to understand that the answers for this work are not very accurate.

In question 6, it is suggested that each child in a group writes his or her own answers and then discusses them with the others in the group. The pupils may well disagree about which unit was 'best'. However, if they notice that the pennies left spaces which were not counted and that the triangles did not give an accurate answer, they will see that squares are the 'best' unit. It will be interesting for the teacher to hear the words used by individual children to explain their choice of unit. One child's words are often more meaningful to another child than those of the teacher.

Introductory activities for Page 33

The children should make and draw shapes. Some of the shapes should be of a specified number of squares. Others should not be of specified area, so the areas can be found by counting squares. Here are a few suggestions:

1 The children could draw a shape with an area of 12 squares on squared paper and then cut it out. A display could be made of the cut-outs.

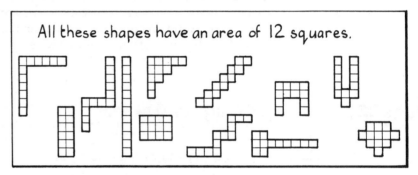

All these shapes have an area of 12 squares.

2 A child could colour a shape with an area of 20 squares on squared paper. When this is completed, a partner could count the squares to check if the shape has the correct area.
3 The children could draw a rectangle and count its area in squares. They could then draw a square and count its area as a number of squares.
4 The children could draw their own shapes made up of squares and find the area of each. Again, a partner could check each area.

Page 33	Counting squares	Area Using squares

Materials squared paper and coloured pencils

The teacher could use Page 33 to check on the children's understanding of area and on their ability to express area as a number of squares. The examples give practice in finding areas by counting squares and drawing shapes of a given area.

In question 3, it should be suggested that the 'large shape' is one made up of whole squares. This prevents the children having to decide which squares to count for an approximate answer. However, for the brightest pupils, teachers may wish to give this challenge as an additional example.

Page 34	Comparing areas	Area Comparison

Materials coloured pencils including red and blue

The examples on this page link previous work on greater and smaller areas to work on areas expressed as a number of squares.

The pupil could either draw a larger shape and then count the squares to find the area, or count the squares in the original shape, then make a shape with a greater number of squares. The teacher might like to demonstrate these two ways of drawing a larger (and smaller) shape than a given one using a large sheet of squared paper.

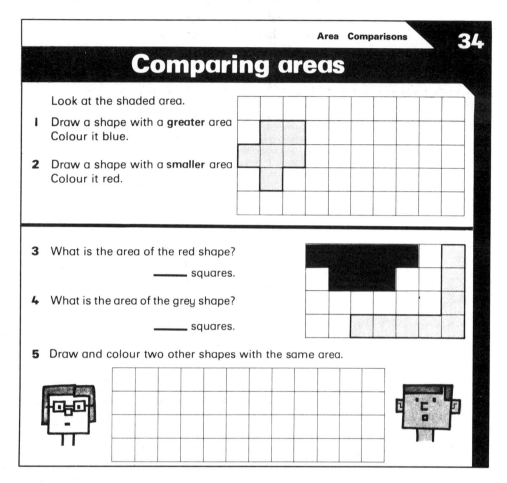

In question 1, the children have a limited amount of grid for two shapes. However, as they are asked to draw the larger shape first, and the smaller can be as small as one square, there is unlikely to be any difficulty. Questions 3, 4, and 5 emphasise that shapes which look different can have the same area. In question 6, the children should be encouraged to estimate the smaller area by *looking* at the shapes. Only after doing this should they proceed to find the area of each shape by counting squares.

Additional activity

Card 30 (and part of 29) in the *Teacher's Materials Pack* provides an area game called 'Cover the Picture' which would be relevant for use at this point.

Measure cards 52, 54, 56, 58, and 60

These six cards give the children additional experience in measure work. Cards 52 and 54 combine work on length and pictorial representation. Cards 56 and 58 give practical experience in handling objects and using a balance to compare weights. Card 60 provides further practical activity in filling and pouring.

Introductory activities for Cards 52 and 54

These two cards are designed to integrate the language of length with measurement using metres and half metres and interpretation of graphs. In order to answer some of the questions the children will need to know certain dimensions of their classroom, namely the length and the height in metres. It is suggested that these measurements are obtained in a practical activity before the children attempt the cards and that they be displayed, perhaps with other measurements on the classroom wall.

> Our classroom measurements.
>
> Length ——→ about 11 metres
> Breadth——→ about 6 metres
> Height ——→ about 2½ metres

Card 52	Vehicle lengths

Materials   none

The graph shows the length in metres of three vehicles. Some children may need help with the word 'vehicle'. By reading the horizontal axis of the graph, the children can state the length of each vehicle. To make the lengths more meaningful, the children are asked to compare them, in questions 1 and 2, to the length of their classroom. In questions 3 and 4 the difference between two lengths has to be found. The answers should be obtained by using the graph, thus avoiding written calculations.

The language of length used includes 'length', 'long', 'longer', 'longest' and 'shortest'. If desired, additional questions may be asked to extend this language, for example, 'How much shorter is the car than the van?'.

Card 54	Heights of clowns

Materials   none

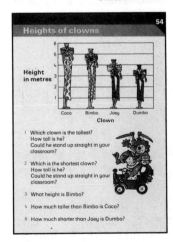

The graph on this card shows the heights, to the nearest half metre, of four clowns. By reading the vertical axis of the graph the children can state the height of each clown. Again, to give more meaning to these heights, the children are asked in questions 1 and 2 to compare certain heights with the height of their own classroom. Note that in question 3 Bimbo is $5\frac{1}{2}$ metres in height and in questions 4 and 5, where the difference between two heights has to be found, half metres are again involved. In these questions the answers should be obtained by using the graph.

The language of length used includes 'height', 'tall', 'taller', 'tallest', 'shorter', and 'shortest'. If desired, additional questions using this language can easily be created, for example, 'What is the difference in height between the tallest and the shortest clown?'.

Card 56   Heavier and lighter

Materials   three parcels, each as colourful as possible and labelled with the names Alan, Betty, and Charles; two-pan balance

In this card, three objects are ordered to find the heaviest and the lightest. In the first instance the pupils estimate by handling the objects, then the balance is used to check their estimated order.

The difference in the weights of the parcels should not be too obvious but should be identifiable when the balance is used.

Children may require help before they realise that the parcels must be compared two at a time, one in each hand. The teacher should demonstrate and discuss this procedure. This may mean three separate comparisons to give the estimated order. It should then be suggested that their estimated order be used as a guide when checking the comparisons using the balance. An additional example with another three parcels, perhaps made up by classmates and with their names on, would give further practice.

Card 58   Ordering jars

Materials   three identical empty jars, for example, jam jars or coffee jars; sand, peas, and marbles – enough of each to fill a jar; two-pan balance. A flat tray, for example, from supermarket food, could be placed under each jar when the pouring is being carried out.

The child has to fill each jar with a different substance. Many children will need guidance in this task.

The child may decide that one jar is the heaviest (or lightest) and then compare it with each of the others. This is probably a more satisfactory strategy than picking up pairs at random. However, this should be discussed by a group as the task is carried out, or when they are telling the teacher their findings.

Having established an order by handling, the children should use the two-pan balance to check if their estimated order is correct.

Card 60   More or less

Materials   three mugs – each labelled with a name (Ann, Bill, Carol are suggested), water or some other pouring material such as sand

The children may well be at the stage where one dimension influences their perception of volume. It will be interesting for the teacher to note if, for example, height is the criterion which a child uses to give an estimated order. The children may have to be reminded to pour carefully so that as little as possible is spilled.

The children may like to repeat this activity using three of their own mugs.

Solid shapes Pages 35 to 39

Content and development

In Workbook 1 the children carried out informal sorting and building activities to help them describe, recognise, and name solid shapes. The shapes dealt with were the cube, cuboid, sphere, triangular prism, egg-shape, cylinder, and cone.

In this workbook the children carry out activities through which they gain experience of the *faces* of solid shapes. The solid shapes dealt with are the cube, cuboid, cylinder, cone, and triangular prism. The flat shapes associated with these are the square, rectangle, circle, and triangle.

This work is extended in Stage 2 of *Primary Mathematics: A development through activity*, where the edges, both straight and curved, and the corners of solid shapes are considered.

Introductory activities for Pages 35 to 39

Before the children are asked to do Pages 35 to 39, the teacher should discuss with them shapes they have previously met, in particular, the cube, cuboid, cylinder, cone, and triangular prism.

The aim of this preliminary work is to ensure that the children can recognise and name both the solid shapes and the flat faces of the solids. There should also be some discussion of the fact that the cylinder and cone have curved surfaces which cause these solids to roll in different ways.

Here are some suitable activities:

1 Blind man's buff   The children take turns at feeling shapes set out on the table. They name each shape as they feel it. Instead of using a blindfold, one child could put a solid into the hands of another whose eyes are closed.

2 Match   Each child in a group is given one of these name cards:

| cube | cuboid | triangular prism | cone | cylinder |

The child then has to pick up the appropriate solid shape from the shape table and hold card and shape aloft. The shapes are then replaced on the table, the cards are re-allocated, and the activity repeated. This could be made into a knock-out competition, with the last child to match card and shape being eliminated each time.

3 Wall chart   A child could be asked to draw round *one* face of a cube. Other children would then be chosen to repeat this for the remaining faces. All the children could then discuss the resulting shapes. From this activity they should learn that a cube has six square faces, all the same size.

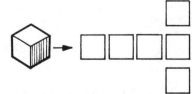

This activity and discussion could then be repeated for other solids, the cuboid, triangular prism, cylinder, and cone. Finally the drawn faces could be labelled.

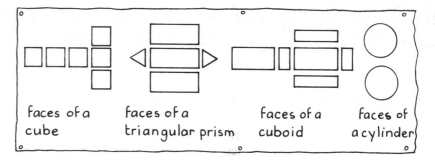

faces of a
cube

faces of a
triangular prism

faces of a
cuboid

faces of
a cylinder

4 What is it?   One child thinks of a particular solid shape, for example a triangular prism, and describes the faces: 'There are five faces altogether. Three are rectangles, which are all the same. Two are triangles, which are both the same. What is it?' The other children have then to name the shape.

It is interesting to see the order in which children supply the necessary information. Thinking what information to give and the best order in which to give it, should improve with practice and through listening to each other.

Page 35   Faces of a cube   Solid shapes   The cube

Materials   at least 27 wooden or plastic cubes (Cuisenaire or Tillich cubes would do), pencil, crayon

This should be a straightforward exercise. The children should realise that there are six square faces, all the same size. Although they are only asked to draw two of them, they should appreciate that if they draw round each face in turn they will finish up with six identical squares.

The children might like to colour the squares they have drawn.

Questions 4 and 5 are concerned with building cube shapes from small cubes. These are more difficult questions and teachers may decide that some children should not attempt question 5.

Some children may not at first appreciate that *four* small cubes do not make a cube shape. Viewed from the *top* a square is seen, but viewed from the *side* a rectangle is seen. Another layer of small cubes is required.

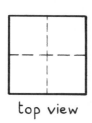

top view

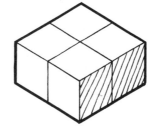

side view

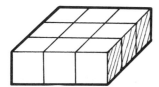

In the case of the larger cube, three layers are needed, each layer containing nine small cubes. It is hoped that the diagrams on Page 35 will help children to see this.

Page 36   Faces of a cuboid   Solid shapes   The cuboid

Materials   a wooden or plastic cuboid with three different edge lengths (like a matchbox), pencil, crayon

The children should notice that a cuboid, like a cube, has six faces. They should find that, for a cuboid of the type suggested for this activity, the faces are all rectangles. There are three pairs of identical rectangles, two like A, two like B, and two like C.

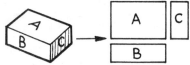

Some cuboids have two square faces. Cuisenaire rods are like this. The children should appreciate that, in the case of a cube, *all* the faces are identical squares.

Later, the children will learn that the cube is a special cuboid but, as far as the present course is concerned, we refer to these shapes as follows:

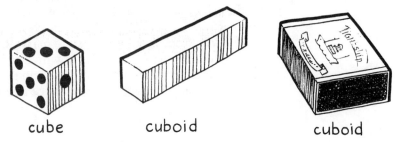

cube   cuboid   cuboid

Page 37   **Cylinder and cone**   Solid shapes   Cylinder and cone

Materials   a cylinder and a cone, preferably made of wood or plastic; pencil; crayon

In the case of the cylinder, the children should learn from the activity that this solid has two flat faces which are identical circles. If they have room they might try drawing round both faces of the cylinder. This should result in two circles of the same size.

They should also see, by rolling the cylinder along the table, that it has a curved surface and can roll in a straight path. The cone, which also has a curved surface, rolls in a circular path. It has one flat face, which is a circle.

Page 38   **Triangular prism**   Solid shapes   Triangular prism

Materials   a triangular prism, preferably made of wood or plastic, though a Toblerone packet would do; pencil; crayon

In this activity the children should find out that the triangular prism has five flat faces – two opposite faces which are identical triangles and three rectangular faces.

The prism which the children use will probably have triangular faces which are equilateral triangles. This will mean that the three rectangular faces are also identical in shape and size.

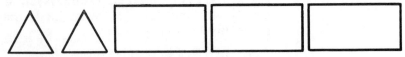

A triangular prism which has triangular faces which are *not* equilateral triangles might have faces like this:

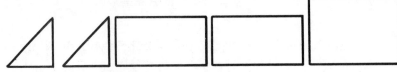

It is enough for the children to appreciate that there are two triangular faces and three rectangular faces.

Page 39   Faces of solid shapes   Solid shapes   Faces

Materials   a cube, cuboid, cylinder, cone, and triangular prism

This page tests the children's knowledge of the faces of the five solids. The teacher may have to guide those children who do not notice that *two* matching lines are required for the circle and *two* for the rectangle.

There is a reference at the foot of the page to Shape Cards 62, 64, 66, 68, 70. Teachers should note that these cards do not deal with solid shapes but are concerned with the flat shapes which are the faces of the solids dealt with in Pages 35 to 39.

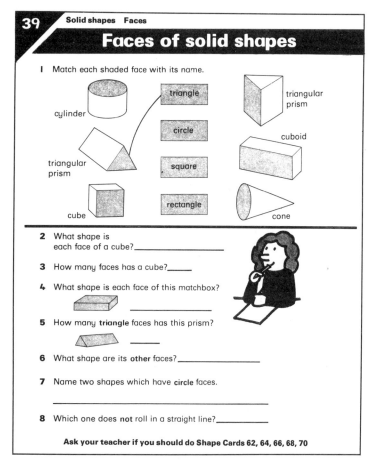

Additional cards concerning faces of solid shapes

Here are two cards which the teacher could make. They should help consolidate the children's knowledge of the faces of solid shapes.

Shape cards
62, 64, 66, 68, and 70   Puzzle cards

These five cards provide some extra activities involving shape. Some of the activities may be more suitable for abler children and could be used at any time.

Card 62   Shapes graph

Materials   none

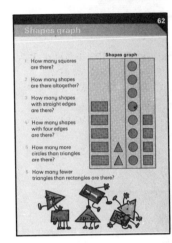

The children have to answer questions about the shapes shown on the graph and their properties.

In question 3, the children should count all the rectangles, triangles, and squares.

The word 'fewer' in question 6 may pose problems for some children. They may need help to see that they are meant to compare the number of rectangles and triangles and find the difference. They should be able to say how many *more* rectangles there are and the teacher can relate this to 'How many fewer triangles'.

Pupils should be encouraged to make use of the graph to answer the questions. For example, in question 6 they could count the difference of 3 rather than find $5-2$.

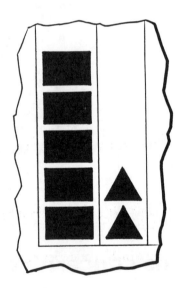

Cards 64 and 66   Counting triangles and squares

Materials   none

These cards try to explain how to count all the triangles or squares in drawings where the shapes overlap. This is a difficult idea and may need some explanation from the teacher. It may not suit less able pupils.

In question 2 on each card, reasonable sketches rather than accurate drawings should be expected.

Card 68   A shape puzzle

Materials   two cardboard or plastic shapes cut from a square thus:

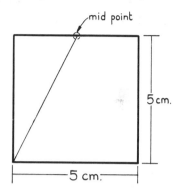

The aim of the card is that the children visualise and also experiment to make the shapes shown. Shapes of the size specified above will fit on top of the drawings on the card but there is no reason why a larger square should not be used with the children making larger versions of the required shapes beside the card. The shapes can be kept in an envelope, perhaps attached to the card with a paper clip.

The shape shown below may cause some difficulty, as the triangle has to be turned over.

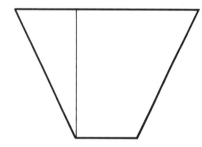

This card may be more suitable for able children.

Card 70   A puzzle with rectangles

Materials   four small rectangles of the size shown below

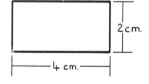

The aim of this card is that the children should experiment with fitting the rectangles together to make the shapes shown. Rectangles of the size given above will fit exactly on top of the diagrams on the card. Other larger rectangles whose length is exactly twice their breadth could also be used, with the children making larger versions of the shapes on the card without fitting on top. Dominoes may provide suitable rectangles.

This card may be more suitable for able children.